Evaluating
Second Language
Courses

Evaluating Second Language Courses

Dale Griffee

ELS Language Center
Lubbock, Texas

Greta Gorsuch

Texas Tech University

INFORMATION AGE PUBLISHING, INC.
Charlotte, NC • www.infoagepub.com

Library of Congress Cataloging-in-Publication Data

A CIP record for this book is available from the Library of Congress
http://www.loc.gov

ISBN: 978-1-68123-593-6 (Paperback)
        978-1-68123-594-3 (Hardcover)
        978-1-68123-595-0 (ebook)

Cover illustration:

Pflug, Christiane. (1966). *Kitchen door with Ursula* [Oil on canvas, 164.8 × 193.2 cm].
Winnipeg, Canada: Collection of the Winnipeg Art Gallery

Acquired with the assistance of the Women's Committee
and The Winnipeg Foundation, G-66-89

Photographer: Ernest Mayer

Used by permission.

Printed in the United States of America

Contents

Foreword

As Griffee and Gorsuch explain in their preface, the need for this book arose (a) because interest in evaluation seems to be increasing, both inside and outside of the foreign and second language teaching/learning fields, (b) because the existing books on evaluation in our field typically cover large-scale evaluation based on extensive evaluation projects conducted by their authors, and (c) because (a) and (b) leave teachers having to adapt large-scale strategies and techniques to meet their much smaller classroom level evaluation needs. In response, *Evaluating Second Language Courses* was primarily intended to provide classroom teachers and teachers-in-training with a significant resource that they can use in evaluating and improving their own language teaching and courses.

However, just because it is designed to help practicing teachers, does not mean that it leaves out important theoretical considerations. Indeed, this book pinpoints fundamental connections between theories and models of evaluation and practical evaluation practices. To that end, the authors offer two solid and innovative tools.

The first tool is a model for course goal validation that they call the SOAC model (i.e., the **S**takeholders, **O**utcomes, **A**ssessments, **C**urriculum model, attributed to Griffee & Gevara, 2011), which can be used for evaluation at both the program and course levels. The components of the model, include the *world, stakeholders*, the *evaluand*, and *outcomes, assessment*, and *curriculum*. Each of these components is defined at length and then the authors focus on

Evaluating Second Language Courses, pages ix–xi
Copyright © 2016 by Information Age Publishing
ix

the relationships among them and how those relationships can help teachers think about and proceed through any evaluation project.

The second tool is a template (in Chapter 9) that they call RAPs (i.e., **R**eading and **A**ssessing Evaluation **P**ublications), which readers will find particularly useful for critically understanding and weighing the quality of articles in the (language) evaluation literature. The authors encourage readers to use RAP to glean information from such articles that is relevant for their own course evaluation activities and search for tips on how to effectively write-up their own course evaluation reports.

Evaluating Second Language Courses provides full and complete coverage in its ten chapters by addressing the following issues:

- what course evaluation is;
- available models of SL course evaluation;
- the importance of stakeholders and outcomes, the real world, and outcome validation;
- needs analysis, the world and stakeholders, and needs analysis;
- the roles of curriculum, outcomes, and course logic;
- the links among curriculum, stakeholders, and formative evaluation;
- how curriculum, assessment, and instrument validation fit together (including tests & quizzes);
- the relationships among curriculum, assessment, and data collection validation (including classroom observations, interviews, & questionnaires);
- the connections among outcomes, assessment, and summative evaluation;
- and finally, strategies for critically reading and assessing evaluation publications.

In addition, the book has a number of useful supplementary features including (a) a table of contents, (b) brief previews at the beginning of each chapter to tell readers what to expect, (c) discussion questions at the end of most main sections within the chapters, (d) application tasks in each chapter that will help readers apply what they have learned to their own settings, (e) references at the end of each chapter, (f) a number of appendices to individual chapters, and (g) four bibliographies in appendices at the end of the book (of publications *of* and *about* evaluation, as well as publications *of* and *about* needs analysis). In addition, (h) key terminology and jargon are highlighted in italics throughout the book and (i) a useful glossary of evaluation terminology is supplied at the end.

One of the most important characteristics of this book is the well-organized, straightforward, and accessible writing style, with its many clear and concise definitions, easy-to-understand descriptions, and practical examples drawn from the literature. Unlike many co-authored books where the reader senses shifts in style back-and-forth between the two authors, this book blends the sections each of them wrote into a single, seamless, coherent whole. In addition, while the authors do draw on the literature a great deal, they carefully weave those sources together with their own insights on evaluation and needs analysis to create a cohesive, logical, systematic whole in such a way that the reader is not ever aware of the process.

In short, *Evaluating Second Language Courses* is just the sort of thing that second and foreign language teachers have long needed because it provides them with the background, basic information, and resources necessary for them to conduct effective and efficient evaluations in the language courses they teach. In addition to teachers, I'm sure that needs analyses, evaluators, and curriculum developers of all sorts will also find this book useful and informative whether they are dealing with ESL, EFL, or other languages at the course or program level. In short, I highly recommend this book.

Reference

Griffee, D. T., & Gevara, J. R. (2011). Standard setting in the post-modern era for an ITA Performance Test. *Texas Papers in Foreign Language Education, 15*(1), 3–16. Retrieved from http://studentorgs.utexas.edu/flesa/TPFLE _New/Index.htm.

—**James Dean ("JD") Brown**
Kaneʻohe Bay, Hawaiʻi

1

What Is Course Evaluation?

*If we never encounter new possibility for thought and action, we never question the
lack of development of those possibilities in ourselves.*
—Erickson and Schultz (1994, p. 482)

This chapter introduces *course evaluation*[1] for teachers, and moves evaluation
from something slightly threatening done at the last minute for external reasons, to something done for reasons more valid to teachers. Teachers can "assign worth" (evaluate) to parts of a course for reasons of their own, and they
can use results of their evaluation to communicate to others about their course.
Key terms are introduced, such as *outcomes*, which refer to what *foreign language*
and *second language* students should accomplish as a result of participating in
a course. Research and evaluation are compared, and while they share some
things, evaluation is a valid field of scholarly inquiry in its own right. The chapter finishes with a course evaluation plan form for readers to use.

The quote by Erickson and Schultz is intriguing because it suggests
that the purpose of evaluation is to think about the possibility for new

1. For all terms in *italics*, see Glossary.

Evaluating Second Language Courses, pages 1–16

1

thought and action. The purpose of this chapter is to raise new possibilities for thought and action by teachers who wish to know in more depth what they are currently doing in classrooms, and how they might change what they are doing to bring about better outcomes. We think one road to follow is course evaluation. Evaluation gives teachers power and authority. Doing evaluation and getting results (data) from this process gives teachers a way to talk to other teachers, principals, and administrators about their courses based on more than hunches, experience, and intuition. There is power in having data that means something to others outside the classroom, and being able to talk about what the data might mean. In addition, to evaluate their own classes is one way for teachers to overcome the isolation of the classroom, and to join a larger community of teachers, scholars, and researchers. Finally, as Erickson and Schultz (1994) point out, evaluation is a way of encountering new possibilities for thought and action, which encourages change based on something more than enthusiasm and good intentions.

Getting Started

Here are some terms that are used in our field, and as such will be used in this book. Most major terms we use also appear in the glossary for this book. These terms appear in italics the first time they are mentioned in a chapter. Second language refers to a language taught to nonnative speakers of the language in places where the language is consistently and widely used outside of the classroom, such as English in the United States or the United Kingdom, or Turkish in Turkey. Foreign language refers to any language taught to nonnative speakers of the language in places where it is not consistently or widely used outside the classroom. This would be, for example, French, German, or Russian taught in the United States, and English or Chinese taught in Russia or Japan. When thinking of the cognitive learning processes involved in learning another language (in other words, what happens inside learners' heads), it would be correct to use the term second language learning because these processes are encouraged, we hope, in classrooms regardless of geographic location.

Nonetheless, as language educators we have worked in various countries where the language we taught (English) was viewed differently by the societies and education systems in which we worked. Thus we know that in terms of course design and teaching and evaluation, geographic location does matter. Course outcomes of a second language course may relate more to learners using the language to get by and function in a society where the language is used, for example as health care workers in a U.S.

hospital. Thus the outcomes of such a course might include communicating with patients on health topics and with insurance companies on financial issues. In a foreign language setting where the language may be viewed as academic content, or as a means of cultural or intellectual enrichment, we may be looking at a course where the learning outcomes focus on mastery of particular grammatical structures, or gaining experience with literary genres (Swaffar & Arens, 2005). Course outcomes, or the things the course is supposed to accomplish, are particularly important for teachers and course evaluation, and will be discussed in more detail in later chapters. Because we intend this book to be used by teachers of any language in both second language and foreign language learning settings, we use the terms interchangeably.

There is one more term commonly used in our field that is relevant to course evaluation. This is *curriculum*, which in the context of this book we take to mean all the ways a second language course or program responds to a perceived learner need. This includes class exercises, textbooks, handouts, lectures, how often classes are scheduled to meet and for how long, teaching methods, etc. The larger field of second language curriculum was historically concerned with developing a *syllabus*, which traditionally is a specification of what content or skills are to be focused on in a course, and in what order. An example would be a grammatical syllabus that specifies grammar forms, or a functional syllabus that specifies communicative functions (Dubin & Olshtain, 1986; Nunan, 1988). Syllabus now more commonly indicates a document, typically focused on a single course, which outlines information about the course, such as required materials, and includes a statement of course goals or outcomes. Later writers in curriculum use curriculum development models that take us to a still-current focus on learner outcomes and arranging instruction to bring learners to these outcomes (see Brown, 1995; Richards, 2001). We agree with Brown (1995) that a curriculum is only as good as the evaluations that should regularly be done on it. We also think evaluation has a strong scholarly tradition of its own apart from curriculum. Evaluation has its own unique purposes and uses. We discuss this now.

Evaluation is a term commonly used by evaluation professionals to refer to the evaluation of any program including education, medical, criminal justice, and social action by government or private persons. In this book, we use evaluation to mean the process by which we collect information and assign a judgment of worth to parts of a course, an entire course, or several related courses that comprise a program. This book focuses on evaluation at the level of a single course. We would like to state at the outset that the idea of worth means more than simply being good or bad. We do not wish to promote such blanket conclusions, and we do not believe evaluation is necessarily for the purpose of deciding a course or part of a course is good or bad. The process of assigning worth, in our minds, has more to do with understanding well a course or part of a course. In illuminating our own understanding of what a course does and how, we can create nuanced decisions about what could change, what ought to change, and what needs no change.

Throughout this book we will pose discussion questions that are designed to give you a break from taking in information and time to mull over the concepts by yourself or with others.

DISCUSSION QUESTION 1

What kind of teacher are you currently? Second language? Foreign language? If you are not currently teaching, answer in terms of when you taught in the past. For readers who have not yet taught, reflect on the last language class you took as a learner. What language was being taught, and where? Would you consider the class to have been a second language or a foreign language course? Why?

DISCUSSION QUESTION 2

How did you become a teacher? If you have not taught, reflect on why you think you might want to teach. How will you become a teacher? How will you get a job teaching?

DISCUSSION QUESTION 3

What is your main challenge? Do you think evaluation may help you with this challenge? Again, if you have not taught, think about a past language course you have taken. What challenges do you think there might have been to offering the course you took?

Evaluation as a Process of Collecting Information and Making Decisions

It is helpful to see evaluation as something other than grudgingly writing up a report for a supervisor or giving out an end-of-semester questionnaire to students. Course evaluation is a dynamic, generative process with distinct purposes and stages, much like the classes we teach. In evaluation we collect information (or data) so we can make decisions, again, much like we do in teaching. According to Brown (1989, p. 223) "evaluation is the systematic collection and analysis of all relevant information necessary to promote the improvement of a curriculum, and assess its effectiveness and efficiency, as well as the participants' attitudes within the context of the particular institutions involved." Taking up the theme of collection, Posavac and Carey (1985, p. 5) state that evaluation is

> a collection of methods, skills, and sensitivities necessary to determine whether a human service is needed and likely to be used, whether it is sufficiently intense to meet the need identified, whether the service is offered as planned, and whether the human service actually does help people in need.

McDavid and Hawthorn (2006, p. 3) emphasize evaluation as a process, noting that "evaluation can be viewed as a structured process that creates and synthesizes information intended to reduce the level of uncertainty for *stakeholders* about a given program or policy." Scriven (1991, p. 139), also seeing evaluation as a process, says that evaluation "refers to the process of determining the merit, worth, or value of something, or the product of that process."

Decisions that are made from an evaluation thus include ways to improve a program and explain a program, as well as highlighting the value of a program to various stakeholders when necessary. This book focuses primarily on evaluation as a means of understanding and improving a language course or program, hence our focus on decision points, or specific suggestions, that arise from an evaluation. This is what we mean when we say that course evaluation is a process by which we assign a judgment of worth to a course or parts of a course. The idea of worth is related to the decisions the evaluation is going to be used to make, in other words, the purpose of an evaluation. Much of this text will highlight how to determine the purpose of a course evaluation.

What Is Course Evaluation?

To reiterate, course evaluation is a process by which we collect information and assign a judgment of worth to a course or parts of a single course. Many books on evaluation in second and foreign language education mention *program evaluation*, but not really course evaluation. This may be partly because many evaluation professionals outside our field, like some of those we cited just previously, write in terms of evaluating whole programs with broad aims as opposed to a single course. And up until now, evaluation writers in the second and foreign language field have read and borrowed from the professional evaluation field (as we do ourselves), or have been most concerned with evaluating programs made up of multiple courses such as a Spanish foreign language program in the United States (e.g., Sanders, 2005). We focus on evaluation at the level of the course because we think that ordinary teachers have a place in evaluation as a field of scholarly activity, and that they will benefit personally and professionally from doing course evaluation.

Why Course Evaluation?

Teachers might engage in course evaluation for external or internal reasons. External means that the reason comes from outside the course. For example, your immediate supervisor tells you that you have to evaluate all or part of a course you are teaching for a report she wants to put together. This is not a welcome reason for doing an evaluation because it ignores you and your reasons. Another external reason is that an accrediting agency or some "higher" party in your school requires evaluation of your course. Again, this is not a good reason for conducting a course evaluation because teachers all too often write an evaluation report without much thought, just to get it done and over with to please a nameless and faceless agency. This purpose is often associated with *summative evaluation*, which is done for accountability. A third external reason is more positive and shows why course evaluation can be useful for teacher networking and professional growth. For instance, a teacher or professional in your school or at another school may wish to know about your course as a way to reflect on his or her own course.

Internal means that the reason for course evaluation comes from you. This implies that you understand what you are evaluating and why you are evaluating it. This purpose might be more associated with *formative evaluation*, which is done to more clearly understand a course and to improve a course using more local viewpoints, such as those of students in the course. Cronbach (1963, p. 675) says, "The greatest service evaluation can perform is to identify aspects of the course where revision is desirable." In other words, we evaluate a course to improve it. See Appendix A for a bibliography of articles and book chapters reporting on actual evaluations, both summative and formative.

DISCUSSION QUESTION 4

Are you teaching? If so, which course could you evaluate? If you are not teaching, what course could you "borrow" to try a small evaluation on? Hint: Do you have any friends or classmates who are teaching?

What Teachers Know and Do Not Know

We teachers know that some aspects of our course are working, and know (or at least suspect) that some are not. The problem is to identify which is which. Another problem is that even though Cronbach published his article in the early 1960s, nobody in second or foreign language education seems to have read it. As a result, we are not usually expected or encouraged to engage in evaluation, which means that we are not in control of our improvement. And even if we do want to evaluate our courses, we have not been prepared. What we are prepared to do is continue a never-ending search for the perfect textbook and the right exercises for our students that we never seem to find. This text may not definitively solve those problems, but it will start you on your journey into course evaluation, which may provide some answers you need.

What Can Be Evaluated?

There are three basic options. For a classroom teacher, the first and most obvious option is that we can evaluate the whole course. Such a course evaluation would consider the course purpose and outcomes, usually found in some form in the course syllabus or a document that we create and hand out to students and our supervisor. We refer to course aims, goals, and objectives later in this book as outcomes. Course evaluations with this scope would also likely consider all persons defined as stakeholders (students, their parents, students' employers, teachers' supervisors, school administrators, etc.), and the *curriculum* (what materials are used, what is done in classes, the teaching philosophy of the teacher, etc.). Finally, such course evaluations would consider the tests in a course and how those tests are used. In this book we use the term *assessment* for tests.

A second option for evaluation is focusing on a specific part of the course, perhaps a *curricular innovation*, which is a principled change to a course to bring about some worthwhile change in students' learning. Examples are transforming a university business degree taught in Austrian German to one taught in a foreign language (English; Unterberger, 2012), or diversifying the types of English foreign language vocabulary exercises used in a high school course in Taiwan (Lu, 2013), or introducing a new culture component into a German foreign language program at an American college (Rogers, LeCompte, & Plumly, 2012). Such a smaller-scope course evaluation might also be an investigation of the needs of stakeholders, such as the self-efficacy of American college-level learners of foreign language Spanish, Russian, French, German, Italian, Japanese, Arabic, and Chinese in the final course of their foreign language requirement (Gorsuch, 2009); or novice foreign language Spanish teachers' needs for integrating practical theory into lesson planning (Dupuy & Allen, 2012).

A third option would be to evaluate several related courses that comprise a program. This would in effect be a program evaluation. This might be as simple as investigating the linkages between materials (curriculum) used in first, second, and third year high school, and university preparation foreign language courses (Riazi & Mosalanejad, 2010); or shifts in goals (outcomes) between the lower- and upper-division Spanish, French, or German foreign language courses of a modern language university department (Rava, 2000). As a final example, such an evaluation might focus on tests (assessments) used in an English second language program designed to prepare international students to teach in freshman college science and math classes (Griffee & Gevara, 2011).

DISCUSSION QUESTION 5

Which of the three options are you thinking of? Answer either as if you will evaluate your own course as a teacher, or evaluate the course being taught by another teacher/classmate/colleague.

Evaluation Is a Special Form of Research

Language teachers are more familiar with research than evaluation, in the sense that research is a kind of "default" activity that everyone has heard about. Even if teachers do not know research and its workings well, they have heard of it. This is less true for evaluation. The difference between research and evaluation is important yet easy to miss in that there is overlap between them. As a result we may unconsciously slip into calling our course evaluation work research, and thereby omit key components of evaluation.

Overlapping Areas of Evaluation and Research

Evaluation and research overlap in at least four significant ways (Mathison, 2008). First, both use what could be called social science research methods including *data collection instruments*, for example questionnaires and tests; and *research designs*, for example experimental design and case study design. Both evaluation and research include a concern for data collection instrument design and validation evidence, which is a careful process for questioning whether a data collection instrument actually captured the information the investigator intended.

Second, evaluation and research work in systematic and objective ways. In other words, both are scientific orientations, which stress a combination of creative insights based on data and the analysis of that data.

Third, both evaluation and research strive toward generalizability, where evaluation or research findings have applications in many settings and situations. Although generalizability is overtly sought by researchers, evaluators are perhaps more predisposed to learn local, directly useful information from their investigations, than to apply it to other situations. Fourth and finally, both evaluation and research practitioners use theory to explain their results.

How Evaluation and Research Do Not Overlap

Although evaluation and research overlap, they are different in four crucial ways. First, course evaluation identifies multiple stakeholders and takes their concerns into account. In course evaluation students are not research participants or subjects, but key stakeholders. Second and foreign language teachers have a long history of caring a great deal about their students, but not actually taking them into account at the outcome, curriculum, and assessment levels. This is because we conceive of them as participants (a research perspective) rather than costakeholders (an evaluation perspective).

Second, course evaluation relies on a locally conducted *needs analysis* to relate various stakeholders' needs to each other and to inform course goals. An evaluation without a needs analysis would render the evaluator blind to the direction of the evaluation. Third, evaluation uses an *evaluation purpose* and an *evaluation model.* An evaluation purpose refers to whether an evaluation should be used for accountability, or to inform and illuminate (House, 1993). An evaluation model refers to beliefs about what the components of evaluation are, and how the components relate to each other. In contrast, research uses *domain theory* such as second language reading comprehension theories or second language acquisition models (Griffee, 2012). Course evaluation, while still using research design and data collection instruments, needs the framework provided by an evaluation purpose and an evaluation model to guide the evaluation. Finally, course evaluation is used to make policy recommendations, whereas research typically concludes with a call for more research or is used to motivate further, related research. Evaluation requires practical and useful actions: "An evaluation that is not used is in some important sense a failure" (Alderson, 1992, p. 298). We will refer to these evaluation-driven actions later as decision points. The extent any of these four unique aspects of evaluation are missing from an evaluation is the extent the evaluation is more research than evaluation.

DISCUSSION QUESTION 6

What is something you now know about evaluation as a unique field that you did not know before? Does this change how you might describe your course evaluation plans to another person?

A Reasonable Timeline

All teachers informally and intuitively evaluate their classes. We think it is our second nature. When teaching a foreign language at schools in Japan, we could walk into a classroom on the first day and say "Good morning." From the responses (an answer, a look of bewilderment, an attempt to hide), we could estimate students' general levels of proficiency, or perhaps their willingness to engage in the speaking activities we had planned. That first-day, rather intuitive, evaluation took 3–5 seconds, but how long might a more systematic evaluation take? In Chapter 2 we will introduce a course evaluation model and outline six areas that can be investigated in depth. So, about how much time should you plan for any one of them? Mitchell (1992) supplies a word of warning: Any evaluation takes about twice as long as you expect. So a simple formula is $ET = R \times 2$ where ET is evaluation time, R is a reasonable length of time, and 2 is twice as long as you expect. While our formula is a little tongue-in-cheek, it is also true-to-life: If you think a more ambitious course evaluation project will take one semester, it is more likely to take two semesters.

DISCUSSION QUESTION 7

How long do you think your course evaluation will take? How much time per week can you give it?

DISCUSSION QUESTION 8

What times during a semester would like be "most busy" for your course evaluation? What times during a semester might your course evaluation work be done at a more relaxed pace? If you do not currently teach try posing these questions to someone who is teaching now. What are his or her perspectives on "busy" or "relaxed" times during a semester?

Helpful Questions to Ask Before Starting an Evaluation Project

The purpose of the questions we give here is to orient you to the various roles we play as a teacher, evaluator, or researcher. Knowing about these roles affects why we do a course evaluation project, and what we do. This orientation helps us at the planning stage on questions such as what we intend to ask and why, how we will collect data, how we will interpret it, and who we will communicate our conclusions to for what purpose. We think that if you ask a question, an answer sooner or later will come. One reason course evaluation projects take longer than expected is that we often are not clear at the beginning what we want to do, in other words what questions we wish to ask, what we wish to investigate. As a result, we do not plan well and are caught off guard later when we are at our busiest, losing focus and purpose. Hence we offer the questions in Table 1.1.

The background for these questions comes from three sources: Beretta (1992, p. 264), Mitchell (1992), and Lynch (1992). Beretta reflected on lessons learned from his evaluation of a second language education project in Bangalore, India. Beretta wished that at the very beginning he had known more clearly: (a) the purpose of the evaluation; and (b) what uses were to be made of the findings, in terms of who the conclusions are communicated to for what purpose. Beretta had the role of a jet-in-jet-out (JIJO) external evaluator, meaning that he had some distance between himself and the possible consequences of his evaluation findings. Nonetheless, knowing more clearly the "why" and "what uses" would have helped him to define what he needed to do earlier in the process. Needless to say, these are helpful questions that teachers in their own roles can ask when evaluating their own courses.

Mitchell (1992) conducted an evaluation on a bilingual program in Scotland. The local school board and teachers wanted to preserve the native Gaelic language in an English-speaking country, and to implement a child-centered teaching curriculum. Mitchell and her colleagues (again, external evaluators) found themselves caught between the interests of a local board of education operating at the school and classroom level (two sets of stakeholders), and a national board of education interested in national policy (another set of stakeholders). As a result, the national board did not

TABLE 1.1 Helpful Questions to Ask Before Beginning an Evaluation Project	
1	What is the purpose of the evaluation? Why do the evaluation?
2	What uses will be made of the evaluation findings?
3	Who might wish to know the evaluation findings? Who are the potential audiences? At what level of concern do they work?
4	What kinds of data might these audiences (including you, the teacher/evaluator) appreciate or value? Interviews? Observations? Test scores?
5	What kinds of answers can quantitative data tell us, and what kinds of answers can qualitative data tell us?

accept the validity of the local evaluation data and conclusions. Mitchell's situation made us wonder if all evaluation projects have not one, but three possible aspects. The first aspect might be a local concern, at the level of classroom or school. A second aspect could be a possible research concern, for instance, how does interaction between second language teachers and learners contribute to child-centered instruction? This level of concern would be somewhere between classroom and a level beyond classroom and school. A third and final aspect might be a national or global interest, which is a level of concern beyond the classroom and school. We also wondered if it might be the case that the higher—in the sense of more global—the evaluation reporting, the more likely that decontextualized, quantitative data and analysis might be appreciated. Such data might be seen as speaking to many teaching situations. Conversely, at a more local level, evaluators reporting more contextualized, qualitative data might be better appreciated. Such data might seem to have a better "fit" to evaluators right there in the locale. Thus, even if the purpose of an evaluation is clear, and the use of the results may seem clear, we might ask, who, outside our immediate evaluation audience, might wish to know the findings? Further, what kind of data is appreciated or valued by them?

Finally, Lynch (1992) did an evaluation of a college foreign language reading program in Mexico. Lynch (an external evaluator) concluded that evaluation workers (teachers, researchers, and evaluators) had to be able to match the purpose of their evaluation with the *evaluation questions*. Evaluation questions, or EQs, are specific statements of the scope and intent of the evaluation. In other words the evaluation purpose needs to "drive" the evaluation questions, which in turn drive the data collection. Lynch concluded that both quantitative and qualitative data work together in the sense that we need to be able to answer the question of what happened (quantitative data), and why it happened (qualitative data). Thus, in addition to asking questions of why, what use, and who, we might ask what kind of answers can quantitative data tell us, and what kind of answers can qualitative data tell us?

DISCUSSION QUESTION 9

Thinking of Beretta, Mitchell, or Lynch, which of these evaluators' experiences "speaks" to you? What advice would you like to get from the evaluator? What would you like to learn from him, her, or them?

Another way to visualize these questions is using Table 1.2, which illustrates three levels of possible concern (local purpose, research concern, and global interest) against general groupings of data we can collect, such as decontextualized quantitative data, and contextualized qualitative data.

TABLE 1.2 Three Levels of Course Evaluation Concerns and Two Kinds of Data

	Local purpose	Research concern	Global interest
Decontextualized quantitative data			
Contextualized qualitative data			

We have found Table 1.2 to be helpful to think through what our own concerns are at the local level, and what kind of data we thought would be most helpful to us. We became interested in evaluating our instructor and test rater training for a second language English course in the United States. The course curriculum included a complex spoken performance test to be rated by two instructors, hence the need for test rater training. For our own purposes, we considered using interviews with the instructors and their students (qualitative data collection). But then Table 1.2 proved its worth to us by causing us to think through who else might be interested in our findings, and what kinds of data we might wish to collect to answer the question of how well our instructor training and test rater training were doing. As it turned out, an external reason appeared for doing the evaluation: We began to hire qualified nonnative English speaking instructors for the course at the same time we began instructor and test-rater training in earnest. Several administrators wanted to know how we were justified in hiring nonnative speakers. Rather than relying on our heartfelt, experience-based, local, and contextualized knowledge of how teacher qualifications trump native-speaker status, we used Table 1.2 to plan quantitative data collection in the form of a well-designed survey. We designed the survey on well-established second language teacher qualities that we also felt we emphasized in our instructor training. After administering the survey to the students, we could, if needed, examine student ratings of the nonnative English speaking instructors as teachers and use the resulting quantitative data to address global concerns expressed by the administrators. In other words, the issues raised in Table 1.2 helped us visualize our course evaluation in broader terms, which as it turned out, we needed to do.

We think the questions in Table 1.1, particularly Number 1, might seem easy to answer, but our experience tells us that upon reflection, none of them are easy to answer, nor do they have fixed answers. We think you will change your mind and revise your answers as you learn while doing a course evaluation. You can also use the Appendix to help you begin planning your course evaluation.

APPLICATION TASK: A Course Evaluation Plan

We suggest you begin this task, completing the form at the end of this chapter, while you have access to other teachers in your program. Perhaps you are having regular working meetings or you are taking a graduate class. You can consult your colleagues and confirm or clarify your answers. Your colleagues may have additional suggestions after you have filled out your answers in tentative form. You can continue working on the task afterwards and then find ways to report your findings to your colleagues during a working meeting or a class.

A COURSE EVALUATION PLAN: GETTING STARTED

Name: _____ Date: _____

I. Describe the course you plan to evaluate in terms of:
- Official name and course number.
- Time and location.
- Purpose and goals as mentioned in the syllabus.
- Number and description of students.
- Textbook being used.
- Other relevant information (frequency and length of class meetings, classroom description, etc.)

II. Are you interested in (check one)
- ☐ evaluating all of the course
- ☐ evaluating part of the course
  - – A goals validation study (Chapter 3)
  - – A needs analysis (Chapter 4)
  - – A course logic study (Chapter 5)
  - – Any aspect of the course curriculum (Chapters 2 and 6)
  - – Any aspect of the course assessments (Chapters 2 and 7)
- ☐ evaluating a group of courses (a program)
- ☐ if none of the above speak to you, can you state in a few sentences what you are interested in.

III. Answer as many of the initial evaluation questions as you can.
1. What is your local, classroom purpose for this evaluation?
2. Is there a research issue that could be investigated? There does not have to be one, but is there a possible one?
3. Is there a global interest that might be served? Again, there does not have to be one, but is one possible?
4. What kinds of data do you plan to collect?
5. What data collection instruments (DCIs) such as interviews, observations, a questionnaire, tests could provide that data?

References

Alderson, J. C. (1992). Guidelines for the evaluation of language education. In J. C. Alderson & A. Beretta (Eds.), *Evaluating second language education* (pp. 274–304). Cambridge, England: Cambridge University Press.

Beretta, A. (1992). What can be learned from the Bangalore evaluation. In J. C. Alderson & A. Beretta (Eds.), *Evaluating second language education* (pp. 250–273). Cambridge, England: Cambridge University Press.

Brown, J. D. (1989). Language program evaluation: A synthesis of existing possibilities. In R. K. Johnson (Ed.), *The second language curriculum* (pp. 222–241). Cambridge, England: Cambridge University Press.

Brown, J. D. (1995). *The elements of language curriculum.* Boston, MA: Heinle & Heinle.

Cronbach, L. J. (1963). Course improvement through evaluation. *Teacher's College Record, 64,* 672–683.

Dubin, F., & Olshtain, E. (1986). *Course design.* Cambridge, England: Cambridge University Press.

Dupuy, B., & Allen, H.W. (2012). Appropriating conceptual and pedagogical tools of literacy. In G. Gorsuch (Ed.), *Working theories for teaching assistant development* (pp. 275–315). Stillwater, OK: New Forums Press.

Erickson, F. & Shultz, J. (1994). Students' experience of the curriculum. In P. W. Jackson (Ed.), *Handbook on research on curriculum* (pp. 465–485). New York, NY: Macmillan.

Gorsuch, G. J. (2009). Investigating second language learner self-efficacy and future expectancy of second language use for high stakes program evaluation. *Foreign Language Annals, 42*(2), 505–540.

Griffee, D. T. (2012). The role of theory in TA and ITA research. In G. Gorsuch (Ed.), *Working theories for teaching assistant development: Time-tested & robust theories, frameworks, & models for TA & ITA Learning* (pp. 39–61). Stillwater, OK: New Forums Press.

Griffee, D. T., & Gevara, J. R. (2011). Standard setting in the post-modern era for an ITA performance test. *Texas Papers in Foreign Language Education, 15*(1), 3–16.

House, E. (1993). *Professional evaluation: Social impact and political consequences.* Newbury Park, CA: Sage.

Lu, M. (2013). Effects of four vocabulary exercises on facilitating learning vocabulary meaning. *TESOL Quarterly, 47*(1), 167–176.

Lynch, B. (1992). Evaluating a program inside and out. In J. C. Alderson & A. Beretta (Eds.), *Evaluating second language education* (pp. 61–99). Cambridge, England: Cambridge University Press.

Mathison, S. (2008). What is the difference between evaluation and research—and why do we care? In N. L. Smith & P. R. Brandon (Eds.), *Fundamental issues in evaluation* (pp. 183–196). New York, NY: Guilford.

McDavid, J. C., & Hawthorn, L. R. L. (2006). *Program evaluation & performance measurement: An introduction to practice.* Thousand Oaks, CA: Sage.

Mitchell, R. (1992). The independent evaluation of bilingual primary education: A narrative account. In J. C. Alderson & A. Beretta (Eds.), *Evaluating second language education* (pp. 100–140). Cambridge, England: Cambridge University Press.

Nunan, D. (1988). *Syllabus design*. Oxford, England: Oxford University Press.

Posavac, E. J., & Carey, R. G. (1985). *Program evaluation: Methods and case studies* (2nd ed.). Englewood Cliffs, NJ: Prentice-Hall.

Rava, S. (2000). The changing face of the intermediate language curriculum. *Foreign Language Annals, 33*(3), 342–348.

Riazi, A.M., & Mosalanejad, N. (2010). Evaluation of learning objectives in Iranian high-school and pre-university English textbooks using Bloom's taxonomy. *TESL-EJ, 13*(4). Retrieved April 10, 2013, from http://www.tesl-ej.org/wordpress/issues/volume13/ej52/ej52a5/

Richards, J. C. (2001). *Curriculum development in language teaching*. Cambridge, England: Cambridge University Press.

Rogers, N.J., LeCompte, L., & Plumly, V. (2012). Articulating the curriculum through cultural themes: A literacy and genre approach to teaching protest, rebellion, and the reevaluation of the past. *Die Unterrichtpraxis, 45*(1), 40–52.

Sanders, R. (2005). Redesigning introductory Spanish: Increased enrollment, online management, cost reduction, and effects on student learning. *Foreign Language Annals, 38*, 523–532.

Scriven, M. (1991). *Evaluation thesaurus* (4th ed.). Thousand Oaks, CA: Sage.

Swaffar, J., & Arens, K. (2005). *Remapping the foreign language curriculum*. New York, NY: Modern Language Association of America.

Unterberger, B. (2012). English-medium programmes at Austrian business faculties: A status quo survey on national trends and a case study on programme design and delivery. In U. Smit & E. Dafouz (Eds.), *AILA review* (Vol. 25): *Integrating content and language in higher education* (pp. 80–100). Amsterdam, the Netherlands: John Benjamins.

2

Models of Second Language Course Evaluation

Evaluation models[1] are introduced in this chapter, with ideas on what a model should do for a course teacher/evaluator and why evaluation needs a model to begin with. Depending on what model an evaluator uses, the purpose, scope, and direction of the evaluation changes entirely. Four evaluation models used in second language education are described. Finally, the *stakeholders, outcomes, assessment,* and *curriculum* (SOAC) model is introduced and briefly explained. The SOAC (pronounced soak) model is explored in many of the remaining chapters in the book.

A n evaluation model is a plan or a theory that has the function of guiding a teacher/evaluator on how to plan and do a course evaluation. In the quote at the beginning of this chapter, Eisenhower suggests that "life

---

1. For all terms in *italics*, see Glossary.

Evaluating Second Language Courses, pages 17–32
Copyright © 2016 by Information Age Publishing
All rights of reproduction in any form reserved.

happens" and can shred a plan without warning, which is likely true. But we also wholeheartedly agree with him that the process of planning is indispensable for focusing ideas on what to accomplish and how to proceed. Thinking more about the tension between plans (a product) and planning (a process) leads to consideration of categories such as the **expected**, the **unexpected**, **accountability**, and **insight**. An evaluation model is designed to deal directly with issues of the expected results and accountability, but can deal only indirectly with the unexpected and insightful. Yet, especially for classroom teachers, the unexpected and insight may be as valuable in an evaluation as the expected and accountability issues—maybe even more so.

In the context of course evaluation, evaluation models are not distant things in a different, abstract world. Rather, they are real and practical things of our world that help us focus our thinking and planning to do the very real and practical undertaking of a course evaluation. An evaluation model should thus accomplish at least three things:

1. An evaluation model should list and describe all major areas of a course
2. A model should suggest important relationships between areas in a course to evaluate
3. A model should give us ideas on where to begin

By areas of a course, we mean the basic building blocks of a course, such as the curriculum, outcomes, assessments used in the course, and stakeholders. These course areas can be consciously related to each other in order to do course evaluation. One course evaluation project might be to examine the congruence of the course assessments to the course curriculum, for example. As will be seen later in this chapter, these course areas are in fact components of a course evaluation model we propose: the stakeholders, outcomes, assessment, and curriculum (SOAC) model.

DISCUSSION QUESTION 1

Can you think of one or two questions you would like for a course evaluation to answer? What course areas do your questions seem to focus on? Do any of your questions seem to focus on two course areas at the same time? What might the relationship between the two areas of a course be?

Why Use an Evaluation Model?

Without an evaluation model, a teacher/evaluator is likely to fall back on a research design such as the experimental design (Henry & Roseberry,

1998) or a set of learning principles (Mitchell, 1992, p. 103) as the default evaluation position. If, say, the experimental design is used, this would limit the teacher/evaluator to the types of questions, data collection, and analyses that an experimental design promotes. This might work for some course evaluations where the teacher/evaluator wishes to pose limited *evaluation questions* (EQs), such as "Does this type of instructional treatment with Group X result in better scores on XX measure compared to Group Y who has not had the instructional treatment?" An experimental design would not be appropriate for broader EQs, which are far more common in evaluation. These would be questions such as "What are the *goals* of this course? How did they come about? Are they effective? Are they consonant with the needs or values of learners, teachers, and school administrators? Are the goals met effectively? What can be improved?" For a typical course evaluation many more kinds of *data collection instruments* (interviews and questionnaires, for instance) and *data collection protocols* (deciding to observe a class multiple times, for instance) would be needed than would comfortably "fit" in an experimental research model. Significantly, in course evaluation we wish to focus on a course without having to arrange a control group that does not "have" the course, as in an experimental design. Although courses are sometimes compared in evaluation, it is rare that two language courses taken as a whole are so similar that you could use one as an experimental group and another as a control group.

Evaluation Model Orientations

An evaluation model is a theory about what the components of a course or program are, and how they relate to each other. An evaluation model guides the planning and processes of an evaluation. Evaluation models fall into general orientations, which point to an evaluation purpose. For instance is an evaluation for accountability purposes, or to inform and illuminate details of how a course works? This may not seem like much of a difference, but in fact these two different purposes imply vast differences in what evaluation questions (EQs) will be asked, what data will be collected, and how the data will be interpreted and reported, and finally, used. For instance, Madaus and Kellaghan (2000) describe evaluation models such as "objectives/goals-based" and "cost-based evaluation" (pp. 26–27), which assume that an evaluation is conducted for the purpose of comparing a course with some predetermined, externally set "bottom line." Using such "factory model" evaluation models, assigning worth to a course would involve assuming that "no part of the curriculum process is unique and each part is reproducible" (Madaus & Kellaghan, 2000, p. 21). This implies that each part of a course could be boiled down to a quantifiable variable, such as learners' "time on task" or "amount of time spent interacting in the L2" or "percentage of teacher's use of L2 in classes." The results from the data would be reported for the benefit of external others to show that a course was still worth offering, or that a set of course goals was being met.

In contrast, a "responsive" or "illuminative" evaluation model "orients more directly to program activities than to program intents" (Madaus & Kellaghan, 2000, p. 29) and accounts for "how it [a *curricular innovation*] is influenced by the various school situations in which it is applied" (p. 30). This is the insight referred to earlier. Various parts of a course curriculum are not seen as an objective reality, and many parts of courses are more complex than we think and should not be reduced to a quantifiable variable. Thus, in order to account for this complexity, "time on task" should not be treated as something equal when done by two different instructors with different teaching philosophies and outlooks on learning. Observations of time on task and interviews of learners and instructors would be needed to understand how this aspect of a course operated, and how, on its own merits, it affected the experiences of learners in the course. Such data would be used for teachers/evaluators' immediate use and edification rather than some more distant administrators trying to decide to continue funding a course.

There are many evaluation models described in the mainstream evaluation field (see for example Shadish, Cook, & Leviton, 1991; Stufflebeam, Madaus, & Kellaghan, 2000; Stufflebeam & Shinkfield, 2007). Stufflebeam (2000) lists, describes, and evaluates 22 models or approaches he characterizes as the product of the 20th century expansion of the field of evaluation. He underscores how different evaluation models are influenced by "their authors' beliefs and experiences" (Stufflebeam, 2000, p. 34) with different strengths and shortcomings. In this chapter we present an evaluation model (stakeholders, outcomes, assessments, and curriculum) designed for second and foreign language courses, which we think will provide structure and direction for teachers/evaluators working on a variety of EQs for a variety of purposes.

DISCUSSION QUESTION 2

What sort of orientation of evaluation models do you think you would like to use? Given the few aforementioned examples, which general orientation of evaluation models seems to be connected to the EQs you are interested in?

DISCUSSION QUESTION 3

How might you look for or at least be open to the unexpected?

Evaluation Models in Second Language Education

Four evaluation models from the second language education field are described here in roughly chronological order. These models are useful in that they demonstrate the historical connections between evaluation in our own field and that of general evaluation. In describing these historical models, foundational concepts in course evaluation are described and reinforced (see Chapters 1 and 9). See Appendix B for a bibliography of articles, book chapters, and books about evaluation, many of which include evaluation models.

Hargreaves' Proto-Model

Hargreaves (1989) presented a well-developed checklist, which can be interpreted as a proto-evaluation model, or a model in the making. Each aspect of the 12 points on the checklist is called a "factor" and can include any number of teaching situations. The model does not precisely serve as a guide to posing EQs or planning data collection, or relating the major areas of a course evaluation to each other. For its time, however, the proto-model brought up key considerations for a course evaluation. We work with many of the same considerations in current second language course evaluation, and in this book. See Table 2.1.

In the checklist, Item 1 referred to target audience, which we would call stakeholder identification. Item 2 on the checklist called upon readers to identify an evaluation purpose, which was stated as either summative (for

TABLE 2.1   Hargreaves' Evaluator's Checklist
1. Identify target audience
2. Identify evaluation purpose
3. Determine evaluation focus (causes, and intended and unintended effects)
4. Name evaluation criteria
5. Decide evaluation method
6. Develop data collection plans
7. Identify who is going an evaluation
8. List resources for doing an evaluation
9. Consider time factors
10. Determine what to do with evaluation findings
11. Present the findings (results)
12. Follow up

Source: Adapted from Hargreaves (1989)

accountability) or formative (for illumination and improvement). Item 3 focused on identifying causes (say, a textbook) and effects (changes in learning), suggesting a traditional reliance on the tried-and-true experimental research design. Item 4 directed the evaluator to choose criteria for assigning worth to whatever was being evaluated. Item 5 broadened the notion of evaluation criteria by suggesting criteria be divided into global criteria supplied by experts external to the program and locally developed criteria based on the program being evaluated. Item 6 in the checklist called for evaluators to identify their data collection instruments and data collection protocols (a working plan for collecting data). This item was called "means/instruments" in the checklist, and called for identification of data to be collected before the course evaluation, such as a data collection protocol for document retrieval. This item also called for identification of data to be collected during the course evaluation, using such *data collection instruments* as tests or observation checklists to show changes in learners' language learning or use.

Item 7 in the checklist involved listing agents, or all those involved in doing the evaluation and the roles they played; and Item 8 called for an identification of resources to conduct the course evaluation including people or money. Item 9 called for planning how much time it might take to do a course evaluation, and trying to ensure that it was done quickly enough so that improvements suggested by the evaluation could be made while the course was still under way (see Formative Evaluation, Chapter 4). Hargreaves noted that doing evaluation takes much more money and time and effort than most evaluators think, suggesting an assumption that he thought it would be teachers doing an evaluation without much previous experience. Item 10 called for ensuring that all parties concerned agreed on what sort of decisions could be made based on the findings before beginning the course evaluation. In other words, would the recommendations (decisions) based on the findings be "mandatory and binding" or "advisory" (p. 43)? Item 11 called for a consideration of how to present the results to different stakeholders. Finally, Item 12 called for a follow-up on how recommendations suggested by the evaluation were implemented.

Genesee and Upshur's Strategy for Classroom-Based Evaluation

Genesee and Upshur (1996, p. 43) proposed what they called a strategy for classroom-based evaluation involving comparisons of five key aspects of second language education. Each comparison was meant to represent a possible evaluation study. Their first comparison was input factors (teacher abilities or time allocated to the class) with instructional purposes (the rationale for the course or program). The second comparison was between instructional purposes and instructional plans (*syllabuses* and stated instructional approaches). The third comparison was between instructional plans and instructional practices (the instruction that actually took place). The fourth comparison was of input factors and instructional practices, and the fifth and final comparison was of the actual course outcomes and instructional purposes (the course or program rationale). Genesee and Upshur's thinking was that these comparisons were "central components of instruction" (p. 36) and that teachers might find aspects of "input factors" they could change and then evaluate. This model was complex because it attempted to capture the complexity of second and foreign language classroom activities and processes, which form the building blocks of courses and programs. For all the richness of the model and its then-timely placement of evaluation activities directly in classrooms, the model may assume a lot of evaluation experience on the part of teachers/evaluators.

Lynch's Context-Adaptive Model

Lynch (1996) offered his context-adaptive model, which was composed of seven steps. Some of these steps were articulated as very detailed checklists, most notably the model component in which the program is described. This model was more oriented to program evaluation, or the evaluation of multiple courses thought to comprise a program of second language study. The model was presented as consecutive steps, perhaps to represent the order in which a program evaluation was to be carried out. The first step was identification of the evaluation audience and goals of the evaluation. The second step was to describe in detail the program (called a "context inventory," Lynch, 1996, p. 5), for example, the availability of valid and reliable tests, and the intensity and duration of classes. The third step called for constructing a preliminary thematic framework of stated concerns of stakeholders (the evaluation "audience") to focus the evaluation. For instance, only a new instructional approach might be evaluated across classes, or the program evaluation might focus on only the portions of the program that involved second language reading, because these were the issues stakeholders were concerned about.

The fourth step was deciding on types of data collection, which were seen as constrained and guided by elements of the context (the program). For instance if program staff were hostile to the evaluation or if valid tests were not locally available, these might change how data would be collected. Thus, an evaluator may reduce the number of classroom observations, or focus more of his or her time on developing locally valid tests. The fifth and sixth steps were data collection and data analysis, which called for efforts to ensure validity of data collection processes. The data collection processes were organized conceptually into data used for a summative report (assigning worth to end results) and data used for a formative report (assigning worth to ongoing processes). The final, seventh step was to create and submit one or more evaluation reports to predetermined audiences for the program evaluation. This model, with its focus on describing the program context, reflected the author's making sense of the chaos that confronted him when evaluating a foreign language program he had little advance experience with. This from-the-outside-looking-in perspective was intriguing and was timely in that several "outsider" evaluations of foreign language programs were being done including Beretta (1986) working in India, and Alderson and Scott (1992) working in Brazil.

Norris's Utilization-Focused Evaluation

Norris (2008) promoted utilization-focused evaluation consisting of four steps. By utilization focused, Norris meant that he was primarily concerned that the evaluation process and results would actually be used to improve programs so that "specific intended users" could address "priority questions" (p. 78). In the first and second steps, stakeholders were to be identified and then quizzed about their needs or concerns in order to narrow down and agree on the use of the evaluation. In the third step, he called for a determination of design and evaluation methods. In a fourth and final step, he called for the results to be reported but with the key condition that "local expertise of primary intended users" be called upon so that "evaluation outcomes can be used in program-meaningful ways" (Norris, 2008, p. 82). This reflected his concern, still current in general evaluation circles, that evaluations be useful to educators and other evaluation stakeholders (Madaus & Kellaghan, 2000; Mangan, 2013).

DISCUSSION QUESTION 4

In looking at these three historical models is it possible to see the basic areas of a course we mentioned earlier, those of curriculum, outcomes, assessments, and stakeholders? They may not be stated exactly as curriculum, for example, but appear nonetheless under different names. What are other names for the course areas?

DISCUSSION QUESTION 5

We understand our descriptions of these historical models are limited. Nevertheless, given the short descriptions, which of these models attract you? Why? What does an evaluation model need to be so it is most useful to you?

The SOAC Course Evaluation Model

The SOAC model is specifically aimed at second language evaluation (Griffee & Gevara, 2011). SOAC stands for stakeholders, outcomes, assessment, and curriculum. We use the terms course evaluation and program evaluation interchangeably because even though this book focuses on course evaluation, we believe the model has utility for evaluation at both the levels of course and program. See Figure 2.1.

We will spend some time now defining the components of the model, including the world, stakeholders, the *evaluand*, and outcomes, assessment, and curriculum. We also suggest relationships between the components and how these relationships offer ways to think about and proceed with different course evaluation projects: The relationships are the arrows and lines in the model.

World

The world is something outside the course or program, but which is relevant to the course in the sense that it affects the course by making the

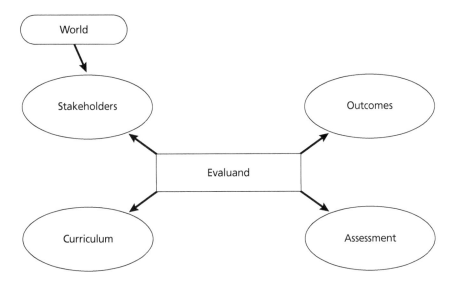

Figure 2.1   The SOAC model for second language evaluation.

course necessary or shaping what the course ends up being. For instance, if a university wants to increase undergraduate student enrollments over time (e.g., Cook, 2011), all of the new undergraduate students are going to need to enroll in required courses such as chemistry and biology labs, and math classes. Those labs and classes are going to need instructors, which in the United States are, by and large, nonnative English speaking graduate students in chemistry, biology, and math. In order to ensure more international teaching assistants come to Texas Tech but more importantly also qualify to teach in terms of their English communication ability, the current ITA (international teaching assistant) preparation course will need to be offered more. The current course will perhaps also need to be changed to accommodate more ITAs per class. A course evaluation might be needed to know whether larger classes can still result in acceptable outcomes (ITAs communicating in English better), or to suggest new, more effective instructional methods. Thus the world might be thought of as the environment, a problem, the real world, reality, a situation, or society. The world is everything, yet is not course stakeholders. Rather, it is more the circumstances in which stakeholders find themselves, hence the arrow going from the world to stakeholders in the SOAC model (Figure 2.1). The world provides a motivation, but perhaps not the only motivation, for both research and course evaluation.

DISCUSSION QUESTION 6

How would you describe the world from where you are right now as a language teacher, language learner, or graduate student? What is a course you are teaching or taking now, and how did the world make the course necessary?

Stakeholders

This component includes persons or groups interested in the existence and results of a course. Stakeholders would include teachers, students, and supervisors, but could also refer to parents, faculty, school administrators, future employers, textbook publishers, and the government. Each stakeholder group has their own values and concerns. The stakeholders' component also includes institutional policies where the evaluand exists. Finally, needs analysis is an important part of the stakeholders' component, because a needs analysis is the means and method by which a teacher/evaluator constructs the identity of stakeholders for the purpose of the course evaluation. Another way to look at this is to see a needs analysis as suggested by the relationship between the stakeholders' component, and the outcomes and world components of the model (Chapter 4). Note the arrows connecting the three components through the evaluand.

DISCUSSION QUESTION 7

In your own words, what is the difference between stakeholders and the world? How does the world affect stakeholders, such as you, a teacher or learner?

DISCUSSION QUESTION 8

Can you identify some of your stakeholders?

DISCUSSION QUESTION 9

Which stakeholders are usually not included?

Evaluand

The evaluand component represents that part of the course or program we are interested in evaluating, such as the materials, or the course outcomes, or the system of placement of students into a class. The teacher/evaluator is the person doing the course evaluation. For most second language teachers/evaluators, the evaluand is usually a course or part of a course, or a program, such as a study abroad program. Note that the evaluand is at the center of the four main components of the model: stakeholders, outcomes, assessment, and curriculum. The SOAC evaluation model posits that whatever is being evaluated, it is composed of the four main components; hence, the arrows pointing from the four SOAC model components to the evaluand. It is these four areas of interest, and their relationships to each other with reference to the evaluand, that guide the course evaluation. This idea will be developed in later chapters of this book.

DISCUSSION QUESTION 10

What do you think will be the evaluand in your course evaluation?

Outcomes

The outcomes component includes what are referred to as *goals*, course *objectives*, or learning outcomes. Goals, or some similar term, are usually listed in a course syllabus and announce to stakeholders: This is what I want to do and you can hold me accountable for it. The outcomes component also includes considerations of course purpose, mission statements, policy recommendations, how much time there is for a course to meet, and teaching staff number and qualification constraints, all of which may form parts of a course evaluation. This component also includes writing course evaluation reports in the sense that the report itself will be used to describe outcomes to whoever is interested (stakeholders, including the teacher/ evaluator). The outcomes component has a significant relationship with curriculum (note the arrow from one component to the other through the evaluand). Considering the two together suggests that course evaluation investigate whether the outcomes and curriculum are in accord. In other words, is the curriculum up to supporting the outcomes? We will explore this relationship in Chapter 5 by considering a *course logic* study.

Assessment

Assessment is a complex component, but we will describe the basic aspects here. We also take up assessment in a more detailed way in later chapters. Overall, assessment is concerned with measurement, in the sense of having a direct relationship with the course outcomes. In essence, when we state outcomes for a course, we then must find the most appropriate, clear, and credible ways to understand and describe learner and instructor activity to investigate whether course outcomes are met. Note here the relationship, depicted by arrows, between assessment and outcomes in the model. For instance, if one course outcome is that college-level foreign language learners should be able to write with reasonable grammatical accuracy in French, then assessments must be designed and used to discover whether learners met the outcomes. In the case of Adair-Hauck, Willingham-McLain, and Young (2000), foreign language learners were given three writing assessments that presumably measured grammatical accuracy: One at the beginning of the semester, one in the middle, and one at the end of the semester. Tests such as these are data collection instruments that require validation and reliability estimation to ensure they are collecting the data the teacher/evaluator thinks they should collect, and doing so consistently.

There is a strong element of credibility here, in the sense of whether a teacher/evaluator has adequately demonstrated to stakeholders and readers of evaluation reports whether his or her data collection instruments, and indeed their evaluation design, is valid. In Chapter 7, Chapter 8, and especially Chapter 10 on reading and assessing evaluation publications (RAPS), we provide multiple criteria for judging the clarity and credibility of the assessments used in evaluation reports. Against these criteria, Adair-Hauck, et al. (2000) would be commended for providing evidence that two raters agreed on learners' French writing test scores. This evidence suggests learners are being measured consistently. But then they would be criticized for not providing the actual tests in an appendix with more practical explanations of what the evaluators thought their tests were measuring and how that related to the course outcomes. Evidence would be lacking here as to whether the tests (data collection instruments) were accurately and clearly measuring learners' progress toward course outcomes.

Curriculum

Finally, the curriculum component includes all the ways the course or program responds to circumstances in the world, which are then interpreted as a learning need by stakeholders. Curriculum is often used as another word for a course or program itself because it contains all aspects of the course including materials, class exercises, textbooks, handouts, lectures, and relevant domain theories, such as the belief that input and learner interaction bring about acquisition). Curriculum also includes time available, formal teaching methods (such as the direct method, or the communicative method), and teacher theories. Teacher theories are implicit beliefs held by teachers on what ought to take place in the classroom. Complete descriptions of a curriculum are essential for a course evaluation in that the very process of describing brings about clarity about the aspect of a course that is being evaluated (the evaluand) and the evaluation questions (EQs). As described earlier, the curriculum component has significant relationships with outcomes and other components, each of which suggests a course evaluation project, which will be explored in more detail in subsequent chapters.

DISCUSSION QUESTION 11

With which SOAC component are you most familiar?

DISCUSSION QUESTION 12

With which SOAC component are you least familiar?

DISCUSSION QUESTION 13

What might account for your answer to either Question 7 or 8?

Course Evaluation and the Stakeholders, Outcomes, Assessment, and Curriculum Evaluation Model

Based on the stakeholders, outcomes, assessment, and curriculum (SOAC) model, course evaluation can be defined as the process of identifying whether and how course outcomes, consistent with stakeholder values, and measured by locally validated data collection instruments, are accomplished by a curriculum. Each component of SOAC includes multiple facets as we have suggested in our previous descriptions. For example, curriculum can include anything from classroom exercises to textbooks to teacher's talk. The components are open-ended and yet limited in number. Compare the number of components in SOAC to the historical evaluation models described earlier in this chapter. If every possible aspect of course evaluation were identified in the SOAC model, it would be overly complex. Thus, the important relationships between the components that create a basis for specific activities for course evaluation would be less apparent. In subsequent chapters we will more closely define each component, but more importantly, how the components are related to each other. It is in considering the relationship between say, outcomes and curriculum, which helps form evaluation questions (EQs) and guide the course evaluation.

DISCUSSION QUESTION 14

Does the definition of course evaluation make sense to you? Can you explain it to a colleague or classmate?

APPLICATION TASKS: Explaining a Component of the SOAC Model to a Colleague

First task idea: Examine one or more of the five second language evaluation models against the three criteria given on p. 26. How do the models stand up against the idea that a model should identify parts of a course, the relationships between the course parts, and where to begin an evaluation?

Second task idea: Choose one of the components of the stakeholders, outcomes, assessment, and curriculum model that is interesting to you and explain it to your colleagues or classmates. As much as you can, use your own teaching situation or program to illustrate the SOAC component you choose to describe. Make notes of anything you had trouble explaining, or of questions your colleagues had that you could not answer. Find the answers you need by finding it in this book, or from a senior colleague or faculty member.

References

Adair-Hauck, B., Willingham-McLain, L., & Youngs, B. (2000). Evaluating the integration of technology and second language learning. *CALICO, 17*(2), 269–306. Retrieved from https://calico.org/memberBrowse.php?action=article&id=509

Alderson, J. C., & Scott, M. (1992). Insiders, outsiders and participatory evaluation. In J.C. Alderson & A. Beretta (Eds.), *Evaluating second language education* (pp. 25–60). Cambridge, England: Cambridge University Press.

Beretta, A. (1986). Toward a methodology of ESL program evaluation. *TESOL Quarterly, 20*(1), 144–55.

Cook, C. (2011). Texas Tech once again sets fall enrollment record. *Texas Tech Today*. Retrieved May 3, 2013, from http://today.ttu.edu/2011/09/fall-enrollment-2011/

Genesee, F., & Upshur, J. A. (1996). *Classroom-based evaluation in second language education.* Cambridge, England: Cambridge University Press.

Griffee, D. T., & Gevara, J. R. (2011). Standard setting in the post-modern era for an ITA performance test. *Texas Papers in Foreign Language Education, 15*(1), 3–16. Retrieved from http://studentorgs.utexas.edu/flesa/TP-FLE_New/Index.htm

Hargreaves, P. (1989). DES-IMPL-EVALU-IGN: An evaluator's checklist. In R. K. Johnson (Ed.), *The second-language curriculum* (pp. 35–47). Cambridge, England: Cambridge University Press.

Henry, A., & Roseberry, R. L. (1998). An evaluation of a genre-based approach to the teaching of EAP/ESP writing. *TESOL Quarterly, 32*(1), 147–156.

Lynch, B. K. (1996). *Language program evaluation: Theory and practice.* Cambridge, England: Cambridge University Press.

Madaus, G., & Kellaghan, T. (2000). Models, metaphors, and definitions in evaluation. In D. L. Stufflebeam, G. F. Madaus, & T. Kellaghan (Eds.), *Evaluation models: Viewpoints on educational and human services evaluation* (pp. 19–31). Norwell, MA: Kluwer.

Mangan, K. (2013). Florida colleges make plans for students to opt out of remedial work. *The Week, 55*(4), pp. A4–A7.

Mitchell, R. (1992). The independent evaluation of bilingual primary education: A narrative account. In J. C. Alderson & A. Beretta (Eds.), *Evaluating second language education* (pp. 100–140). Cambridge, England: Cambridge University Press.

Norris, J. M. (2008). *Validity evaluation in language assessment.* New York, NY: Peter Lang.

Shadish, W., Cook, T., & Leviton, L. (1991). *Foundations of program evaluation.* Newbury Park, CA: Sage.

Stufflebeam, D. L. (2000). Foundational models for 21st century program evaluation. In D. L. Stufflebeam, G. F. Madaus, & T. Kellaghan (Eds.), *Evaluation models: Viewpoints on educational and human services evaluation* (pp. 33–83). Norwell, MA: Kluwer.

Stufflebeam, D., Madaus, G., & Kellaghan, T. (Eds.). (2000). *Evaluation models: Viewpoints on educational and human services evaluation.* Boston, MA: Kluwer Academic.

Stufflebeam, D., & Shinkfield, A. (2007). *Evaluation theory, models, & applications.* San Francisco, CA: Jossey-Bass.

3

Stakeholders and Outcomes, the World, and Outcomes Validation

Musashi wrote that the journey of a thousand ri began with the first step.
A stranger in her native country, Cat drew a deep breath
of chill winter air and took the first step.
—St. Clair Robson (1991, p. 50)

This chapter explores in detail the relationships between the SOAC model components the *world,*[1] *stakeholders,* and *outcomes.* This enables us to see a course we teach in an entirely new way by investigating the reasons for the course to exist in the first place. The idea of course outcomes (objectives) is explained and connected to historical thinking in education. This in turn connects us to the field of general evaluation, from which second language course evaluation borrows with great benefit. An outcome validation study is described, and the results of an outcome validation study are given for a second language course taught in the United States.

The next six chapters apply the stakeholders, outcomes, assessment, and curriculum model (SOAC) by describing the components of the

---

1. For all terms in *italics,* see Glossary.

Evaluating Second Language Courses, pages 33–49

model in more detail through an exploration of the relationships between two or more components. Specific types of projects are given for each of the six chapters and are designed to integrate theory (the model) and practice (what teachers/evaluators do). This chapter and the next illuminate the relationship between SOAC model components world, stakeholders, and outcomes. This chapter focuses on outcomes in detail and includes one project, *outcome validation*. The outcome validation project examines existing statements of course outcomes through a critical, empirical process. This project has the aim of clarifying and illuminating existing course outcomes, and understanding them well. A further consideration is: Given limited time and resources, and the sometimes contradictory opinions of stakeholders about the course, are the stated or revealed outcomes the appropriate outcomes to pursue?

These are important first steps, and almost never taken in the second and foreign language education field. Before we evaluate the worth of a course, we need to know the worth of the outcomes. In the quote at the beginning of this chapter, the fictional character Cat begins a long journey in 18th century Japan, which she believes will result in a satisfying revenge. At the outset, she understands she will learn unexpected things. This is what outcome validation reveals to teachers/evaluators who believe they understand thoroughly the course they are teaching, only to find they are in many ways strangers in what they take to be their native country.

DISCUSSION QUESTION 1

Name one or more outcomes of a course you are teaching. It may be easier to think of these as things you want your students to learn, or to understand as a result of participating in your course. Are these outcomes the ones you formulated, or are they outcomes mentioned in a syllabus you "inherited" or had little input into?

DISCUSSION QUESTION 2

If you asked your colleagues, or your supervisor, or faculty members what the outcomes were for your course, would their answers be similar, or might they be something different?

The World and Stakeholders

As we noted in previous chapters, stakeholders are persons who have an interest in the outcomes of a course, and also a course evaluation. Stakeholders are students, policy makers, teachers, colleagues, supervisors, higher-level administrators, and even future employers. Alderson (1992) noted that because various stakeholders may have different values and interests in an evaluation, stakeholder identification is important to help sort out these interests. Teachers may wish to better understand how learners use the assigned materials (evaluation for understanding), while higher-level administrators may wish to know how many learners are satisfied with a course (*summative evaluation*). The reason different stakeholders have different values and interests is a reflection of their living and doing their jobs in what we call the world, which affects each stakeholder group differently.

The world is the set of circumstances that are relevant to a course in the sense that the circumstances affect the course by making the course necessary or shaping what the course ends up being. In Chapter 2 we gave an example of the world as one American university wanting to push up their undergraduate enrollments, thus building a need for more international graduate students (nonnative English speakers) in science and math to provide teaching in more science labs and discussion sections for more undergraduates. Thus classroom-communication-in-English courses for these international teaching assistants (ITAs) became more necessary, and a visible focus of contention. The students (ITAs) in the course valued getting through the course as soon as possible, and getting whatever single "score" they needed to qualify to be science lab instructors. The supervisors of the ITAs in the science departments valued much the same thing, and in addition applied pressure to increase the size of the ITA preparation course classes. The teachers of the ITA course valued multiple, well-defined assessments grounded in language-teaching-field-specific models of communicative competence, and struggled to keep class sizes small. One can see how some of the three different stakeholders' values and conceptions of learner need overlapped, but also how they did not. Each stakeholder group responded differently to the world. Stakeholders' sometimes diverse perspectives can provide significant counterpoints during outcome validation and needs analysis studies, where teachers/evaluators consider the origins or meaning or worth of the outcomes of an existing course.

DISCUSSION QUESTION 3

Why does your course exist? What function does it fill? For whom?

Course Outcomes

By outcomes we mean the aims, *goals*, or *objectives* of a course. Whether we use the term outcome or goal or objective, outcomes are statements about hoped-for changes in learners as a result of participating in a course. In essence, outcomes are statements of intention. Statements of outcomes may be found on course syllabuses or program websites, and are sometimes called course purposes, mission statements, or aims. Outcomes are a key point of our SOAC course evaluation model in that outcomes are the focal lenses through which all other components of the model are viewed. This is why an outcome validation project is so useful. It clarifies the outcomes that the course, and the course evaluation, revolve around. Stating course outcomes, or doing an outcome validation study, does not predetermine an evaluation to be summative, or done for accountability. Doing a course outcome validation study simply makes clearer for us the context of a course. As will be discussed below, there are some educators and researchers who distrust the idea of outcomes, which, perhaps in their minds, means an automatic focus on accountability, or perhaps a rigid and unresponsive approach to teaching and learning.

Some Important History From Curriculum: What Are Course Objectives/Outcomes?

Outcomes are commonly called goals or objectives, which are a familiar part of education and are usually required for syllabus design (Nunan, 1988). Goals and objectives were key concepts in early considerations of education evaluation. Ralph Tyler (1902–1994) is acknowledged as an early and prominent advocate of using objectives (Stufflebeam, 2000). Tyler himself used the term objective, and thus many discussions resulting from his work use the same term. In this book, we use objective, goal, and outcome interchangeably. Tyler (1966) became interested in course objectives and the role they play in evaluation while doing a longitudinal evaluation of high schools called "The Eight-Year Study from 1934 to 1942" (Tyler & Smith, 1942). Tyler further developed his conceptual understanding of objectives as a result of his teaching a curriculum course at the University of Chicago (Tyler, 1949). For Tyler, education was a process that aimed to produce changes in students, and these desired changes could be identified and discussed as educational objectives. A course objective, therefore, can be defined as a desired change in students as a result of their participation in a curriculum.

Tyler was asking educators to clearly state what learning they expected from students, which at the time was not usual. Educators typically used a textbook to create tests, and then asked students to demonstrate knowledge by giving back what was in the textbook. Tyler was asking teachers to think about their students rather than themselves. For instance: When pressed to say their course purpose, teachers might say "We will cover eight major novelists in English and American literature and go over their contributions." The kind of objective Tyler had more in mind was "At the conclusion of the course the student will describe the major contributions of each novelist studied during the semester" (example from Popham, 2013, p. 98). We might add how students would demonstrate what they knew, and to what depth of demonstrated knowledge would be sufficient. In an interview, Tyler recalled how he worked with English teachers to develop learning objectives for their literature classes (Tyler & Nowakowski, 1981). The teachers wanted their students to appreciate literature. Tyler pushed them to say what they had observed in students' behavior that told them students were in fact appreciating literature.

DISCUSSION QUESTION 4

Thinking about a lesson you taught or a textbook chapter you used in class recently, what are two or three things you can say learners might be able to do as a result of being at the lesson or using the textbook pages? How would you know whether learners could do those things?

The Historical Present: Problems With Objectives, and Solutions to the Problems

From the time of Tyler, problems with objectives surfaced, and are still the subject of discussion today. Eisner (1967), Alderson (1992), Stufflebeam (2000), and Richards (2001) are good sources for understanding these problems. A summary of problems, as well as general solutions in the literature, and solutions specific to the SOAC evaluation model are given in Table 3.1.

TABLE 3.1 Problems With Objectives, General Solutions, and SOAC Model Solutions

Problems with objectives	General solutions	SOAC evaluation model solutions
1. Objectives are not themselves evaluated.	Evaluate the objectives.	Do an outcome study and a needs analysis to evaluate outcomes. (Chapters 3, 4)
2. Some objectives do not seem measurable.	Probe the objectives.	Do a course logic study. (Chapter 5)
3. Some objectives are, or should be, abandoned.	Test the objectives.	Do a needs analysis. Chapter 4)
4. Additional objectives become desirable.	Test the objectives.	Do a formative evaluation. (Chapter 6)
5. Unintended consequences are not taken into account.	Throw a wide net in order to consider all consequences.	Use formative evaluation to discern unintended consequences. (Chapter 6)

Problem 1: Objectives Themselves Are Not Evaluated

The first problem is that while measurable course objectives can be devised, and data gotten from them (quiz scores, evidence of changes in student behavior using observation checklists, etc.), the objectives themselves are often not evaluated. It is true in many education settings that we are handed a course to teach where outcomes or objectives are implicitly or explicitly stated. To meet the problem that course objectives are uncritically accepted, we must devise a way to evaluate them. The SOAC evaluation model stipulates an outcome validation study in this chapter, during which course objectives are systematically evaluated from multiple points of view. In this chapter, we describe and explain how to do an outcome validation study and provide an example study. Objectives can also be evaluated by doing a needs analysis (Chapter 4), which relates the world to stakeholders' perceptions of needs in an attempt to see how current course objectives address those needs. Objectives are evaluated in terms of their adequacy to hold in tension sometimes diverging stakeholder perceptions and the demands of the world, which affect each stakeholder group differently.

Problem 2: Some Objectives Do Not Seem Measurable

Some course objectives may not seem measurable. This could point to an objective that is not well defined. Indeed, some of our course objectives, upon closer inspection, turn out to be a bit of a mystery to us and to others. One example is a common wish among teachers that their students develop a more positive attitude about communicating in the second language. This begs the question: What constitutes a positive attitude? For that matter, what proven methods have been shown to bring about more positive learner attitudes in second language courses? Is it something that ought even to be attempted? Answers to these probing questions could reveal how changes in learners' attitudes could be measured, or whether it is even worth doing so. Thus a reasonable solution would be to probe unclear or vague objectives using a course logic study (Chapter 5). A course logic study examines the assumptions of how a curriculum (classes, materials, teaching, etc.) is supposed to bring about desired outcomes. An outcome validation study would also be useful to clarify unclear, seemingly unmeasurable outcomes.

Problem 3: Some Objectives Are or Should Be Abandoned

Some objectives get abandoned, which is seen as a problem by some. This, however, is not necessarily a weakness in terms of the idea of having course objectives. One would hope that in testing or examining course objectives using a needs analysis (Chapter 4), perhaps meaningless or nonfunctioning objectives would be eliminated. If that were the case, a description of the process by which that decision was reached would be appropriate.

Problem 4: Additional Objectives Become Desirable

It is often true that as a course is underway, some additional objectives may need to be formulated. Those who are critical of objectives in general complain that thinking in terms of objectives makes it impossible for courses to change as needed while underway in response to some unexpected development. Perhaps learners were able to do more, or less, in some area of second language use than we thought at the beginning of a course. We disagree, and suggest that existing objectives can be tested, and new objectives formulated using formative evaluation. *Formative evaluation* (Chapter 6) is a process whereby stakeholders, often students in a course, are asked to comment on a course currently underway for the purpose of understanding or changing or improving some aspect of the course.

Problem 5: Unintended Consequences Are Not Taken Into Account

Some believe that using course objectives promotes a narrow base of data collection. This is likely true. Course objectives tend to focus our attention as teachers, as this is what objectives are supposed to do. But other events in the course, perhaps important events, may also occur. These other events, called *unintended consequences*, should be considered or taken into account in a course evaluation. As Scriven (1972) notes, we are interested in evaluating what actually happened in a course, not what the teacher thinks should happen. For example, Lynch (1992) did not find the effect he was hoping for (the effect of a reading program on a target group), but he unexpectedly found that his reading program had a positive effect for general ESL proficiency. This may suggest that an English-for-special-purposes program produces an unintended but positive general proficiency effect.

The idea of unintended consequences presents several questions and tentative answers. First, who is likely to identify or at least become aware of unintended consequences? The obvious answer is stakeholders, but we suggest teachers would notice first, and then students. Second, how might stakeholders recognize an unintended consequence? How would they see, feel, or experience one? We think that for an unintended consequence to be immediately recognized, it must be blatant and obvious, and not subtle or hypothetical. We are not interested in what could have happened. To qualify to be an unintended consequence we would want a certain, in-your-face clarity of an event or events, with perhaps triangulated agreement among stakeholders. For example, if both a teacher and students agree on an effect, the teacher/evaluator would have triangulated evidence of an unintended consequence. Finally, we wonder how data documenting unintended consequences would be collected. One data collection instrument with a long history in course evaluation is the questionnaire. If a questionnaire were used, what questions could we ask that would capture the existence of an unintended consequence? We think that formative evaluation, one of seven studies suggested by the SOAC model, would be a good framework for uncovering unintended consequences.

DISCUSSION QUESTION 5

Have you heard any one of these problems with objectives mentioned at a meeting, or in an article, or at a presentation? What was your response to this problem? How did others respond?

Outcome Validation Study

A key concept to any course evaluation is that of outcomes. In our previous discussion, we identified goals and objectives as common terms used to describe outcomes. As Alderson notes, "It is likely to be the case that any evaluator will have to identify the objectives of a programme" (1992, p. 281). Without identifying, clarifying, and understanding course outcomes, we run the risk of getting hopelessly lost in multiple needs and areas that we could evaluate. Thus we offer an outcome validation study. The purpose of an outcome validation study in the SOAC model is to validate the course outcomes by investigating the relationship between outcomes and stakeholders. Goals or course objectives are statements of intended outcomes. Second language teachers are familiar with the idea of course outcomes, but all too often we do not take them seriously. This may be because outcomes are described in language that seems irrelevant to our actual situation, or it may be because the teacher did not have an active role in creating or stating the outcomes. This is in fact one of the strongest arguments we can make to do an outcome validation study. If the outcomes are presently meaningless, outcome validation will help teachers/evaluators create personal meaning for the outcomes. This does not mean the same thing as agreeing with them.

Steps in an Outcome Validation Study

An outcome validation study involves a two-step process, seen in this articulated and detailed portion (Figure 3.1) of the SOAC model:

First is an investigation of the course outcomes whether they are called outcomes, objectives, purpose, learning outcomes, or goals. Initial questions could include those in Table 3.2.

At this stage the evaluator is gaining clarity on the outcomes themselves, and not asking if the outcomes are consistent with other areas of interest such as stakeholders, assessment, or curriculum. Getting answers on these initial questions is important. A case in point: One teacher of Japanese at our school used these questions to probe the outcomes in a course syllabus he had been given to use. For nearly a year he had taken them to be unchanging, like bedrock. He could not quite see what they had to do with the textbook he had been given to use, and so was keen to do an outcome validation study. In asking himself the initial questions, he realized he had few real answers and thus needed to ask other supervisors and faculty members what they knew. He also looked at past syllabuses for the course. The teacher was surprised to learn that the outcomes had been written in the distant past by someone who had long left the school. They had not undergone revision in any organized way over the years. In looking at the stated outcomes and applying what he had learned in a teaching methods course, he realized that some of them had been written in an audio-lingual method tradition, where learners memorized dialogs and practiced them (see Richards & Rogers, 2001 for a complete description). The answers the teacher found did not fit into a neat

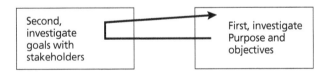

Figure 3.1 An outcome validation model showing the relationship of outcomes to stakeholders.

TABLE 3.2   Initial Outcome Validation Study Questions
1. What is the course purpose? What are the outcomes?
2. Where did the outcomes come from?
3. Who wrote them? Who revised them?
4. Are they clear?
5. Are the outcomes consistent with your understanding of the course purpose?

package, but helped him gain clarity on how the stated outcomes had only a few areas of overlap with what he took to be his own current daily working concepts of the course purpose, and with what various stakeholders in his department had been encouraging him to do (using more communicative speaking tasks and more reading of authentic texts).

DISCUSSION QUESTION 6

What questions would you like to ask the teacher about how he went about finding answers to the initial questions? What do you need to know about going through this process yourself?

The second step of an outcome validation study (Figure 3.1) is to examine the relationship between outcomes and stakeholders. Relevant stakeholders (students, colleagues, supervisors, and faculty members) can be identified, and if possible asked questions that would probe their understanding of the course outcomes. Do they approve of them? Do the outcomes represent what they want to get from the course? Specific questions could include those in Table 3.3.

An Outcome Validation Report Example

We offer here an example outcome validation study report (Box 3.1), which was done for a semester-long ESL course for international teaching assistants (ITAs). The course will be hereafter known as ESL 5310. ITAs are Korean, Chinese, Indian, etc. graduate students in the United States who are pursuing advanced degrees in chemistry, math, or biology. ITAs are supported as graduate students by teaching U.S. undergraduate chemistry or biology labs, or math classes in English, which is ITAs' second language. They are required to take ESL 5310 if they do not pass multiple tests aimed

TABLE 3.3 Follow up *Evaluation Questions* for an Outcome Validation Study
6. Which stakeholders will be consulted?
7. How will the data for this outcome validation study be collected?
8. What are the stakeholders' values and concerns?
9. Are stakeholder values consistent with the outcomes?
10. To what extent do stakeholders understand the outcomes?
11. To what extent do stakeholders agree with the outcomes?
12. Are alternative outcomes possible, and if so, who has the authority to create them?
13. Are the course outcomes adequate as stated, or should they be revised?

BOX 3.1
OUTCOME VALIDATION REPORT FOR ESL 5310

Initial Outcome Validation Study Questions and Responses (see Table 3.2)

1. What are the outcomes, purpose, or course objectives?

The purpose of semester course ESL 5310 and its summer form, the International Teaching Assistant (ITA) workshop as stated in the syllabus is to prepare ITA candidates to promote the learning experiences of Texas Tech University undergraduates and to approve ITA candidates to teach in their respective disciplines. The course objectives are 1). Learners will be able to sustain a presentation on a topic in their field for at least 10 minutes with reasonable spoken fluency, 2). Learners will be able to engage in question and answer sessions after their presentation and demonstrate ability to comprehend and answer questions, and 3. Learners will demonstrate knowledge of discourse intonation and its role in getting U.S. undergraduates to understand learners' intended meaning.

For the purpose of data collection for outcome validation study, the outcomes were restated in simpler terms, as in: 1). Learners will be able to give a class presentation on a prepared topic in their discipline, 2). Learners will be able to speak unrehearsed English including responses to questions, and 3). Learners will be able to understand spoken English in an academic context by building knowledge of and using key aspects of pronunciation.

2. Where did the outcomes come from?

3. Who wrote them? Who revised them?

The purpose and the three objectives were created by the faculty member (the teacher/evaluator) at the school charged with directing the program in consultation with another faculty member who was the former director of the ITA program and who continues to teach in the program. The earliest version of the current goals appeared in 2001. The objectives were revised periodically by both the previous director and the current director.

4. Are they clear?

5. Are the outcomes consistent with your understanding of the course purpose?

The outcomes seem clear to the teacher/evaluator. The objectives are consistent with assessments used in the course, which are a recorded extemporaneous talk responding to questions, a teaching simulation, and a listening test. They appear in his and other instructors' introductory remarks to the students in the course and appear in course syllabuses.

Follow up Evaluation Questions for an Outcome Validation Study (see Table 3.3)

6. Which stakeholders will be consulted?

Two stakeholder groups were involved in this outcome validation study. One group was ITA candidates currently enrolled and the second group was departmental faculty academic advisors, who are the supervisors of the ITAs in their own departments. There were 16 ITA candidates enrolled in ESL 5310 section 1 and 14 candidates enrolled in ESL 5310 section 2. There were three academic advisors from three departments representing over 40% of 2011 ITA candidates: chemistry, math, and physics.

7. How will the data for this outcome validation study be collected?

Because of the number of students (ITAs) to query in all, the teacher/evaluator decided to use a questionnaire. For the academic advisors in the departments, a face-to-face interview based on the questionnaire was decided on.

The teacher/evaluator probed his own perceptions of stakeholder values and concerns through systematically recalling complaints and concerns about the course that had been expressed to him by ITAs, and by academic advisors in writing and in meetings.

Questionnaire: For currently enrolled ITA candidates, the syllabus and course objectives were discussed during the initial class meeting. At the next class meeting, the course objectives were again reviewed and discussed, and a questionnaire was administered (see Chapter Three appendix). Candidates were asked to indicate the extent to which they understood the course objective on a scale of one (understood about 20%) to five (understood 100%) and also to state a level of agreement for each objective.

Interviews: For academic advisors, face-to-face meetings were arranged.

8. What are the stakeholder values and concerns?

9. Are stakeholder values consistent with the outcomes?

Results from the recall procedure done by the teacher/evaluator revealed that some ITAs were worried whether their participation in the course would delay their graduation. They were also worried that their departments would cut off their support if they could not be approved to teach after completing the course.

The academic advisors wanted the ITAs to get finished quickly. They wanted sufficient sections of the course to be offered so their students (the ITAs) could enroll and pass the requirements. They felt the course should have native-English speaking instructors to provide good speaking role models for the ITAs. They wanted ITAs to have good enough pronunciation of English so the advisors would not have to worry about getting complaints from undergraduate student in the labs and classes.

While the values of the stakeholders were not inconsistent with the goals of ESL 5310 some were stated in terms outside the context the teacher/evaluator could operate in, or outside the context of the goals themselves. One example was a student saying that ITAs themselves need to be more proactive to talk more with other English speakers. While this value was consistent with the course outcomes, making ITAs use English more outside of class was beyond the control of the teacher/evaluator.

10. To what extent do stakeholders understand the outcomes?

Descriptive statistics from the ITA questionnaire indicated high scores of "5" for both mode and median for the "To what extent do you understand objective X?" items on each of the three objectives. This indicated a high level of understanding.

Results from the interviews of the academic advisor who were administered the same questionnaire orally revealed high scores of "5" for both mode and median on all questionnaire items.

11. To what extent do stakeholders agree with the outcomes?

Results from the descriptive statistics of questionnaire data from ITA candidates were "5" for both mode and median for all three "How do you feel about objective X?" items. Results on the same items from the academic advisors were "4" which meant they thought each objective "seems fair" indicating a reasonably high level of agreement.

12. Are alternative outcomes possible, and if so, who has the authority to create them?

13. Are the course outcomes adequate as stated, or should they be revised?

The course teacher/evaluator has some latitude in writing and revising course outcomes in consensus with others. Based on the available data, ITA candidates and departmental academic advisors both understood and agreed with the course goals for ESL 5310. Given the available resources (a standard three-credit graduate course could meet twice a week for a total of 180 minutes for 14 weeks) the course outcomes are adequate.

at assessing spoken English communication ability (International Teaching Assistant Workshop, 2014).

DISCUSSION QUESTION 7

Thinking about EQs 8 and 9 in the sample outcome validation study report, some of the values of the ITAs and the academic advisors seemed almost beside the point or unrelated to the course outcomes. What might account for this? Does it mean the stakeholders' values are irrelevant?

APPLICATION TASKS: A Self-Exploration and Inventory, and Doing an Outcome Validation Study

First task idea: Write down your answers to these questions at different points throughout the next week. Keep your pen and pad of paper (or tablet computer or laptop) handy so you can write down answers as you think of them. What is the first step you can take to do an outcome validation study for a course you are teaching? What is a second step? And a third? Reading each evaluation question (*EQs* 6–13), can you think of what first or second steps you need to do to answer each *EQ*? Is there something you are not sure how to do? What is it? Who can you ask for help?

Second task idea: Do an outcome validation study. Keep notes on what issues arose as you did the study. Present your study to colleagues, a supervisor, or a faculty member.

Appendix

Purpose and Outcomes of ESL 5310 Questionnaire

The purpose of ESL 5310 is to prepare ITA candidates to promote the learning experiences of TTU undergraduates and to approve you to teach.

There are three outcomes:

1. Learners will be able to give a class presentation on a prepared topic in their discipline.
2. Learners will be able to speak unrehearsed English including responses to questions.
3. Learners will be able to understand spoken English in an academic context by building knowledge of and using key aspects of pronunciation.

I would like to know if you understand these course outcomes. Circle the number that shows your best answer.

To what extent to you understand outcome one?

Understand 20%	Understand 40%	Understand 60%	Understand 80%	Understand 100%
1	2	3	4	5

To what extent to you understand outcome two?

Understand 20%	Understand 40%	Understand 60%	Understand 80%	Understand 100%
1	2	3	4	5

To what extent to you understand outcome three?

Understand 20%	Understand 40%	Understand 60%	Understand 80%	Understand 100%
1	2	3	4	5

Now I would like to know how you feel about the course outcomes.

How do you feel about outcome one?

Hate it	Don't like	Maybe OK	Seems fair	Very reasonable
1	2	3	4	5

How do you feel about outcome two?

Hate it	Don't like	Maybe OK	Seems fair	Very reasonable
1	2	3	4	5

How do you feel about outcome three?

Hate it	Don't like	Maybe OK	Seems fair	Very reasonable
1	2	3	4	5

References

Alderson, J. C. (1992). Guidelines for the evaluation of language education. In J. C. Alderson & A. Beretta (Eds.), *Evaluating second language education* (pp. 274–304). Cambridge, England: Cambridge University Press.

Eisner, E. (1967). Education objectives-help or hindrance. *School Review, 75*(3), 250–260.

International Teaching Assistant Workshop. (2014). *Standards for approval to teach.* Texas Tech University, Lubbock, Texas. Retrieved from http://www.depts.ttu.edu/classic_modern/ita/ApprovalTeach.pdf

Lynch, B. (1992). Evaluating a program inside and out. In J. C. Alderson & A. Beretta (Eds.), *Evaluating second language education* (pp. 61–99). Cambridge, England: Cambridge University Press.

Nunan, D. (1988). *Syllabus design.* Oxford, England: Oxford University Press.

Popham, W. (2013). *Objectives.* In D. Flinders & S. Thornton (Eds.), *The curriculum studies reader* (4th ed.; pp. 95–108). New York, NY: Routledge.

Richards, J. C. (2001). *Curriculum development in language teaching.* Cambridge, England: Cambridge University Press.

Richards, J. C., & Rogers, T. S. (2001). *Approaches and methods in language teaching* (2nd ed.). Cambridge, England: Cambridge University Press.

St. Clair Robson, L. (1991). *The Tokaido road.* New York, NY: Ballantine Books.

Scriven, M. (1972). Prose and cons about goal-free evaluation. *Evaluation Comment, 3*(4), 1–4.

Stufflebeam, D. L. (2000). Foundational models for 21st century program evaluation. In D. L. Stufflebeam, G. F. Madaus, & T. Kellaghan (Eds.), *Evaluation models: Viewpoints on educational and human services evaluation* (pp. 33–83). Norwell, MA: Kluwer.

Tyler, R. W. (1949). *Basic principles of curriculum and instruction.* Chicago, IL: University of Chicago Press.

Tyler, R. W. (1966). New dimensions in curriculum development. *Phi Delta Kappan,* (48), 25–28).

Tyler, R. W., & Nowakowski, J. R. (1981). An interview with Ralph Tyler. In G. F. Madaus and D. Stufflebeam (Eds.), *Educational evaluation: Classical works of Ralph W. Tyler* (1989; pp. 243–272). Boston, MA: Kluwer.

Tyler, R. W., & Smith, E. R. (1942). Purposes and procedures of the evaluation staff. In *Appraising and recording student progress* (pp. 3–34). New York, NY: Harper.

4

The World, Stakeholders, and Needs Analysis

Necessity is the law of time and place.
—Latin proverb

This chapter explores the relationships between the *world*,[1] *stakeholders* and *outcomes* in a somewhat different way than in the previous chapter, with the end result here being a *needs analysis*. What learners' needs are taken to be is not simple and changes greatly when viewed by different stakeholders. Differing stakeholders' views are underscored by a description of learner needs as seen in general education and in second language education. Some needs analyses are published, and the form that these published reports take are compared to general research reports. A key difference is outlined, that needs analysis reports treat "results" as statements of learner need, and treat the "discussion" as recasting those needs into course outcomes or *objectives*. Through this comparison is demonstrated the process of doing a needs analysis.

---

1. For all terms in *italics*, see Glossary.

Evaluating Second Language Courses, pages 51–69
Copyright © 2016 by Information Age Publishing
51

This is the second of six chapters in which the stakeholders, outcomes, assessment, and curriculum evaluation model (SOAC) is applied to second and foreign language classrooms. We are interested here in continuing our examination of the relationship between SOAC components world, stakeholders, and outcomes, and this takes us into the territory of learning needs. The project in this chapter is a *needs analysis*, which sharply focuses teachers'/evaluators' knowledge of how stakeholders' conceptions of learner/learning need are shaped by the world (the circumstances that created or shaped the course) and sometimes end up as outcomes. The previous quotation illustrates how what we think is a need ("necessity") is shaped in particular contexts, the places in which teachers must live, work, and make their decisions. An *outcome validation* study (Chapter 3) and a needs analysis are together indispensable for us to learn which outcomes are worthwhile and which are needed.

DISCUSSION QUESTION 1

When starting out teaching a course, have you had an idea what learners need? Thinking about that time, now give yourself a full 2 minutes to make a list. Quite literally, time yourself and take the full 2 minutes. How many needs are there?

DISCUSSION QUESTION 2

If you are not teaching at this time, make a list about yourself. Take a full 2 minutes and write a list of your own learning needs, perhaps in terms of a course you are taking or recently took.

DISCUSSION QUESTION 3

Given the list of learning needs you just made for either Discussion question 1 or Discussion question 2, choose only two. Why those two? How did you decide?

Outcomes, Outcome Validation, and Needs Analysis

The purpose of a needs analysis in the SOAC course evaluation model is to continue the validation of the course outcomes by investigating the relationship between the world, stakeholders, and course outcomes. First, some history on needs analysis (NA). According to Richards (1984, p. 3), needs analysis arose from a major shift in perspective in language teaching, basically from a focus on language itself to a more functional use of language. Richards also credited the origin of needs analysis to the influence of *communicative language learning theory*, which posited that a second language is learned most effectively through using the language with others. This idea was applied to pedagogy, and also to *criterion-referenced tests* in the testing and evaluation field. Criterion-referenced tests are tests made for learners in a specific course. In order to make teaching, courses, and tests align with how learners need to use a second language, teachers need to know what learners need. We would add to the list of influences bringing about needs analysis an important subfield: the English for special purposes movement (Hutchinson & Waters, 1987, p. 53). From this subfield arose a whole new sensibility about how to design and assess second language programs devoted to English for drilling oil, airline pilot English, and English for restaurants, hospitality, and tourism. See Appendix C for a bibliography of needs analysis reports.

Although it is seen by some as possible to conduct a needs analysis with no consideration of a course or course outcomes (see for example Jasso-Aguilar, 2005; Long, 2005), in the SOAC model a needs analysis continues the validation of the course outcomes begun by the outcome validation study, adds the world to the mix, and further validates the course outcomes by analyzing stakeholders. In other words, needs analysis as it is described here, must have a context, and that context is a course (see Figure 4.1). It is part of the SOAC evaluation model that is rendered in greater detail to illustrate the relationships between the world and stakeholders. It is exploring this relationship that will result in a needs analysis. Figure 4.1 also suggests how the results of an outcome validation study (a critical evaluation of the existing outcomes of a course) can be used in an NA.

We contend that in course evaluation a needs analysis must build on the findings of an *outcome validation* study, otherwise an evaluator will get mired down into an endless, unfocused list of learning needs. An outcome validation study examines existing statements of course outcomes and tests them against the teacher/evaluator's understanding of the course purpose,

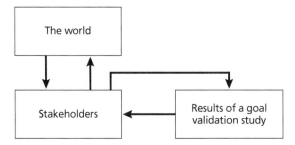

Figure 4.1   A model of needs analysis.

and also against the values of key stakeholders. This relationship is shown as an arrow going from stakeholders to outcome validation study results. Thus the teacher/evaluator begins with the results of the outcome validation study and again consults stakeholders (the arrow from outcome validation to stakeholders), only this time about their conceptions of learning needs for the course. Thus the questions in a needs analysis will be different and will have a different purpose.

An Outline for Needs Analysis

What follows in Table 4.1 is an outline for a needs analysis investigation. Our outline is roughly chronological in the sense of doing the needs analysis and also the format in which a needs analysis report would be presented. We also strongly suggest you study Chapter 10, which fleshes out the needed components of a needs analysis study report. See also Appendix D for a bibliography of sources about needs analysis. Following Table 4.1 is a discussion of each category, one of which—the world—mirrors a component of the SOAC evaluation model. The categories follow the format of a research report or article beginning with the title and ending with an appendix. We include parallel research report categories because we as qualified teachers are sometimes more familiar with them, and thus they may help us better understand the evaluation categories.

TABLE 4.1 Categories for a Needs Analysis Study Compared With Research Report Categories

Needs Analysis	Research Report
Title	Title
The world	Literature review
Definition of need	Literature review
Results of outcome validation study	Literature review
Description of program or course (must include outcomes)	Literature review
Purpose of needs analysis and evaluation questions	Research questions
Describe stakeholders	Participants
Data Collection Instruments	Materials
Analysis	Analysis
State needs	Results
Needs recast as objectives	Discussion
References	References
Appendix	Appendix

Title

For a needs analysis this should be as descriptive of the context as possible, particularly if the report will be published or presented. Second language educators are interested in reading needs analyses that they think have relevance to their own contexts. A descriptive title can provide that "pull." Examples are "Foreign Language Needs of Business Firms" (Vandermeeren, 2005), and "Designing Workplace ESOL Courses for Chinese Health-Care Workers at a Boston Nursing Home" (Uvin, 1996), and "Making a Request for Service in Spanish: Pragmatic Development in the Study Abroad Setting" (Bataller, 2010). As can be seen here, some titles of reports that are in fact needs analyses of varying levels of detail do not include the phrase "needs analysis" in the title.

DISCUSSION QUESTION 4

What are ways you would search for other needs analysis reports? What sources, such as journals, books, etc., would you look for? What search terms would you use? How could you find the many needs analyses that are cited in this book? Look at Chapter 10 for many examples. Could those needs analyses be used to find other, earlier needs analyses? How?

The World

Begin with a consideration of the world and its influences on your course via your stakeholders (see Figure 4.1). Stakeholders include you, the teacher/evaluator. The world is vast and potentially includes everything from relevant literature—including other needs analysis reports—to current political trends. It is necessary, therefore, to be able to focus on the world in such a way as to make it helpful in a needs analysis. While it is true that the world is everything outside a course and its stakeholders, it is not true that everything in the world is relevant to a needs analysis. The job of the teacher/evaluator is to identify the relevant parts of the world that can help them identify problems or circumstances that can be restated as needs. These in turn can be reformulated into course outcomes. Identification of relevant information presented by the world in a needs analysis is not obvious, and it requires a creative leap of imagination. It requires paying attention to research articles, newspaper articles, local radio and television reports, overheard conversations, and recollections and minutes of meetings at a school.

The relationship between the world and stakeholders typically takes one of two forms (the arrows between world and stakeholders in Figure 4.1). In one form, the world impinges on the course stakeholders to the extent that they are made aware of a situation that they are forced to respond to: This relationship in the arrow pointing from the world to stakeholders in Figure 4.1, where some aspect of the world comes to the attention of one or more set of stakeholders who have power to act. For example, in the late 1970s there was an increase in U.S. college students' complaints about the intelligibility of their science course teachers, who were international graduate students in science (international teaching assistants [ITAs]; Zhang, 2012). The local students (stakeholders) complained in the campus newspaper, to the faculty members, and to their parents (other stakeholders). Some of the parents contacted their state-level legislators (still other stakeholders), who created laws requiring universities to ensure ITAs had sufficient English ability to teach (Monoson & Thomas, 1993). Someone doing a needs analysis would need to be aware of this narrative by whatever means, and be prepared to report on it as a relevant context that impacts stakeholders and shapes course outcomes. Note the emphasis on intelligibility in early complaints. This strongly shaped the course content of early ITA preparation ESL courses, which focused on pronunciation (e.g., Smith, Meyers, & Burkhalter, 1992). Later courses, informed by research articles and books on second language learning and discourse (also the world), shifted the focus to language, teaching, and culture (Gorsuch, 2012).

The second form of the relationship between stakeholders and the world can be visualized by the arrow in the model (Figure 4.1) going from stakeholders to the world. It is not so much that stakeholders can change the world, but that teachers/evaluators, as stakeholders, can form a response to the world by engaging in a needs analysis and reporting on an important aspect of the world that is impinging on the course being evaluated. This response forms for the needs analysis what would be a literature review in a research report (see Table 4.1), which provides a context and partial motivation for a research project. By including this information, readers would understand what the teacher/evaluator sees as important and what he or she is responding to.

Definition of Need: Education Philosophies

Berwick (1989) eloquently states why it is necessary to define need when he says, "our perceptions of need develop from what we believe is educationally worthwhile, that needs are not simply 'out there' waiting to be counted and measured" (p. 56). The evaluator's definition of need definitely affects what he or she investigates and the type of information to be gathered (Brown, 1995, p. 38). This would also be true of a researcher who must determine key definitions for his or her study. For instance, someone who defines their area of interest as second language reading fluency will want to collect data on changes in learners' reading speed and comprehension, but not on learners' use of specific grammar points in their writing. How a researcher defines the scope of his or her report would appear in a literature review.

For course evaluators, one good source for narrowing down a definition of need is to consult the education literature. Berwick (1989, p. 53) and Brown (1995, p. 38) concur on four philosophies of needs analysis from the education field: the discrepancy philosophy, the democratic philosophy, the analytic philosophy, and the diagnostic philosophy. Each philosophy, or orientation, poses different questions to be answered in a needs analysis.

The Discrepancy Philosophy

In the discrepancy philosophy, a need is anything that lies between learners' current performance and desired performance. This stance presupposes we can determine the current state of the students, typically through diagnostic or proficiency language tests. Then it is assumed we can state what is desired, and know how to get there. From this teachers can determine course outcomes, and then make a course syllabus. Questions that flow from this approach are: (a) What is the current state of affairs? and (b) What is the desired future state? A typical application of the discrepancy philosophy can be seen in the planning done for a second language academic preparation course taught at a university where future study in some content area will be done in that language.

The Democratic Philosophy

In this philosophy, a need is any change desired by the majority. The democratic philosophy presupposes that students can decide to attend or not attend a language course. Questions that flow from this approach are: (a) How can we identify the group of learners? and (b) How can we identify what they want to do or learn? A typical application is a commercial foreign language school where a group of learners wants language lessons for extended travel and cooking lessons in France.

The Analytic Philosophy

A need as seen here is the next step in learning as analyzed by the experts. The analytic philosophy presupposes that a body, such as a professional committee or government licensing group, exists that has taken responsibility for discussing and publishing what learners need to know. Questions that flow from this approach are (a) Can we identify the governing body responsible for stating the minimum requirements? and (b) How can we determine where students are now? A typical application would appear in a specific purpose second language course, such as English for overseas nurses working in a Texas hospital, or a foreign language Japanese course for tour conductors in New Zealand.

The Diagnostic Philosophy

In this philosophy, a need is anything that would be harmful if missing. The diagnostic philosophy presupposes that learners are in a specific situation, that we know something about that situation, and that we know what language would be helpful or necessary for that situation. Questions that flow from this approach are (a) What is the learner's specific situation? and (b) What is needed by the learner in that situation? A typical application is a survival-oriented class, for example refugees or new immigrants arriving in a country where the second language is used. They will need to find apartments, open bank accounts, and complete job applications.

DISCUSSION QUESTION 5

Which of these four philosophies of need seems most useful to you? In thinking about which questions "flow" from this philosophy, what is a first step you can take to answering the questions?

Definition of Need: Discussions in the Second Language Learning Field

Another source for narrowing down a definition of need comes from the literature offered by curriculum developers in second language education. Learning needs have been the topic of much discussion, which underscores how important it is to think through and provide a definition of need in a needs analysis. Past needs analyses, as exemplified by Munby (1978, p. 52), have been criticized for being too narrowly focused on linguistic items and situations (Benesch, 1996; Brindley, 1989; Hutchinson & Waters, 1987; Pennington & Brown, 1991). Such a narrow concept of learning need, it is suggested, will fail because it does not take into account the characteristics of the learners, their aims, or their values (Allwright, 1984; Nunan, 1989, p. 177). Finally, Coleman (1988) reminds us that needs analysis cannot assume idealized language learners, all of whom have the same needs. So where does this leave us? We still have classes to teach and learners to facilitate. We think it is impossible to reject the idea of developing an objective description of needs. Through principled, critical inquiry needs can be considered, articulated, reconceptualized, and revised. Our ideas are not set in stone, yet they must have a basis, which a needs analysis will provide.

Objective and Subjective Needs

All authors reviewed here seem to agree there is a basic dichotomy of objective needs and subjective needs. Sometimes this seems to depend on which stakeholder is being asked. For instance, Berwick (1989) sees needs as felt needs (wants and desires expressed by students and other stakeholders) and perceived needs (real or objective needs expressed by teachers and other stakeholders). Hutchinson and Waters (1987, p. 55) discuss target needs and learning needs. Target needs are seen as necessities, lacks, and wants. A necessity would be objective, and determined by demands of the target situation as seen by teachers or other qualified experts, such as being able to order a meal in Russian. A lack would also be objective, and represents the gap between what the learner now knows and what the learner needs to know, again as judged by qualified stakeholders. For instance, learners need to be able to give examples in an oral presentation to help their audience connect to a topic, but as yet the learners do not even know they should do so. Finally, a want would be the subjective needs expressed by the learner, such as feeling comfortable conversing socially in Japanese. In contrast to target needs named by Hutchinson and Waters (1987), learning needs refer to creating conditions that will take into account students' knowledge, skills, strategies, motivation, and accustomed ways of studying a second language. This last categorization, learning need, does not fit comfortably under an objective or subjective dichotomy.

Brindley (1989, p. 64) states that objective needs are good starting points and can provide the broad parameters of a syllabus, but once learning begins, things change. Brindley recommends discerning objective needs about the learner's life, such as the use of language the learner will need, and the learner's current proficiency, as would be known by a teacher or some other expert stakeholder. He also recommends considering subjective cognitive needs based on learners' individual personalities, for example confidence; and affective needs, such as wants and expectations.

Finally, Brown (1995, p. 40) lists three types of need dichotomies. The first is situation needs and language needs. Brown's situation needs are posed much like Hutchinson and Waters' (1987) learning needs where there is a consideration of how learners best learn and how they want to learn. Brown's concept of language needs suggests such needs are objective and are discerned by teachers and other second language expert stakeholders. The second dichotomy Brown cites is objective needs and subjective needs. Objective needs focus on observable facts about learners' current abilities and what they need to be able to do with the second language. Subjective needs are something students feel they want (Brown, 1995, p. 41). Finally Brown describes a linguistic needs and learning processes needs dichotomy in which linguistic needs are based on an objective view of the second language itself (learners need to learn nouns, verbs, discourse markers, etc. as judged by a teacher or other expert stakeholder), and learning processes needs, which are subjective and related to learners' motivation.

DISCUSSION QUESTION 6

Have you ever heard a colleague or administrator say that students needed something that seemed impossible or unlikely? How would you account for such statements that were so divergent from your understanding? How would the descriptions of the different types of need given be germane to your account?

Results of an Outcome Validation Study

As described previously, a needs analysis should build on the results of an outcome validation study. This is because learning needs can be quantified but not objectified (Vandermeeren, 2005). In other words, a need is always subjective in the sense that it may vary from course to course and from one time to another time, as in our quotation at the beginning of the chapter. This means a need is partially conditioned by the existing course outcomes at any given time. Briefly reporting the results of an outcome validation study makes transparent to readers the values of the stakeholders that are present in the needs analysis. Research reports would include direct and indirect statements about the context of the research in a literature review (see Table 4.1). A good needs analysis would benefit from the context provided by an outcome validation study.

Describe Your Program or Course

This brief description should begin with a statement of the outcomes of a course. In addition to the outcomes, focus here on the basics: how many times the course meets per week, for how long, and for how many weeks. Describe the kind of teaching that goes on in the course, what types of activities are done, what materials are used, and how students are assessed. Describe how the students come into the course, and what then happens to them after they complete the course. In other words, talk about what kinds of decisions the assessments are used for. Give readers a sense of how the course fits in with other courses in the program, or how the course fits in with the larger educational scene. As we mentioned before, research reports would include a sense of context of the research in a literature review (see Table 4.1). A needs analysis would benefit from a description of the course not only for readers of a report, but as a point of reference for the course evaluator/teacher.

DISCUSSION QUESTION 7

Would you consider any of the information that was suggested to be unnecessary to understanding another teacher's course? Is there any information missing that should be included?

State the Purpose of the Needs Analysis and Your Evaluation Questions

A needs analysis is only as strong as its clarity of purpose and its *evaluation questions* (EQs). In brief, a statement of purpose includes why you are conducting your needs analysis. The EQs are specifically what you would like to know. Stating purpose and research questions are the marks of good research methodology and reporting (see Table 4.1), and the same goes for course evaluation. Alalou (2001, p. 454) wanted to "find out what students expect from the study of foreign languages" for Spanish, French, and German courses in U.S. colleges (the needs analysis purpose). The EQs guiding the needs analysis were (a) "to investigate similarities and differences in language needs among students," and (b) "to determine the extent to which students' perceived needs matched the missions the departments defined for their respective language programs" (p. 455).

Describe Stakeholders

This is analogous to a research report in which participants would be described (Table 4.1). In a needs analysis, a teacher/evaluator would already have defined what they think a need is, and the context of the course that gave rise to existing outcomes. A stakeholders section in a needs analysis describes the needs that are being focused on. Pennington and Brown (1991) pointed out that there are many stakeholders who have a vested interest in the results of a needs analysis, but three groups are primary: students, teachers, and administration. Alalou (2001, p. 455) focused on 525 students in foreign language programs at both the introductory and intermediate level. This statement framed whose needs were investigated and set the stage for how. With such a large group of 525 stakeholders, almost certainly a questionnaire would be used as a data collection instrument. Watanabe, Norris, & Gonzalez-Lloret (2009, p. 11) focused on administrators of college-level German, Spanish, Filipino, Thai, and Japanese programs, including 21 department chairs, language coordinators, and language center directors. This smaller stakeholder group allowed for interviews, another type of a data collection instrument.

State Your Data Collection Instruments

Just as in any good research report on materials (Table 4.1), a good needs analysis needs to describe how the data collection instruments were designed and piloted. Validation evidence should be given, such as instrument reliability. These can be statistical procedures, or other procedures, that indicate that a reader or external other would draw similar interpretations of the data that resulted from using a data collection instrument. For further details see Criteria 12–15 in our reading and assessing publications template in Chapter 10. Here are suggested data collection instruments that could be used for a needs analysis posed from a discrepancy philosophy stance of need. First, "What is the current state of affairs?" Consider using:

- A *criterion-referenced test* or a performance test (writing or speaking samples)
- A questionnaire
- An interview protocol with selected stakeholders (administrators, past teachers)
- A *norm-referenced test* of general second language ability
- Student enrollment records
- Past course documents such as syllabuses, course catalogs, brochures

Second, "what is the desired future state?" Consider using:

- Interviews with teachers and other key stakeholders
- Interviews with past students currently in the future state
- Questionnaires
- Published analyses of trends in the field

Analysis

As with a research report, a section on analyses directly linked to the evaluation questions is key to a clearly planned needs analysis (Table 4.1). Readers want to know what kind of data was collected and how it was related to the EQs (evaluation questions) through the analyses. If quantitative data were collected, descriptions of the analyses need to support an argument for statistical clarity (see Criteria 17a–21a on the reading and assessing publications template in Chapter 10). For instance, if a needs analysis used a questionnaire to capture teachers' agreement or disagreement with a list of proposed learning needs, the EQ would be stated something like, "What were teachers' level of agreement or disagreement with a list of learning needs proposed by future employers of the students?" An analysis section in a needs analysis report ought then to say something like, "To answer EQ1, descriptive statistics for each questionnaire item were calculated, including the mean (the average score) and the mode (the most common score). A high score or an item will indicate agreement, and a low score will indicate disagreement."

If qualitative data were collected, a description of the analysis needs to support credibility (see Criteria 17b–21b in Chapter 10). If a teacher/evaluator used interviews to answer the EQ, "What do ESL teachers in Program XX assume the students need to learn?" then the analysis section needs to say something like "All transcripts were read through and the phrases and sentences which suggested a general thematic relationship to the evaluation question were marked. The transcripts were then read a second time and the marked phrases and sentences were categorized. The categories were confirmed by a colleague not involved in the need analysis."

DISCUSSION QUESTION 8

What aspects of an analysis section are you unsure of? What questions do you have about doing an analysis to answer an EQ and then describing what you did? What resources can you find to answer your questions and address your feelings of uncertainty?

State the Needs You Formulated

In a research paper, this would be the results section. For a needs analysis this would be statements of need. Charts, tables, graphs, and simple statements can be used to tell readers what learning needs emerged from the data and analyses. Mede (2012), in her needs analysis of an English student-teaching program in Turkey, reported on learning needs related to grammar. In interviews, "the student teachers pointed out that the number of grammar hours should be increased in the Language Preparatory Program. They particularly asked for more training on using the grammatical structures accurately while forming complex sentences to express and organize their ideas clearly" (p. 115). In a table on student teachers' perceptions of the program meeting their needs for reading English texts,

Mede stated that 67% of respondents felt agreement that they could "recognize words automatically" and perform other reading tasks requiring speed, but only 3.3% felt they could "read carefully and understand the details of a text" (p. 87).

Recast Your Need

The final step in a needs analysis ought to explain how the needs revealed in the study will be acted on, or not acted on. This is analogous to a discussion section in a research report (Table 4.1). In the case of learner needs that can be acted on, because there are sufficient resources or sufficient will to do so, the needs should be recast as outcomes. This may mean revising current statements of outcomes or adding new outcomes. This may also mean removing other outcomes that will no longer be pursued. While not stated as learner outcomes (what students will learn or be able to do), the latest version of Japan's Ministry of Education (2009) course of study for elementary-level foreign language education notes the following teaching points: "Teachers should mainly set the communication situations and functions listed in the following examples: Greeting, Self-introduction, Shopping, Having meals, Asking and giving directions" (p. 3).

In some cases, a desired outcome of a course will simply be confirmed, but the teacher/evaluator may then elect to devote more time or resources to the outcome, as in Mede (2012).

> Since the structural [grammatical] syllabus was mostly based on controlled activities like gap filling or matching, the [learners] experienced difficulty in performing communicative tasks such as debates or role plays. Thus, the number of the grammar hours should be increased in the program and more communicative tasks should be integrated in the structural syllabus. (p. 151)

As with the previous example, this is not stated as a learner outcome, but is, rather, what we would call a *decision point*. Decision points are an array of specific suggestions for teachers focused on the elements of the curriculum that were investigated in accordance with the evaluation questions (EQs).

Learner Outcomes Versus Teaching Points Versus Decision Points

It is worth focusing, once again, on a salient and currently widespread view of learner outcomes offered by Tyler (1949) and other, later, second language commentators (Brown, 1995; Richards, 2001). The outcomes component in the SOAC evaluation model (see Chapter 2) assumes outcomes are thought of and stated as learner outcomes. Thus, in recasting needs uncovered in a needs analysis, outcomes are to be reconceptualized and then stated as what learners will know or be able to do. In the glossary entry for *outcomes* in this book, we define outcomes as statements of what ought to come about in terms of learner knowledge, ability, or attitude as a result of participating in a course. Thus, while some results of a needs analysis may result in policy recommendations such as "class sizes need to be reduced" and "more books are needed in the library," these are not learner-focused outcomes. Rather, these are decision points, which may result from a needs analysis but are more likely to emerge during *formative* or *summative evaluations*, which result from a comparison between SOAC model components outcomes, curriculum, and assessment.

In some evaluation reports, outcomes of a course may be named "outcomes" and then stated, as in Arnold (2009). For Arnold's extensive reading course for advanced-level learners of German, the outcomes were (p. 348):

- Increase students' motivation to read
- Raise their confidence in their ability to read L2 texts
- Improve their reading ability
- Encourage learners to read for pleasure outside of class

Strictly speaking, even these outcomes are stated almost like teaching points. With some further reading in the report about the pedagogical and theoretical assumptions of the course, additional details emerge that allow for statements of learner outcomes:

- Learners will demonstrate a sustained motivation to read L2 texts through keeping notes and self-reports on how long they searched for texts and read them
- Learners will demonstrate increasing confidence to read L2 texts through self reports of their reactions to a text and recounting the reading processes they use
- Learners will show improved reading ability as demonstrated to their self-reported attention to the formality level, tone, and likely audience of the L2 texts
- Learners will show sustained interest in reading for pleasure outside of class by setting their own reading goals and then achieving their goals

In other evaluation reports, such as Yunos, Rahman, and Ismail's (2013) needs analysis for hotel workers at a resort in Malaysia, course outcomes are referred to but not stated. This requires a teacher/evaluator to patiently search though the authors' descriptions of the pedagogical basis of the course (theme-based learning; Yunos, Rahman, & Ismail, 2013, pp. 19 & 21) and any course syllabuses or outlines provided (see following notes on appendices in needs analysis reports). The authors describe theme-based learning as providing for "ample exposure to repeated topics, phrases, vocabulary, and naturally occurring grammatical structures." This description, coupled with a curriculum outline in the appendix to the report, may be used to restate learner needs as learner outcomes. Here are a few examples:

- Learners will be able to introduce themselves and others, using polite forms as appropriate for a professional hotel setting
- Learners will know and be able to use hotel-related expressions on the telephone, such as leaving messages, making and replying to apologies
- Learners will be able to hear and say some names of nearby places so as to be able to give directions when requested to do so by hotel guests.

Stating learner outcomes takes practice, but it is a rewarding skill to learn and to have. It is upon learner outcomes that curricula (instruction, materials, etc.) and assessments are designed. In the SOAC model, the outcomes and curriculum components are compared in order to describe and evaluate the course logic (Chapter 5). If the learner outcomes are not clearly stated, then it would be difficult to really say whether the course curriculum was up to the task of supporting learners to reach the outcomes.

DISCUSSION QUESTION 9

Taking either the Ministry of Education's recast outcome, or Mede's recast outcome, try writing a student-focused outcome. Start with: "Learners will . . . " or "Learners can . . . at the end of this course."

Reference List

A list of previous published and unpublished documents serves two functions. First, it lets the readers know the teacher/evaluator has sufficient knowledge of the world and has taken into account previous, relevant work. This increases the credibility of the needs analysis and thus its usefulness to others. Second, the references can be used by other evaluators, teachers, administrators, and researchers to do their own work. Thus a reference list represents a body of knowledge. A good reference list should be balanced between reports that are unique and very specialized, but perhaps not widely available, and reports that are published in widely available forums. In Mede's reference list (2012), one can find unpublished doctoral dissertations on very specific topics on needs, which she must have found relevant to her own work on academic English programs in a foreign language setting:

> Kittidhaworn, P. (2001). *An assessment of the English-language needs of second-year Thai undergraduate engineering students in a Thai public university in Thailand in relation to the second-year EAP program in engineering.* (Unpublished doctoral dissertation.) West Virginia University, Morgantown, WV.

At the same time, there are also more general, yet more available works:

> Lepetit, D., & Cichocki, W. (2002). Teaching language to future health professionals: A needs assessment study. *The Modern Language Journal, 86*(3), 384–396.

Appendix

A needs analysis report includes the data collection instruments in the Appendix section, the same as research reports (Table 4.1). Including the interview items, questionnaires, or syllabuses of existing courses adds to the usefulness and credibility of the needs analysis report and its results. Appendices are often key to encouraging other evaluators to replicate the needs analysis, perhaps with modifications, in their own situations.

APPLICATION TASKS: Evaluating a Needs Analysis Report in Two Ways

First task idea: Find a needs analysis report and evaluate it using the reading and assessing publications template for needs analysis (Chapter 10). Examples are in Appendix C, a bibliography of articles and book chapters of needs analysis. Then tell a colleague about the needs analysis, or plan to present it at a teacher's meeting.

Second task idea: Find a needs analysis report that seems relevant to a course you are currently teaching (see Appendix C). After reading the needs and suggested outcomes in the study, write down which seem to accord with your course and which do not. Think about and write down reasons why some needs and suggested outcomes diverge from your understanding of your course purpose.

References

Alalou, A. (2001). Reevaluating curricular objectives using students' perceived needs: The case of three language programs. *Foreign Language Annals, 34*(5), 453–469.

Allwright, D. (1984). Why don't learners learn what teachers teach? The interaction hypothesis. In D. M. Singleton & D. G. Little (Eds.), *Language learning in formal and informal contexts* (pp. 3–18). Dublin, Ireland: IRAAL.

Arnold, N. (2009). Online extensive reading for advanced foreign language learners: An evaluation study. *Foreign Language Annals, 42*(2), 340–366.

Bataller, R. (2010). Making a request for service in Spanish: Pragmatic development in the study abroad setting. *Foreign Language Annals, 43*(1), 160–175.

Benesch, S. (1996). Needs analysis and curriculum development in EAP: An example of a critical approach. *TESOL Quarterly, 30*(4), 723–738.

Berwick, R. (1989). Needs assessment in language programming: From theory to practice. In R. K. Johnson (Ed.), *The second language curriculum* (pp. 48–62). Cambridge, England: Cambridge University Press.

Brindley, G. (1989). The role of needs analysis in adult ESL programme design. In R. K. Johnson (Ed.), *The second language curriculum* (pp. 63–78). Cambridge, England: Cambridge University Press.

Brown, J. D. (1995). *The elements of language curriculum.* Boston, MA: Heinle & Heinle.

Coleman, H. (1988). Analysing language needs in large organizations. *English for Specific Purposes, 7,* 155–169.

Gorsuch, G. (2012). The roles of teacher theory and domain theory in materials and research in international teaching assistant education. In G. Gorsuch (Ed.), *Working theories for teaching assistant development* (pp. 429–482). Stillwater, OK: New Forums Press.

Hutchinson, T., & Waters, A. (1987). Needs analysis. In *English for specific purposes: A learning-centred approach* (pp. 53–64). Cambridge, England: Cambridge University Press.

Jasso-Aguilar, R. (2005). Sources, methods and triangulation in needs analysis: A critical perspective in a case study of Waikiki hotel maids. In M. Long (Ed.), *Second language needs analysis* (pp. 127–158). Cambridge, England: Cambridge University Press.

Long, M. H. (2005). Overview: A rationale for needs analysis and needs analysis research. In M. H. Long (Ed.), *Second language needs analysis* (pp. 1–16). Cambridge, England: Cambridge University Press.

Mede, E. (2012). *Design and evaluation of a language preparatory program at an English medium university in an EFL setting: A case study.* (Unpublished doctoral dissertation.) Yeditepe University, Istanbul, Turkey.

Ministry of Education, Culture, Sports, Science, and Technology. (2009). *Course of study: Elementary school foreign language activities.* Tokyo, Japan: Author. Retrieved June 27, 2013, from http://www.mext.go.jp/component/english/__icsFiles/afieldfile/2011/03/17/1303755_011.pdf

Monoson, P., & Thomas, C. (1993). Oral English proficiency policies for faculty in U.S. higher education. *The Review of Higher Education, 16*, 127–140.

Munby, J. (1978). *Communicative syllabus design.* Cambridge, England: Cambridge University Press.

Nunan, D. (1989). Hidden agendas: The role of the learner in programme implementation. In R. K. Johnson (Ed.), *The second language curriculum* (pp. 176–186). Cambridge, England: Cambridge University Press.

Pennington, M. C., & Brown, J. D. (1991). Unifying curriculum process and curriculum outcomes: The key to excellence in language education. In M. C. Pennington (Ed.), *Building better English language programs: Perspectives in ESL* (pp. 57–74). Washington, DC: NAFSA, Association of International Educators.

Richards, J. C. (1984). Language curriculum development. *RELC Journal, 15*(1), 1–29.

Richards, J. C. (2001). *Curriculum development in language teaching.* Cambridge, England: Cambridge University Press.

Smith, J., Meyers, C., & Burkhalter, A. (1992). *Communicate: Strategies for international teaching assistants.* Englewood Cliffs, NJ: Regents/Prentice Hall.

Tyler, R. W. (1949). *Basic principles of curriculum and instruction.* Chicago, IL: University of Chicago Press.

Uvin, J. (1996). Designing workplace ESOL courses for Chinese health-care workers at a Boston nursing home. In K. Graves (Ed.), *Teachers as course developers* (pp. 39–62). Cambridge, England: Cambridge University Press.

Vandermeeren, S. (2005). Foreign language need of business firms. In M. H. Long (Ed.), *Second language needs analysis* (pp. 159–181). Cambridge, England: Cambridge University Press.

Watanabe, Y., Norris, J. M., & Gonzalez-Lloret, M. (2009). Identifying and responding to evaluation needs in college foreign language programs. In J. M. Norris, J. M. Davis, C. Sinicrope, & Y. Watanabe (Eds.), *Toward useful program evaluation in college foreign language education* (pp. 5–56). University of Hawaii at Manoa, Honolulu, HI: National Foreign Language Resource Center.

Yunos, D., Rahman, S., & Ismail, N. (2013). Developing a theme-based language course for hotel front-line staff. *Creative Practices in Language Learning and Teaching, 1*(2), 18–34. Retrieved from http://www.kedah.uitm.edu.my/CPLT/images/stories/v1n2/Article2.pdf

Zhang, Y. (2012). Rapport management of international teaching assistants in their teaching. In G. Gorsuch (Ed.), *Working theories for teaching assistant development* (pp. 367–392). Stillwater, OK: New Forums Press.

5

Curriculum and Outcomes,
and Course Logic

Education, therefore, is a process of living and not a preparation for future living.
—Dewey (2013, p. 35)

In this chapter, SOAC evaluation model components *curriculum*[1] and *outcomes* are related to each other with the result being a *course logic* study. Course logic studies are rarely done in foreign or second language education, and yet doing one reveals much about how a teacher/evaluator believes a course's curriculum (the books, activities, etc.) brings about the course outcomes. Different teachers from different second language learning traditions may explain how a course "works" to bring about learning quite differently. Graphic organizers adapted from general evaluation, including an impact model, an organizational chart, and a *course logic table* guide teachers/evaluators to collect data on course logic through introspection, interviews, classroom observations, and inspecting course materials.

---

1. For all terms in *italics*, see Glossary.

Evaluating Second Language Courses, pages 71–89

This is the third chapter in which the stakeholders, outcomes, assessment, and curriculum (SOAC) evaluation model is applied to second language classrooms. In this chapter we will explore the relationship between the course curriculum and course outcomes (also called goals or objectives). To accomplish this we will use a course logic study that brings out the assumptions, which are rarely discussed, of how a curriculum is supposed to bring about the outcomes of a course. In other words, how do the class exercises, textbooks, handouts, and teachers' lectures or commentary bring about students' learning? How does students' participation in a course that meets a certain amount of time, several times a week (more or less), for 14 weeks (more or less) bring about their achievement of the outcomes set out for the course? Thus this chapter focuses on the assumed processes of a curriculum, as in Dewey's "process of living," from the previous quotation. This is as opposed to the common conception of a curriculum simply as a set of outcomes and required materials listed on a course syllabus, as in Dewey's "preparation for future living." We posit that a curriculum is functional or dysfunctional to the extent that it answers the question of how teachers and learners, and all aspects of the curriculum, are going to accomplish outcomes.

DISCUSSION QUESTION 1

Think of a course syllabus you read or worked on recently. Are the course outcomes listed? Are required textbooks, etc. listed? Is there any mention of learning processes, or *teaching methods*, or descriptions of how students will learn?

DISCUSSION QUESTION 2

In teachers' meetings or orientations at your school or teacher preparation courses, have you ever heard discussion of why a course should meet for, say, 50 minutes per day, five days per week, for one semester? Was this discussion posed in terms of institutional requirements, or in terms of how such a course duration and intensity brings about learning?

Course Logic

One key step in course evaluation is the articulation of the course logic, which brings into focus the relationship between what it is believed a course should help learners accomplish and whether and how the current course curriculum can support those accomplishments. Genesee and Upshur (1996) come at course logic by modeling a comparison between "instructional purposes" (outcomes) and "instructional plans" (a part of curriculum; p. 43). They note that teachers should "compare materials and activities with interim objectives" and "check whether materials and activities reflect the best current thinking on second language teaching" (p. 42). They stipulate an additional comparison once a course is underway that "asks whether instruction is being implemented as planned" (p. 43), underscoring curriculum as a process and something which learners and teachers/evaluators, experience over a period of time.

We use Figure 5.1 to visualize a way to think about course logic. Figure 5.1 is a more specific examination of portions of the SOAC model, which includes the components outcomes with an arrow pointing to the evaluand (the course) and back, and curriculum with an arrow pointing to the evaluand and back. This means that not only do the outcomes and curriculum influence a course, but the process of thinking about a course, and whether the curriculum can adequately support the course outcomes, can influence the outcomes and curriculum themselves.

Thinking through course logic using a model can be empowering because it presents to us specific ways in which the materials, teaching methods, and other resources at hand may or may not be adequate to help second language learners achieve the outcomes of a course. A consideration of course logic may also lead to needed revisions of course outcomes. For instance, a group of German foreign language educators may decide on a new outcome: Learners will increase their reading fluency (faster reading rate and comprehension) of German texts in order to enhance their agency as independent readers. As the new semester approaches, the teachers add this outcome to their syllabus and identify a stack of German romantic novels they can use as

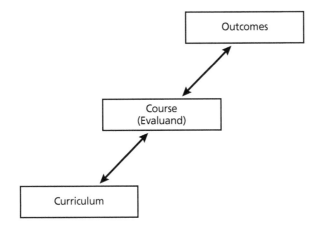

Figure 5.1 A course logic model.

a class set. But one of the teachers approaches the innovation through an examination of the course logic and finds that (a) the course meets only twice a week for 90 minutes each time, (b) the materials on hand (the romantic novels) have too much unknown vocabulary for developing learners' reading fluency, and (c) the teachers are oriented to introducing and drilling grammar rules using carefully selected vocabulary. This last point was observed by the teacher/evaluator when visiting his colleagues' classes and listening to their talk at meetings. The teacher/evaluator concludes that the lack of class time, the established pattern of prioritizing other pressing outcomes, and the lack of appropriate materials will not support the outcome of increasing learner reading fluency given current circumstances. The resources provided by the curriculum do not measure up. Either the outcomes need to change, or the curriculum needs to change.

DISCUSSION QUESTION 3

Do you have a reading component in a second language course you teach? Describe it to a classmate or jot down a description for yourself. Is reading mentioned in the course outcomes? What is reading thought to be for? What does it accomplish for learners?

DISCUSSION QUESTION 4

Can you think of other skills, such as pronunciation, or any area of language not directly related to learning grammar rules or vocabulary, that were discussed for inclusion of a second language course you either taught or were a learner in? What happened to the skill or area of language? Was it taught? Did it appear in the class activities? Why or why not?

Course Logic in Mainstream Evaluation and the Second Language Literature

In the mainstream evaluation field, course logic is also known as program theory, logic model, program model, outcome line, cause map, and action theory (Rossi, Lipsey, & Freeman, 2004, p. 139). This strong conceptualization of whether a program's orientation and resources can achieve an outcome reflects the kinds of high-stakes programs mainstream evaluators work with: drug treatment programs and programs designed to reduce teenage pregnancy. Whatever your views on sex education, course logic brings to the forefront a consideration of whether talking to teenagers about abstinence and self-determination in small groups (one line of logic) or talking to teenagers in how-to-use-detail about condoms and contraceptive sponges in small groups (another line of logic), will result in fewer teenage pregnancies.

Terms such as course logic rarely seem to come up in the second language education literature, even though the kind of detailed information needed to think about course logic may appear in some reports. For example, in an early work on a distinctive teaching methodology (total physical response [TPR]) used in Spanish classes in U.S. high schools, Wolfe and Jones (1982) outlined in detail how the proposed curriculum would work to bring about the outcome of improved student scores on grammar and vocabulary tests. They noted "TPR and similar strategies emphasize that language is acquired implicitly and not learned" (p. 275) and that "TPR is a teaching strategy that uses the imperative form to teach vocabulary and grammar" (p. 274). By using TPR 20 minutes per day and not forcing learners to produce language or focus on other skills such as speaking, writing, and reading, it was claimed that learners acquired Spanish implicitly to the point their test scores would be higher than those of a non-TPR, explicit-instruction group in the same school (p. 279).

In another example, Sanders (2005) was charged to achieve multiple outcomes with a large-scale, university-level Spanish program, including decreasing the cost of instructors, increasing class enrollments, and increasing student learning by increasing "student production by facilitating greater student participation" on computer-mediated communication tasks (p. 524). The author described a detailed rationale for using online chat rooms and mechanical grammar tasks, done outside of class, including a description of one task: "Students also had to individually post summaries about their chat partners … the task required that students exchange sufficient information in chat to be able to write summaries" (p. 526). The depth of these descriptions and their attunement to the learning outcome of increasing learner participation, marks this report as an exercise in course logic even though this term is never referred to. For an additional example for a dual Spanish English immersion elementary school program in the United States, see Sugarman (2008) who, while stating outcomes in terms of what teachers will do and what test scores students ought to achieve, provided detailed descriptions of instruction and the teachers' professional make-up. She then critically evaluated these curriculum resources in light of stated outcomes.

Doing a Course Logic Study

There are three general requirements for an effective course logic study. First, as suggested in the previous section, the teacher/evaluator must describe the course in enough detail that the relationship between the course curriculum and course outcomes is clear. Second, the evaluator needs to estimate the adequacy of the course curriculum to accomplish the outcomes. Finally, the estimation of adequacy needs to be validated. By validated we mean that there is a good degree of transparency or credibility in the teacher's/evaluator's line of thinking. We demonstrate one way to do the validation step in Chapter 6 on formative evaluation. Here, we translate our basic steps into two course "snapshots" suggested by Rossi et al. (2004), which taken together can form a description of a course and outline the relationship between course outcomes and curriculum. These are an *impact model* and an *organizational chart*. The information and the connections between them can then be used to complete a course logic table adapted from Rossi et al. (2004, p. 147) including such elements as inputs (what resources a course provides), activities (what happens in a course), outputs (what a course does in a basic, immediate sense), and outcomes (statements of what learners ought to be able to do or know).

Here is an important note about terminology. We are working with evaluation concepts at this point, not second language acquisition concepts. Thus, inputs does not mean linguistic input that learners get from hearing or reading the second language. In the context of a course logic study, inputs (note the plural form) means what goes into a course, such as instructors, or materials, or even instructor training. In the early stage of a course logic study, inputs will be stated in broad, curriculum planning terms such as theme-based learning, social situations, or learner metacognition. Similarly, outputs in this context does not mean having learners talk and practice, as in comprehensible output in the second language. In a course logic study context, outputs are what the course does, such as learners attending class, or seeking feedback outside of class, or using the online materials provided to them.

The Impact Model

The impact model shows what the teacher/evaluator believes is the causal sequence between curriculum and outcomes. Rossi et al. (2004) note: "Evaluators . . . typically represent program impact theory in the form of a causal diagram showing the cause-and-effect linkages presumed to connect a program's activities with the expected outcomes" (p. 141; see also Stufflebeam & Shinkfield, 2007, on "causal inference"). What follows is an impact model for a second language preparation program for international teaching assistants at a U.S. university (adapted from Rossi et al., 2004). In Figure 5.2, the impact model suggests that in the teacher's/evaluator's

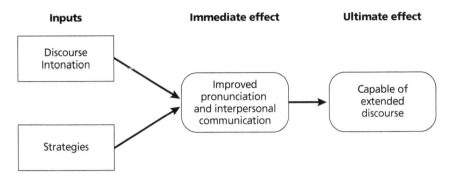

Figure 5.2 An impact model for a second language preparation course for international teaching assistants.

thinking, there are two inputs or "causes" to the course, namely discourse intonation and strategies. Trained instructors, textbooks, and CDs/DVDs attuned to discourse intonation and strategies comprise the input. Discourse intonation refers to an orientation to teaching and learning suprasegmental aspects of North American English pronunciation (thought groups, prominence, and tone choices), which can be used to emphasize and differentiate ideas, begin and end topics, and express social relationships in spoken utterances (Gorsuch, Meyers, Pickering, & Griffee, 2013; Pickering, 2001).

The second input, strategies, refers to classroom communication strategies commonly taught to international teaching assistants (ITA) to compensate for linguistic weaknesses and to facilitate the development of rapport between ITAs and their U.S. undergraduate students. These include doing comprehension checks, using examples to illustrate academic concepts, handling questions from students and using clarification requests or paraphrasing to confirm meaning in student-question sequences, and using transitional phrases in talks (Gorsuch, 2012).

These inputs are believed to cause the short-term effect of improving ITAs' pronunciation and interpersonal communication (also called a proximal or immediate effect). These are also the outcomes of the course stated in very basic terms. The activities associated with the inputs (see Table 5.2) play their part to cause the effects by building ITAs' explicit and implicit knowledge of discourse intonation and strategies through awareness-raising tasks using input with authentic academic discourse, and comprehensible output opportunities with feedback (Gorsuch et al., 2013). The immediate effect of the ITAs' improved pronunciation and interpersonal communication in turn is thought to cause a long-term effect of ITAs being more capable of using English in extended discourse in academic and professional settings (also called a distal or ultimate effect). This long-term effect is believed to come about by ITAs' increased participation in English-using professional communities. This greater participation, in turn, is brought about by feelings of success and greater self-efficacy in the smaller sphere of the classrooms in which ITAs teach physics, math, or chemistry. Self-efficacy is not a feeling, but rather the metacognitive ability to "organize and execute courses of action to attain designated performances" (Snow, Corno, & Jackson, 1995), based on experience (Gorsuch, 2009).

Here is an additional example of an impact model for an undergraduate Russian course taught at an eastern U.S. university (Paperno, 2014). It is possible to extrapolate an impact model from a course syllabus, particularly if the syllabus is fairly complete in its descriptions of outcomes, assignments, and activities. When positing an impact model for a course at a distance, using only a course syllabus, validating the impact model with input from others directly involved in the course becomes even more important. See commentary in both Chapters 5 and 6 on course logic validation.

The first input is online learner preparation, mentioned in the syllabus multiple times. For example, it is stated that learners must memorize two, four-line dialogs from a prespecified online source before each lesson, and must also write an original two-line dialog on a related topic. The syllabus stipulates 40 minutes of preparation before each class meeting based on the online materials. The second input is in-class treatment of learner preparation. This is extrapolated from the class activities described in the syllabus, where learners are told they should be able to recite the memorized dialogs in class without mistakes. Learners build up to doing skits with other learners using the memorized dialogs as a kind of springboard for creative talk. It is mentioned in the syllabus that the memorized dialogs represent useful

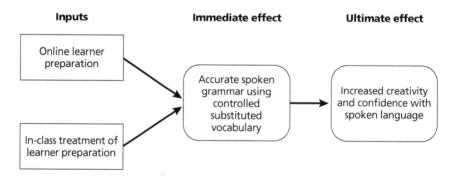

Figure 5.3 An impact model for a foreign language course for U.S. undergraduates.

conversation patterns and that learners can use them as models for their own creativity. The immediate effect of the two inputs seems to aim at accurate spoken grammar using controlled, substituted vocabulary. Learners are told in the syllabus to "pay special attention to using correct grammatical forms of the substitution words" (Paperno, 2014) in the prepared and memorized dialogs. The impact model (Figure 5.3) posits that the two inputs together then cause this immediate effect. The ultimate effect, which is in turn caused by the immediate effect, could be stated as increased creativity and confidence with spoken language. This is evidenced in the stated course purpose to the effect the learners will communicate with spontaneity. Stated learner assessments for the course are the rate of learner participation, and evidence of increasing fluency with unrehearsed conversations.

It may be tempting to overspecify an impact model. Most teachers/evaluators want to put more information into the model, with more explanations and descriptions. This is because they know a lot about the course, and because they experience classrooms and courses as dynamic things. While detailed descriptions will be useful in subsequent stages of mapping out course logic, at this stage of the game what is required is a level of thought at the level of a model with overarching concepts. At this initial stage of plotting out an impact model, it is best to keep things at a basic level and ask: "What are the main causes of learning in the course?" "What can these causes of learning be called?"

Working with the basic ideas at the conceptual level of a model is a significant strategy for maintaining clarity for oneself and also for establishing validity for the course logic study. If administrators or other persons external to the evaluation see the impact model and "get it" after a brief explanation from the evaluator, then we can say the model is more likely to be capable of validation. In fact, teachers/evaluators should be keeping a diary about doing the impact model and the organizational chart (Figure 5.3). This should include notes of their own thought processes and dilemmas, but even more importantly, records of how administrators and colleagues reacted to the impact model.

DISCUSSION QUESTION 5

Without looking at the description of the impact model in Figure 5.2 or Figure 5.3, explain one of the models to a colleague or a classmate. What part of your explanation did you struggle with? Could you explain the impact model with different inputs and outcomes for a different course?

The Organizational Chart

An organizational chart is used by a teacher/evaluator to think through what mainstream evaluators call the activities of a course. In contrast with an impact model (Figures 5.2 and 5.3), an organizational chart invites descriptive detail on what processes occur to support the course and the outcomes from the outside the classroom, and what processes occur to support the learners and the outcomes inside the classroom. Rossi et al. (2004) note "the plan encompasses both the functions and activities the program is expected to perform" (p. 142). Activities in the context of a course logic study means what happens to support a course (such as instructor training) and what happens in the course itself to support students to achieve course outcomes (instruction). Functions refers to who does the activities and why (see Figure 5.4).

The organizational chart in Figure 5.4 represents three groups who do the necessary functions of the course: a course coordinator, instructors, and students (the "target population," Rossi et al., 2004, p. 145). The course coordinator is represented by one box representing one function, with function being a label for why activities are done or what they build up to. The course coordinator's function here is that of giving "course direction, support." Thus the activities that the course coordinator does, such as establishing and monitoring course outcomes, and training instructors and graduate student teaching assistants (TAs), function to support the activities done in the ESL course by the instructors. Note the arrows from left to right. This suggests that the course coordinator's function and activities are necessary to adequately support the instructors and their in- and out-of-classroom activities.

The instructors are represented by four boxes, suggesting a line of logic which assumes there are four functions to the course: (a) helping learners develop explicit knowledge of discourse intonation and strategies through input, noticing; (b) helping learners develop implicit knowledge of discourse intonation through input, noticing; (c) leading learners to practice discourse intonation and strategies through comprehensible output; and (d) providing opportunities for feedback on use of discourse intonation and strategies. Discourse intonation means suprasegmental pronunciation including thought groups, prominence, and tone choices. Strategies means using comprehension checks and the like to develop rapport with U.S. undergraduates. In-class activities under each function are thought to support that function. For instance, Figure 5.4 suggests a line of logic that "Recursive listening tasks linking meaning, form" presented to ITAs as opportunities for input and noticing will help build learners' explicit knowledge of

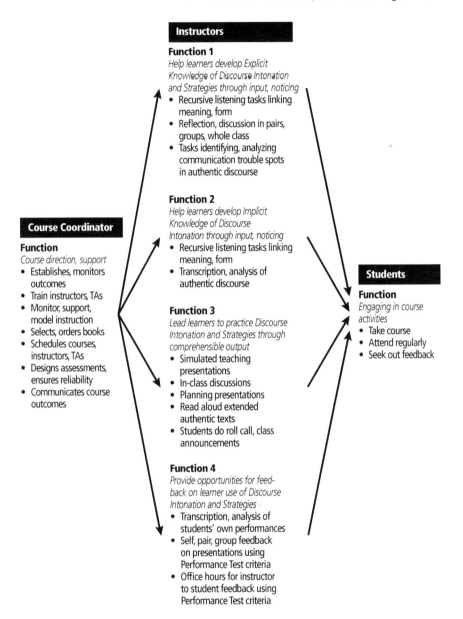

Instructors

Function 1
Help learners develop Explicit Knowledge of Discourse Intonation and Strategies through input, noticing
• Recursive listening tasks linking meaning, form
• Reflection, discussion in pairs, groups, whole class
• Tasks identifying, analyzing communication trouble spots in authentic discourse

Function 2
Help learners develop Implicit Knowledge of Discourse Intonation through input, noticing
• Recursive listening tasks linking meaning, form
• Transcription, analysis of authentic discourse

Function 3
Lead learners to practice Discourse Intonation and Strategies through comprehensible output
• Simulated teaching presentations
• In-class discussions
• Planning presentations
• Read aloud extended authentic texts
• Students do roll call, class announcements

Function 4
Provide opportunities for feedback on learner use of Discourse Intonation and Strategies
• Transcription, analysis of students' own performances
• Self, pair, group feedback on presentations using Performance Test criteria
• Office hours for instructor to student feedback using Performance Test criteria

Course Coordinator

Function
Course direction, support
• Establishes, monitors outcomes
• Train instructors, TAs
• Monitor, support, model instruction
• Selects, orders books
• Schedules courses, instructors, TAs
• Designs assessments, ensures reliability
• Communicates course outcomes

Students

Function
Engaging in course activities
• Take course
• Attend regularly
• Seek out feedback

Figure 5.4 Organizational chart for a second language preparation course for international teaching assistants.

DI and strategies. The arrows—from left to right leading to students—suggests that the activities set up by the instructors, such as self, pair, group feedback using the performance test criteria support the activities done by the students on the far right hand side of the model. As with the activities under the course coordinator's single function, the activities done by the instructors under the four functions are needed to adequately support the students and their activities. Finally, the students are represented by a single box that ascribes to them one basic function, that of "Engaging in course activities." This means taking the course, attending regularly, and seeking out feedback. All three of these activities are assumed to be necessary for learners to do in order to engage in the course.

Functions in an Organizational Chart for a Second Language Course Logic Study

The main benefit of specifying the functions of instructors and others in an organizational chart comes from having to link course activities to what they are supposed to accomplish for learners. In other words, teachers/evaluators need to know why given activities are done. In grouping activities into functions, teachers/evaluators are establishing and focusing their assumptions about how the activities support learners. In an organizational chart the functions stand in for course outcomes. They are not the outcomes themselves, yet they represent what the teacher/evaluator thinks has to happen in a course so that learners can accomplish the outcomes. In the case of Figure 5.4, the four instructor functions are stated in terms of robust findings from second language acquisition research, namely that learners need comprehensible input (Functions 1 and 2), they need to notice forms in the input (Functions 1 and 2), and they need to engage in comprehensible output (Function 3). An additional learning theory unpinning the feedback function in Figure 5.4 comes from the international teaching assistant (ITA) education field, namely that feedback on performance is needed to build ITAs' metacognition (Function 4), thus enhancing their ability to self-regulate and self-monitor (Gorsuch, 2012).

Not all teachers use learning theories such as input, noticing, comprehensible output, and metacognition to think about their teaching, and thus the way they ascribe functions, and the activities that support them, may be different. Their organizational charts will have different content. An evaluator, if he or she is not the teacher of the course, needs to take this into consideration. See Table 5.1, which uses two studies introduced earlier in this chapter.

Mapping out an organizational chart generates much detail that will assist the teacher/evaluator to create a final product, a course logic table. As noted earlier, teachers/evaluators should be keeping a diary about doing the impact model and the organizational chart. This should include notes of thought processes and dilemmas, but even more importantly records of

TABLE 5.1 Different Ways of Ascribing Activities and Functions in a Course			
Teacher/ Evaluator's tradition	Activities that support the functions	Functions ascribed to a course	Course outcomes
Total Physical Response (Wolfe et al., 1982)	Teacher presents new language as commands, students respond physically (*stand up, sit down, run*), then allowed to repeat new language verbally	Acquiring grammar, vocabulary through listening	Improving implicit knowledge of grammar and vocabulary
Computer-assisted language learning (Sanders, 2005)	Synchronous computer mediated communication tasks (chat), evaluated and discussed in face-to-face class time In-class group-work on poster sessions Automated exercises on WebCT	Facilitating greater student participation Processing input and monitoring output Students producing more language Learning grammar and vocabulary, and increasing comprehension through drill-like repetition	Improving oral performance

how administrators and colleagues reacted to the impact model and the organizational chart. Such stakeholders may offer useful commentary on the adequacy of a curriculum to bring about course outcomes, which is the whole point of a course logic study. For instance, someone looking at Figure 5.4 might say, "The functions and activities for the course do not seem like very much. Do you really spend all of your class time doing just those things?" A teacher/evaluator would note this response and then start thinking about (a) whether he or she included enough detail about the functions and activities in the organizational chart, and (b) whether the amount of time allocated to the course (twice a week, 90-minute sessions) would allow for additional functions and activities. Considering course intensity and duration (how often the course meets and for how long) as a curriculum resource is not often done and will be discussed in more detail.

DISCUSSION QUESTION 6

Describe and explain the model in Figure 5.4 to another person. What parts were easy to explain? Why? Which parts were difficult? Why?

DISCUSSION QUESTION 7

ooking at Table 5.1 can you think of other functions that the listed activities would support? Can you think of other activities suggested by the functions?

The Course Logic Table

Using information and ideas generated by the impact model and the organizational chart, teachers/evaluators can now complete a course logic table. The table is a way to organize key points of a course curriculum for the purpose of assessing the adequacy of the course curriculum to accomplish the outcomes. On p. 85 is a course logic table (Table 5.2) for an English as a second language preparation program for international teaching assistants at a U.S. university.

While there are no arrows in the table (as in Figures 5.3 and 5.4) there is a general orientation from left to right, where inputs are used to bring about activities that in turn results in an output, which we hope results in short- and long-term outcomes. One important addition to this chart has to do with the duration and intensity of a course, found under inputs, as time available is a resource for the course. This ITA preparation course follows a typical duration and intensity model of graduate content courses at the university where it is offered. That is to say, graduate courses in history or chemistry at the school are all configured to be worth three credit hours, which in the estimation of the school requires 37.33 contact hours per semester. This is an inescapable element of curriculum, particularly when working with second language learning, which is slow and not the same as content knowledge learning. It is likely that many second language courses stipulate too many functions, activities, and outcomes for the time that is available to the course. A course logic table, and the processes that lead up to it, can be used to argue for more frequent and longer class meetings while still keeping an eye on the inputs to the course. More and longer class meetings may require that instructors be paid more, or for the materials or instruction to change.

Teachers/evaluators can use the course logic table (Table 5.2), and their notes from constructing an impact model (Figures 5.2 and 5.3) and an organizational chart (Figure 5.4) to assess and validate their course logic. The three documents and the evaluator's notes and new understandings of the course comprise the course logic study.

TABLE 5.2 Course Logic Table for an English as a Second Language Preparation Course for International Teaching Assistants

Course Inputs	Functions and Activities	Course Outputs	Short-term outcomes	Long-term outcomes
Organizing concepts of Discourse Intonation and Strategies Course coordinator Trained instructors Textbook, CDs/DVDs designed for ITAs Locally developed and validated assessments based in current second language communicative competence theory ITAs identified by academic departments for course participation; some ITAs self-select Classes meet twice a week for 80 minutes each for 14 weeks (37.33 hours total)	Functions: Course provides classes on building implicit and explicit second language knowledge of DI and Strategies using second language acquisition theories stipulating opportunities for input, noticing, comprehensible output, and theories of adult metacognition development. Activities: Recursive listening tasks, pair/group/whole class discussions and tasks, simulated teaching presentations with pair/group and instructor/student feedback using course assessment criteria, transcription and analysis tasks	ITAs take course, attend regularly, seek out feedback on spoken performances	Outcome summary: Improved ITA pronunciation and interpersonal communication Stated course outcomes: 1. Learners will be able to sustain a presentation on a topic in their field for at least 10 minutes with reasonable spoken fluency. 2. Learners will be able to engage in question and answer sessions after their presentation and demonstrate ability to comprehend and answer questions. 3. Learners will demonstrate knowledge of discourse intonation and its role in getting U.S. undergraduates to understand learners' intended meaning.	Outcome summary: ITAs capable of extended discourse in academic and professional settings

Assessing and Validating Course Logic

In mainstream evaluation (evaluation as a field in its own right external to second language education), some commentators suggest creating a panel of reviewers who review the course outcomes and assess the likelihood that the curriculum can support learners to attain the outcomes. Validating the course logic simply means a teacher/evaluator has collected persuasive evidence from multiple sources as to the logical clarity and soundness of the course logic. Putting together a panel is probably too cumbersome and time consuming for teachers/evaluators working on their own. Nonetheless, teachers/evaluators have much to gain by going to a handful of knowledgeable stakeholders to assess their impact model and organizational chart, and most importantly their course logic table.

Here are some general suggestions for assessing and building up a validation of course logic:

1. By doing a course logic study, a teacher/evaluator has likely made their own assessment as the adequacy of the course curriculum to support stated learner outcomes. For the purposes of asking others to assess the course logic teachers should not mention their own assessment until a reviewer has said all they wish to say. In fact, the teacher need not mention their assessment at all.

2. Select two or three reviewers from different levels of administrative experience, for instance one instructor/colleague, and one departmental chairperson or an associate dean. Once it becomes clear the teacher/evaluator is focused on the course logic and not asking for more resources or undermining the person who wrote the curriculum, reviewers at higher administrative levels can offer useful insights.

3. Choose one knowledgeable reviewer from outside the school in which the course is offered.

4. The teacher/evaluator should make notes based on reviewers' comments.

5. Using notes from sessions with reviewers, the teacher/evaluator should critically evaluate their own assessment. Is there a pattern to reviewers' comments? Have reviewers' comments brought up new insights on the curriculum and or the outcomes? Were there particular issues or descriptions of the outcomes or curriculum that reviewers seemed unclear on?

6. Revise and write down an assessment of the course logic based on the course logic study and reviewers' comments if appropriate.

Here are some additional suggestions on building up a validation of course logic:

7. Teachers/evaluators can present their assessment of the course logic to a group of colleagues during informal or formal faculty meetings. Make note of the audience's comments. Do they generally concur with the assessment? If not, why not?
8. Do additional reading in the literature to find both confirmatory and non-confirmatory evidence for the assessment. What have other teachers/evaluators found while doing course evaluation or needs analysis of their programs?

DISCUSSION QUESTION 8

f you showed your course logic model to your immediate supervisor, what might his or her reaction be? What might cause you concern?

APPLICATION TASKS: Making Choices About Curriculum Change and Preparing for Course Logic Validation

First task idea: Taking the example from earlier in the chapter about the German-language teachers who wanted to include a new reading fluency outcome but could not do so with the current curriculum, write down the positive and negative points about either choice: (a) change the course curriculum or (b) change the outcomes of the course. Which choice is more compelling? If Letter a, note how the teachers would need to change the course curriculum in order to accommodate the new reading fluency outcome. For instance, can more appropriate materials for reading fluency be located? How? Can class time itself be increased? How? If Letter b, note what teachers might have been thinking of when they discussed German reading fluency as a worthwhile outcome. What will be the effect on learners, and teachers, if the course outcomes remain focused on grammar and vocabulary?

Second task idea: Write a script of how you would present a course logic study (an impact model, etc.) for review by another person for the purposes of assessment. LaRocco (2012) used "epoche," a kind of conscious focusing of purpose, before interviewing people for her study on intercultural communication. She noted, "[I] took a few minutes before each interview to think about the topic and research question and to clear my mind of thoughts and reactions to the topic" (p. 622). If your purpose is to get a clear picture of another person's assessment of course logic through a comparison of outcomes and curriculum, what specific focus statements can you use to prepare yourself for the interview? How would you keep yourself, and the reviewer, focused on your purpose?

References

Dewey, J. (2013). My pedagogic creed. In D. Flinders & S. Thornton (Eds.), *The curriculum studies reader* (4th ed.; pp. 33–40). New York, NY: Routledge.

Genesee, F., & Upshur, J. (1996). *Classroom-based evaluation in second language education.* Cambridge, England: Cambridge University Press.

Gorsuch, G. (2009). Investigating second language learner self-efficacy and future expectancy for second language use for high-stakes program evaluation. *Foreign Language Annals, 42*(3), 505–540.

Gorsuch, G. (2012). The roles of teacher theory and domain theory in materials and research in international teaching assistant education. In G. Gorsuch (Ed.). *Working theories for teaching assistant development* (pp. 429–482). Stillwater, OK: New Forums Press.

Gorsuch, G., Meyers, C., Pickering, L., & Griffee, D. (2013). *English communication for international teaching assistants* (2nd ed.). Long Grove, IL: Waveland Press.

LaRocco, M. J. (2012). Chinese international teaching assistants and the essence of intercultural competence in university contexts. In G. Gorsuch (Ed.), *Working theories for teaching assistant development* (pp. 609–654). Stillwater, OK: New Forums Press.

Paperno, S. (2014). *Russian 1104: Course description.* Ithaca, NY: Cornell University. Retrieved from http://russian.dmll.cornell.edu/index.cfm?MainFrameURL=description&Section=currentclasses&CourseID=RUSSA1104-101&LinkID=RUSSA1104-101

Pickering, L. (2001). The role of tone choice in improving ITA communication in the classroom. *TESOL Quarterly, 35*(2), 233–255.

Rossi, P. H., Lipsey, M. W., & Freeman, H. E. (2004). *Evaluation: A systematic approach* (7th ed.). Thousand Oaks, CA: Sage.

Sanders, R. (2005). Redesigning introductory Spanish: Increased enrollment, online management, cost reduction, and effects on student learning. *Foreign Language Annals, 38*(4), 523–532.

Snow, R., Corno, L., & Jackson, D. (1995). Individual differences in affective and conative functions. In D. Berliner & R. Calfee (Eds.), *Handbook of educational psychology* (pp. 243–310). New York, NY: MacMillan.

Stufflebeam, D., & Shinkfield, A. (2007). *Evaluation theory, models, and applications.* San Francisco, CA: Jossey-Bass.

Sugarman, J. (2008). *Evaluation of the dual language program in the North Shore School District 112, Highland Park, IL.* Washington, DC: Center for Applied Linguistics.

Wolfe, D., & Jones, G. (1982) Integrating total physical response strategy in a level I Spanish class. *Foreign Language Annals, 14*(4), 273–279.

6

Curriculum and Stakeholders, and Formative Evaluation

I must do something to keep my thoughts fresh and growing. I dread nothing so much as falling into a rut and feeling myself becoming a fossil.

—James Garfield, self-educated school teacher, American Civil War veteran, and 19th century U.S. president

This chapter explores the relationship of SOAC model components *curriculum*[1] and *stakeholders*, where stakeholders comment on how a course is functioning, typically while the course is underway. This is *formative evaluation*, and two actual formative evaluations are recounted here: those of an English course and a German course. Teachers/evaluators are guided through formative evaluation in practical detail while capturing a balance between data collection sufficient to mean something and a respect for teachers'/evaluators' limited time and energy.

Here is the fourth chapter in which the SOAC evaluation model (stakeholders, outcomes, assessment, and curriculum) is applied to second and *foreign language* courses. In this chapter we will explore the relationship

---

1. For all terms in *italics*, see Glossary.

Evaluating Second Language Courses, pages 91–132
Copyright © 2016 by Information Age Publishing

between the course curriculum and the stakeholders of the course, which is best captured in a *formative evaluation*. A formative evaluation is typically done while a course is taking place, and answers the question of whether and how the curriculum (the class exercises, textbooks, PowerPoints, homework assignments, and teachers' talk and explanations) is supporting *second language* learners' attainment of the course outcomes. The stakeholders most often consulted are the learners, but other stakeholders can be consulted, including supervisors, the course teacher, and teachers of the same or similar courses at a school. It should be noted that a formative evaluation can also be done at the end of the course, with the purpose of making *decision points* (suggestions or comments) for when the course may be offered again. Regardless of when a formative evaluation is done in relation to the course time span, there are ways to create a balance between collecting enough data so as to be informative, and accommodating a teacher's/evaluator's limited time and energy.

DISCUSSION QUESTION 1

Have you ever asked your students, or anyone else involved in a course you were teaching, what they thought about the course?

DISCUSSION QUESTION 2

If you are not now teaching, but were given the chance to teach a course, what questions might you ask the students, or others, about how the course was going?

DISCUSSION QUESTION 3

Has anyone ever asked you to comment on a course someone else was teaching? What stakeholder were you? What did you say?

Invariably, the process of doing a formative evaluation unearths ways of improving the course curriculum, which through a reflective process results in a set of decision points for teachers to consider. Decision points are suggestions for teachers/evaluators focused on the elements of the curriculum that are investigated in accordance with the *evaluation questions* (EQs). Examples of decision points resulting from a college-level German foreign language course formative evaluation are:

1. Consider allowing use of smartphone technologies for students to find vocabulary for individual purposes, with instruction on how to wisely discern needed information in the definitions.

2. Consider having learners ask questions during an already-existing activity, that of the instructor showing photographs on a Power-Point presentation and talking about the pictures.
3. Consider aiming at vocabulary recycling at least 80% of the textbook lists in future lessons.
4. Consider focusing on common words that appear more frequently in the book to recycle as opposed to proper nouns, which do not occur frequently in use.
5. Consider using the PowerPoints as an opportunity to recycle vocabulary if the book does not.

These decision points resulted from the teacher's EQ: What activities are done in the classroom that involve explicit vocabulary instruction? These decision points and the EQ are living instances of the thoughts of 19th century educator James Garfield, quoted at the beginning of this chapter. Many teachers want to remain fresh and creative, and to uncover effective and timely ways to support learning outcomes. Formative evaluation serves teachers/evaluators to do this in ways that are relevant to how well a curriculum supports course objectives using stakeholders' perspectives as significant points of reference. The project for this chapter will be a formative evaluation, where teachers/evaluators form EQs for a course, collect data, and write decision points to consider. Two formative evaluations are used as illustrations: one a graduate-level, second language English class and the other a college-level German foreign language class.

DISCUSSION QUESTION 4

Consider the five decision points and the teacher's EQ previously listed. What would you guess is one of the stated outcomes of the German course? Do the decision points seem oriented to the outcome?

What Is Formative Evaluation and Where Is It in the SOAC Model?

One way to get a grip on doing a formative evaluation is to relate it to the SOAC model (see Chapter 2). Formative evaluation can be seen in the partial SOAC model in Figure 6.1.

Formative evaluation is a process whereby stakeholders (often students in a course) are asked to comment on a course curriculum (the teaching, the materials, learners' independent work, etc.), typically currently underway, for the purpose of changing or improving some aspect of the course (Wiliam, 2011). Formative evaluation can include quiz scores, learner or

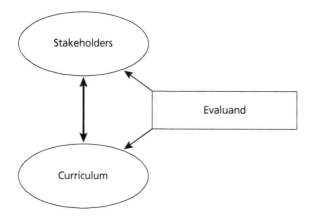

Figure 6.1   The SOAC model and formative evaluation.

teacher observations, or comments that suggest that specific processes in the curriculum are promoting learner achievement of outcomes, or are not as effective as they could be. As will become more clear, the real struggle is deciding what to include in a formative evaluation, which by its nature must be lean, nimble, and focused if teachers/evaluators are to answer evaluation questions (EQs) to provide useful information while the course is still underway, or during all-too-brief breaks between course terms. We approach this struggle by discussing why a formative evaluation might be done by demonstrating how *course logic* can be used to focus our EQs. We also detail what to do if a teacher/evaluator has not previously worked with course logic. Finally we introduce a formative evaluation plan table which will bring clarity to a formative evaluation. For more on course logic, see Chapter 5.

Why Do a Formative Evaluation?

In asking "Why do a formative evaluation?" there are two things that make formative evaluation somewhat different from *summative evaluation*: First, formative evaluation is typically done while the course is under way. The purpose of formative evaluation in this sense is to propose changes (decision points) to implement before the course is over, allowing for needed "mid-course corrections" to take place (Isaac & Michael, 1997; Wiliam, 2011). It is true that decision points can be used for a course to be offered the next year or next term, but formative evaluation has strong value to a course while it is still being held. Gorsuch and Sokolowski (2007) taught nonnative English speaking college lab instructors to write and administer short questionnaires to their freshmen students about the instructors'

English used for teaching. The questionnaires were handed out at three points during the semester, and were slightly different each time as each instructor discovered unique aspects of their instruction they wanted students' perspectives on. Many of the lab instructors changed their teaching and second language talk in positive, observable ways on the basis of the freshmen students' successive comments when it most counted—before the course was even half over.

Second, formative evaluation is well suited to capturing the processes of a curriculum. It is one thing to retrospect over someone's teaching once a semester is over and done, and yet another thing to observe and comment on that person's teaching in real time, as it is taking place over successive class meetings. In the former case, a teacher's instruction, which took place throughout a course, might simply be reduced to two or three categories of half-remembered impressions. In the latter case, a teacher/evaluator can see whether and how German vocabulary items are recycled over a period of time, or whether students' attendance at spoken English feedback sessions is adequate at the beginning of a course. The beginning of the course is when feedback on second language performance is most valuable, considering the inherent slowness of second language learning processes (see for example, Teachers of English to Speakers of Other Languages, 2010). Various authors in second language evaluation might term this way of looking at formative evaluation as "illuminative evaluation" in which an evaluation "seeks to provide a deeper understanding of the processes of teaching and learning that occur" (Richards, 2001, p. 289; Kiely & Rea-Dickins, 2005; and see also Ellis, 1997 for his description of an evaluation actually done by a teacher/evaluator). If we are to focus intensely on whether and how a curriculum supports course outcomes in the eyes of various stakeholders, viewing the teaching, learning tasks, and independent learner activities as real-time processes confers significant advantage.

There is some discussion in second language education that suggests that formative evaluation should be defined as an evaluation that takes place for reasons internal to a teacher/evaluator (see Chapter 1). For instance, a teacher/evaluator may wish to know whether her PowerPoint presentations on grammar are seen as helpful or needed by learners. The same teacher may think that direct correction of students' utterances in class is needed to attain course outcomes, which are to accurately learn German grammar rules. The teacher may also wonder whether she is hurting students' feelings by correcting them, and whether this is demotivating. However, as a mainstream evaluation counterpoint to the idea that formative evaluations are done for internal reasons, see Wiliam (2011) for descriptions of large-scale formative evaluations done for external reasons. A second language education example might be some external party, such as a supervisor or researcher, wanting information about how well or how easily teachers can use a required textbook to provide needed feedback to second language students, where the feedback is deemed a main means of learner attainment of outcomes (see Figure 5.4 and Table 5.2). See Appendix A for a bibliography of articles and book chapters of evaluation reports, some of which are formative evaluations.

DISCUSSION QUESTION 5

Make a list of 10 things you think need to take place in a second language course in order for students to learn, including what students have to do and what teachers have to do. Can all of those things take place during a single class meeting, or even during regular class times?

DISCUSSION QUESTION 6

Does the teacher's job change from the beginning of a second language textbook chapter or unit to the end of a textbook chapter or unit? Do the students' jobs change? How? Why would one day of teaching or studying be different than another day?

As mentioned earlier, one key task for a teacher/evaluator is to focus the scope of a formative evaluation. Thus, while teachers experience a course curriculum as rich and having many aspects of interest, they need to narrow down what they choose to evaluate.

DISCUSSION QUESTION 7

Out of the list you made for discussion question 5 or your thoughts from discussion question 6, which one item or area is of most interest to you? Why?

Using Course Logic to Focus a Formative Evaluation

In this chapter, two examples of formative evaluations are given. The first one, which is detailed, is a formative evaluation of a graduate-level second language English course taught at a U.S. university. ESL 5310 is designed for international teaching assistants (ITAs) who have not yet been approved to teach. The course has been described in Chapters 3, 4, and 5. In Chapter 5, we introduced an impact model (Figure 5.2), an organizational chart (Figure 5.4), and course logic table (Table 5.2). These are organizing graphics used to bring together the results of a course logic study, which is a study of the assumptions of how the ESL 5310 curriculum is thought to bring about learners' attainment of course outcomes. Teachers/evaluators who have done a course logic study may find the results to be useful for determining the scope of a formative evaluation and thus posing EQs. Course logic is after all a detailed hypothesis, posed in terms of the curriculum itself as to how the curriculum works.

The best way to use an existing course logic study to frame a formative evaluation is to assess or review it (see Chapter 5). In other words, has the course logic study captured what a curriculum likely does to bring students to the outcomes? Table 6.1 shows the steps of a course logic assessment and validation actually done for ESL 5310. Note there is some overlap with the suggestions given for course logic validation found at the end of Chapter 5.

Steps 1 and 2: Selecting and Interviewing Knowledgeable Stakeholders

As our first step we worked to review our ESL 5310 course logic study by selecting and interviewing three knowledgeable stakeholders: a department chairperson, an administrator in the department but with no personal stake in the course, and a senior ESL 5310 instructor. The first two stakeholders were individuals who had ultimate administrative responsibility, or accountability, for the course. They had heard many teachers talk about their courses over the years, mediated many student complaints, and mentored many teachers with low end-of-semester evaluations. Thus they thought of the many courses offered in the department in broad, almost business-like ways. When reviewing the ESL 5310 course logic model, it was they who posed specific questions about the TAs, who were graduate students assisting the instructor, and their roles in the course as depicted in the course logic model (see Figure 5.4 and Table 5.2 in Chapter 5). Did the TAs have enough knowledge or support on how to instruct students in a high-stakes course? This emerged as a significant unintended consequence of the course logic of ESL 5310, and not surprisingly, emerged later in the evaluation (see Table 6.9). The third stakeholder had experience with ESL

TABLE 6.1 Course Logic Assessment, and Using the Results to Focus a Formative Evaluation
1. Selecting and interviewing knowledgeable stakeholders
2. Keeping a running memo of stakeholders' reactions to the course logic
3. Using the memo to review and introspect, and to identify gaps in course logic or other areas of emerging interest
4. Prioritizing and choosing one or two curriculum areas to focus on
5. Writing evaluation questions for the formative evaluation

5310 as an instructor, but was also disinterested in a healthy way in that he did not have a strong emotional stake in the curriculum. It was he who commented about a lack of clarity of the students' role in the course logic model (Figure 5.4 and Table 5.2). What responsibilities or resources did the students have to improve their English outside of class?

The three stakeholders were each shown the impact model (Figure 5.2), the organizational chart (Figure 5.4), and the course logic table (Table 5.2) one at a time and were asked three questions for each graphic: (a) Are the proposed inputs, activities, and outputs, and the relationships between them conceptually clear? (b) Is anything missing? and (c) Is the curriculum up to supporting the course outcomes? Notes of stakeholders' responses were written down in a running *memo*. A memo is simply a word processing document or notebook in which a teacher/evaluator can keep brief, daily notes about the evaluation in progress.

DISCUSSION QUESTION 8

Who are the stakeholders in a course you are involved in as a teacher or a student? Which stakeholder would you choose to comment on the course logic? Why? Even if you have not formally worked on articulating the course logic, you probably have some idea of how to describe how your course works.

Step 3: Keeping a Running Memo of Stakeholders' Reactions to the Course Logic

We returned to the memo once every few days with fresh eyes and added additional insights based on the responses of stakeholders to the course logic model and also based on introspection. We were able to identify gaps in the course logic and also some emerging areas of interest. Here are excerpts from the memo:

> TAs and our training activities with them need to be modeled. Do they know how to give feedback to students?

> Query: Is the textbook, and other materials, being used in ways that support course outcomes?

> Students' "job" needs to be more descriptive. Do they use office hours? What do they use them for?

> Explore out-of-class activities which would amount to 37.33 hours outside of class.

> Query: Will additional out-of-class activities just end up being more work for teachers?

Step 4: Using the Memo to Review and Introspect, and to Identify Gaps in Course Logic or Other Areas of Emerging Interest

It is tempting to investigate everything in a curriculum. But for a formative evaluation to be done while a course is underway, it has to remain limited in scope. A teacher/evaluator needs to prioritize and choose one or two areas of the curriculum to evaluate. What are the areas of a curriculum? In Chapters 2 and 5, we identified the following: instruction (lectures, activities, teacher theories underpinning activities, and assignments); materials (textbooks, handouts, CDs, software); schedule (how often a class meets and for how long); participants' roles and responsibilities (what teachers and students are supposed to do); tests (quizzes, unit tests); facilities (the classroom, libraries); and course transparency (course syllabuses, and descriptions of course requirements and assignments). We illustrate these while discussing three strategies for prioritizing which curriculum areas to write evaluation questions for (Table 6.2).

The first strategy is to identify what seems urgent. Are students complaining loudly and refusing to use a required textbook (materials)? Has a supervisor given feedback that important assignment descriptions and grading criteria for them on a syllabus seem unclear (course transparency)? Has a teaching evaluation done in a previous semester indicated low ratings on how well an instructor explains concepts in class (instruction)? In the context of the course logic assessment done for ESL 5310, the instructor/ stakeholder felt alarmed that students were not working on their English outside of class, and not visiting during office hours (participants' roles and responsibilities). The resulting lack of students' progress and their apparent attitude of indifference made him feel inept and demotivated as a teacher.

A second strategy is to identify what gives discomfort. Are students doing fine with their grammar exercises, but not as well on end-of-unit tests demanding free talk (instruction, and possibly tests)? Such a mismatch might give the teacher discomfort because of the gap between practice activities that ought to help, and the reality of little transfer from one small task to another large task. In ESL 5310, instructors and TAs remarked that

TABLE 6.2 Strategies for Prioritizing Which Curriculum Areas to Investigate
1. Identify what seems urgent, and seriously challenges professional or personal values, or runs counter to institutional values or policies.
2. Identify what causes discomfort, and somewhat challenges professional values or *teacher theory* about what constitutes effective ways to learn.
3. Identify what is interesting or absorbing, and causes interest and anticipation.

students came to office hours without focused questions and seemed more interested in simply giving the same presentation over and over with little appreciable improvement (participants' roles and responsibilities, and possibly instruction if it is believed tutoring ought to take place during office hours). This caused discomfort. The two administrators/ stakeholders interviewed for the course logic assessment wondered at the same time whether the TAs had enough training to know how to conduct useful office hours and give feedback (instruction). If TAs knew better how to conduct office hours, they might not be at the mercy of students who insisted on engaging in activities that were not apparently helpful.

A third and final strategy is to identify what is simply interesting or absorbing. Some teachers/evaluators may be interested in using language learning lab (LLL) facilities because the school has a new LLL or because students have said they like a particular language learning program (facilities and possibly materials). Other teachers/evaluators teaching a course that meets only twice a week might be interested in exploring whether reviewing ought to be done by students outside of class in assigned study groups (schedule and possibly participants' roles and responsibilities). During the ESL 5310 course logic assessment, we became interested in if and how the textbook and other classroom materials (materials) were being used by instructors and TAs during students' office hour visits (instruction), and how principled changes in these practices might support course objectives better. We were interested in whether using the textbook during office hours might focus students' attention more effectively on the outcomes (participants' roles and responsibilities), and whether the textbook might prove an effective tool for supporting the TAs to conduct office hours and give feedback (materials and also instruction).

DISCUSSION QUESTION 9

Which of the three strategies in Table 6.2 do you find most compelling? Why?

For the formative evaluation for ESL 5310 we settled on materials as the main curriculum area to be studied. While our running memo helped us identify four or five topics of emerging interest, we focused on those that caused discomfort to teachers and TAs, namely the lack of student focus in class and during office hour visits. We also focused on what seemed interesting, namely exploring ways the textbook and other materials were used in class, which might then be transferred to office hour visits, and also for training TAs how to give feedback to students on their spoken performances. It is true that curriculum areas have overlap. When thinking about textbooks and office hours, does not instruction also suggest itself as a curriculum area to explore in a formative evaluation? There is no easy answer to this except to think about it in terms of greater focus on one area and less on another. If a teacher/evaluator chose one primary area such as materials, they may be asking "What are the various materials used? Do students think using them helps them reach course outcomes?" Descriptions of instruction taking place using materials may be noted down in a formative evaluation, but the materials are the primary focus.

Step 5: Writing Evaluation Questions for the Formative Evaluation

When composing evaluation questions (EQs), it helps to recall what a formative evaluation does. Among other things, a formative evaluation looks at how well curriculum processes support course objectives using stakeholders' perspectives. Thus a formative evaluation ought to capture curriculum processes, suggesting *what* questions and *how* questions. A formative evaluation can also assign value, or direction, to these curriculum processes from multiple perspectives in light of desired course outcomes, suggesting *how well* and *are XX satisfied* questions. Here are the EQs for the ESL 5310 formative evaluation:

EQ 1: What materials do instructors, TAs, and students use in class? What materials do they use out of class? How do they use them?

EQ 2: How well do the materials used in class support the course outcomes? How well do the materials used out of class support the course outcomes? Are instructors, TAs, and students satisfied with the materials?

While our purpose was to focus on students' office hour visits (one part of out-of-class time) we felt we needed to identify effective and favored materials used in class. Such materials and practices, if not already used during office hours, might be most adaptable to out-of-class use. We felt the stakeholders who would offer the most direct information were the instructors, the TAs, and the students. Further, in order to keep the formative evaluation doable, we kept to these three stakeholder groups.

How to Focus a Formative Evaluation When You Do Not Have an Existing Course Logic Study

Many teachers/evaluators will not have done a course logic study. Working with course logic is rare. Therefore, teachers/evaluators will not have an

TABLE 6.3   Doing an Exploratory Interview and Using the Results to Focus a Formative Evaluation
1. Do an exploratory interview
2. Review the interview at least twice and keep a running memo of reactions to the responses
3. Use the memo to review and introspect, and identify areas of emerging interest
4. Prioritize and choose one or two curriculum areas to focus on
5. Write evaluation questions for the formative evaluation

existing model to review or assess in order to generate focal points for a formative evaluation. This was the case with a formative evaluation we did with a second-year undergraduate German foreign language course at a U.S. university. As we describe here, not having a course logic study to assess does not mean a teacher/evaluator will have any shortage of topics to explore. The question again will be to focus the scope of the formative evaluation. Many of the steps are similar to what an evaluator would do to produce evaluations questions (EQs) based on a course logic assessment. See Table 6.3.

Step 1: Doing an Exploratory Interview

This exploratory interview is based on the SOAC evaluation model with an emphasis on the curriculum and stakeholders sections of the model. Note how we touch on materials, instruction, roles and responsibilities, etc. in the interview items. The interview can be done by another person at the behest of a teacher who wishes to have someone do a formative evaluation of his or her course, or by the teacher himself or herself as a self-inventory. In either event, we suggest the person answering the questions to say aloud and record their responses, and to speak at length. The verbal responses can be transcribed and then reviewed. We find the process of transcribing the responses to increase an evaluator's depth of review and introspection done with the responses. See Table 6.4 for the exploratory interview. Items can be added as necessary to reflect the local context, or items related to the teacher's internal reasons for doing the evaluation. For example, we added an item about a new tutoring program being offered to students in German and other foreign language classes in the department.

We highlight some of the instructor's responses about the German course here.

> **Evaluator:** Could you describe the outcomes of your course in your own words?

TABLE 6.4   Exploratory Interview Items
Could you describe the outcomes of your course in your own words?
Who cares about the course outcomes? Who are your stakeholders?
Which stakeholders are you concerned about? Why?
Please describe your lessons.
Please describe your materials.
How do the lessons and materials contribute to course outcomes?
Please describe your course schedule.
What is your job with the course?
What is the students' job?
What is the supervisor's or director's job?
Who else has a job to do?
Please describe your tests. How do you assign grades?
Are the tests used in class or for any other instructional purpose? A focus for instruction?
Please describe the facilities for the course.
What part do your office hours play in the course?
Do you use the course syllabus to communicate with students?
What function does the course syllabus play?
What are you concerned about with your course?
What would you like to examine in the course as it pertains to the studying/learning experiences students have in your course?
What would you like to examine in the course as it pertains to the teaching experiences you have in your course?

Instructor: They should be able to speak about normal daily personal issues. Have a daily conversation with a friend, or a non-formal conversation. And also they should be able to read a text that is not too hard and grasp the overall topic and main arguments, they should be able to write a text, a short essay and also personal stuff that it related to their own lives. They should have some knowledge about German culture, how life is in Germany.

Evaluator: And those are stated on the syllabus?

Instructor: Uh-huh more or less.

Evaluator: What would you like to examine in the course as it pertains to the studying/learning experiences students have in the course?

Instructor: Yeah, that transition that goes from grammar vocabulary things they learn to actually using it and being able to survive in a real-life situation, and how this prepares them for those situations.

Evaluator: What would you like to examine in the course as it pertains to the teaching experiences you have in the course?

Instructor: Well my interest is in vocabulary teaching and learning, and how I can make it, how I can provide a good way for my students to learn vocabulary so that it sticks. I'm convinced that a big part of the students' job is to learn vocabulary, but how can I help them, what can I do in the class to just help them with that.

Evaluator: What does learning vocabulary have to do with students doing their jobs in the course?

Instructor: Well it's the basis. They need that for any language production whatsoever. They go to the country, if they want to read texts, if they want to write texts, if they want to write emails later in German, if they want to communicate to somebody, if they want to talk about things with their friends. They need to have vocabulary that is big enough to build on. We have cases and endings.

Evaluator: If learners had basic verbs and nouns, would they sound stupid if they didn't have the right endings?

Instructor: Yes. They need so much help with the endings. They have to know the gender for nouns in order to determine the endings, and also the adjectives take different endings.

Note that while the evaluator/interviewer starts out with the basic interview items shown in Table 6.4, she follows up with questions to clarify the instructor's responses.

Steps 2 and 3: Reviewing the Interview and Identifying Areas of Emerging Interest

The interview responses for the German course formative evaluation were reviewed three times over the period of a week and impressions were written down in a running memo. A memo, once more, is simply a word processing document in which the evaluator kept brief, daily notes about the evaluation. Before actually returning to the interview responses and the memo for review, the evaluator spent a few minutes recalling what was in the responses and memo to reach some points of focus, something akin to what LaRocco (2012, p. 622) reported doing when dealing with large amounts of interview data: "I took a few moments before each interview... to think about the topic... and to clear my mind of thoughts and reactions to the topic." Reaching this state of mind, and then reviewing the responses and the memo to confirm or add information, helped to identify emerging areas of interest. Here are excerpts from the memo:

Week one:

Once we have defined one or two areas of curriculum concern I can design DCIs [data collection instruments] and a plan for collection and analysis. Important for instructor to have input and concur. Consensus will be one method of validating the DCIs.

Week two:

In terms of what she (the teacher) experiences: "How I can provide a good way for my students to learn vocabulary so that it sticks. I'm convinced that a big part of the students' job is to learn vocabulary, but how can I help them, what can I do in the class to just help them with that."

She seems to want to investigate these issues in terms of: (a) what learners will need to be able to do in the next German course in the sequence, and (b) what learners need to be able to do in real life.

One other possible area also has to do with what she thinks learners must be able to do in the next German course: "What kind of activities I choose also. Do I want them to write things down, do I want them to speak and have an oral activity, or do I want them to work by themselves or with partners or in groups. A decision would be how much instruction they need from me, how much I can have them work independently." This seems to have to do with getting learners to integrate explicit knowledge into real-use situations such as reading texts, or writing e-mails, or having simple discussions in German about texts.

My next steps are to (a) go over the transcript with the teacher, (b) validate it, and then (c) confirm what areas to focus on for the FE (formative evaluation). We need to come up with EQs and a data collection plan.

Three days later:

I met briefly with the teacher yesterday and she confirmed the points (previously listed) were of greatest interest to her.

Steps 4 and 5: Prioritizing a Curriculum Area on Which to Focus, and Writing Evaluation Questions

Of all the areas of interest emerging from the review of the exploratory interview responses and the memo, the instructor seemed most focused on the curriculum area of instruction and participant roles and responsibilities, with two issues either causing discomfort or feelings of interest: her instruction of vocabulary, and how students worked on their own with vocabulary outside of class. These were important to the instructor because she anticipated a shift in course outcomes for the last course in the required 2-year program that the students would take next. This last course would require students to be independent readers of longer texts, among other things, for which they would need vocabulary. She wondered whether the course she taught would adequately prepare students for their next course. The areas of interest suggested a focus on her (the instructor) and the students as stakeholders.

Following the reasoning that a formative evaluation ought to capture curriculum processes of interest (what) and then assign value to these curriculum processes from multiple perspectives (how well), in light of desired course outcomes, the following evaluation questions (EQs) were posed:

> **EQ 1:** What activities are done in the classroom that involve explicit vocabulary instruction?
>
> **EQ 2:** What activities do learners do outside of class in which they are self-instructing vocabulary?

DISCUSSION QUESTION 10

In both instances, using an existing course logic study and working without an existing course logic study, keeping a memo has a large role in keeping track of a teacher's/evaluator's ideas and emerging themes. If you used a memo, what would it look like? What problems do you foresee in keeping and using a memo? If a memo is not kept, what other ways could a teacher/evaluator keep track of his or her ideas?

Planning Data Collection for a Formative Evaluation

Establishing evaluation questions (EQs) for a formative evaluation is the first major step. EQs provide direction for data collection and analysis. When doing a formative evaluation for a course, the greatest value of a data collection plan is to save time and prioritize evaluation activity. Planning is key for teachers/evaluators who are busy getting on with their lives as well as doing a formative evaluation. In addition, having a plan for data collection allows for review. No plan is set in stone and any aspect of it can be changed, should the teacher/evaluator decide to abandon, change, or add an EQ. Or, a teacher/evaluator may decide that after interviews with numerous stakeholders and multiple classroom observations, he or she has enough representative information and does not need to do a questionnaire after all. We address the issue of teacher/evaluator time and energy later in this chapter under the heading, "how much data to collect."

We offer a formative evaluation data collection plan template for the second language course, ESL 5310 (see Table 6.5). A blank template for

TABLE 6.5 ESL 5310 Formative Evaluation Data Collection Plan

Stakeholders → / Curriculum ↑	Instruction	Materials	Schedule	Participants' roles and responsibilities	Tests	Facilities	Course transparency
Teacher (1)	EQ1: 1 interview, 2 class observations, collect all materials and 3–5 lesson plans EQ2: 1 interview, 2 class observations				EQ1: 1 interview, 2 class observations, collect all materials and 3–5 lesson plans EQ2: 1 interview, 2 class observations		
Students (14)	EQ1: interview 2, collect materials, survey 14 EQ2: interview 2, survey 14				EQ1: interview 2, collect materials, survey 14 EQ2: interview 2, survey 14		
Supervisor							
Administrator							
Others? TAs (6)	EQ1: interview 2, 2 class observations, collect all materials and 3–5 lesson plans, record 2–3 office hours, survey 6 EQ2: interview 2, survey 6				EQ1: interview 2, 2 class observations, collect all materials and 3–5 lesson plans, record 2–3 office hours, survey 6 EQ2: interview 2, survey 6		
Curriculum ↑		Textbook, SPEAK-like questions, repeated reading, other student-selected materials	Note: Class meets twice a week for 14 weeks, 80 minutes each class. Office hours twice a week		TA presentation test and practice listening test used as materials		Course transparency (syllabuses, descriptions of assignments)

readers to use can be found at the end of this chapter in an Appendix. For the remainder of the chapter we will primarily focus on the ESL 5310 formative evaluation, although we provide examples from the German formative evaluation as well.

Curriculum Areas

Along the bottom of the table we list the curriculum areas we mentioned earlier, including instruction, materials, schedule, participants' roles and responsibilities, tests, facilities, and course transparency. Our EQs for ESL 5310 focused on materials and so under material we listed materials that we thought were likely used in the course and should be included in the formative evaluation. These were: textbook, SPEAK-like questions, repeated reading, and other as yet unknown student-selected materials. We also listed two materials under tests because they were used in class as instructional materials: The ITA Presentation Test, and practice listening test items. Even though we were not doing a formative evaluation on schedule issues, we noted how often the class met, for how many weeks, and how long each class meeting was, which would figure later on while we developed our *data collection protocols*. Data collection protocol refers to a detailed working plan for a specific type of data collection in an evaluation, such as interviews.

Listing things such as textbook and repeated reading to the plan identifies documents and other materials a teacher/evaluator wants to focus on. These can then become focused items on *data collection instruments* (DCIs) such as lists of questions for interviews, or things to focus on for classroom observations. Having a colleague observe a teacher's class with an idea of what to look for (materials, in the case of ESL 5310) will result in more complete information as the observer notes classroom talk or activities that involve the materials being used. The same holds true for situations where a teacher/evaluator video- or audio-records his or her own class for self-observation. Information about the number of class meetings for the course will have a role in the planning process to determine how many times a teacher/evaluator may want to have his or her class observed, video- or audio-recorded for self-observation.

Stakeholders

Along the left side of the table, we list possible stakeholders to collect data from. These are teachers (or instructors), students, supervisor, administrator, and others. There may be a seeming overlap between these categories, particularly between supervisors and administrators. Supervisors and administrators may be differentiated in terms of their roles or "distance" from the course. Supervisors have more direct responsibility to oversee the course and may have deep knowledge of the course, while administrators are more removed in terms of responsibility for, and knowledge of, the course. For our formative evaluation we had no supervisor for the course and felt any administrator would lack sufficient familiarity with the materials or the course to offer information on the specifics of materials being used in class. For our formative evaluation, then, we decided to focus on three sets of stakeholders who were teachers, students, and TAs (written under "others"). We felt they would have the most direct information to offer. We felt that the curriculum area we chose (materials) had potential impacts on them. We also noted down the total number of each stakeholder group: There was 1 instructor, 14 students, and 6 TAs. Having these numbers written down in the stakeholders' column helped us plan how many interviews we wanted to do, or whether data collection using a survey might be necessary. For instance, it is easier in terms of data analysis to have 14 students complete a survey than to interview all 14. See the discussion below about data collection protocols, and how much data to collect.

Assigning EQs to Cells in the Table

Defining the curriculum areas to work on and the stakeholders whose perspectives we sought, helped us identify cells in the table to assign EQs to. This had two functions: (a) to demonstrate we had sufficiently focused our EQs, and could likely answer them adequately, and (b) to help us think of what kinds of data we needed to collect, about what parts of the curriculum from which stakeholders. In Table 6.5 we can see only six cells are filled, suggesting good focus. Two curriculum areas were indicated, materials and tests (where the tests are used as instructional materials), and three sets of stakeholders were identified. Through introspection we determined that both EQ1 (what materials used) and EQ2 (adequacy and effectiveness of materials, and satisfaction with materials) could be addressed by asking for information from the instructor, the TAs, and also the students. We considered not assigning EQ1 to the student cell, in that the instructor and the TAs together could potentially provide comprehensive information on what materials were being used (EQ1). This would shorten any interviews or surveys needing to be completed by students. In the end, however, we realized only students could provide us with information on their use and manner of use of unassigned materials.

Deciding How to Collect Data, and How Much Data to Collect: Data Collection Protocols

In collecting data for a formative evaluation, the challenge is to find a balance between what can be done by a busy teacher/evaluator and what ought to be done to ensure that there are enough data to meaningfully explore the curriculum area of interest, and stakeholders' responses to them. This means deciding how to collect data and how much to collect. The idea of "how to collect" data has to do with designing a data collection instrument, and what we also call a data collection protocol. Data collection protocol refers to a detailed working plan to collect a particular type of data for an evaluation with reference to the data collection plan (Table 6.5). A single evaluation project may have multiple data collection protocols. In Table 6.5, there are plans to interview stakeholders, observe classes, and collect materials, thus suggesting at least three data collection protocols that need to be developed.

Data collection protocols take planning one step beyond what can be shown in Table 6.5. Data collection protocols answer questions such as: "How will I approach students to ask for an interview?" "What will I ask?" and "What if I don't get useful information from the interview?" A data collection protocol often includes an actual data collection instrument, such as a questionnaire or a quiz, or a list of questions for an interview. A data collection protocol for document retrieval would include listing what documents to collect, for example lesson plans, class handouts, photocopied pages of textbooks, etc. Developing a protocol need be nothing more complicated than jotting down details on the actual data collection plan. When designing a data collection instrument, which is of course more involved, a teacher/evaluator can establish a list of questions for, say, an interview, and add items as needed to a sheet of paper or a word processing document.

DISCUSSION QUESTION 11

Write down your own example of a data collection protocol. What type of data collection does it involve? Will you need to create a data collection instrument? What will be your first step?

How to collect data also has to do with what types of data may result from a data collection protocol. One way to look at this is to think of what data collection can "see." It may sound strange to refer to data collection as "seeing" anything. Yet different types of data collection tend to yield different levels of detail, and different kinds of information, about what we are interested in. A recording and a transcription of students engaged in a task will result in rich detail in the form of transcribed or summarized spoken utterances that can then be interpreted. At the same time, such recordings and transcriptions are like snapshots, taken at one point in time of just a few people, as opposed to an entire class of 10 or more students. So this kind of data collection protocol will see deeply but will then only see briefly a few people at one point in time. Two or three classroom observations in a row, in contrast, will see certain broad themes or blocks of activities taking place and will result in written descriptions noted down by the teacher/ evaluator. Every person in the class, and what they do, can be seen broadly, but without full details of what each person is saying or doing. At the same time, because multiple observations are being done, the themes in the data are not snapshots, but can be followed over time. From such observations, a teacher/evaluator may see patterns in how different pages or activities within in a textbook are used by the teacher or by the students, and how. These considerations of what data collection protocols can see is the main reason we argue earlier in the book for triangulation, where two or more kinds of data collection types or data collection instruments (DCIs) are used to see different sides of the relationship between curriculum and stakeholders.

The idea of "how much" has to do with considerations like how many classes to observe, such as one class meeting, one week of class meetings, or multiple classes comprising one unit. How much also has to do with how many stakeholders to get different types of information from, how many quiz scores to collect (one set of scores, or scores from three or more successive weeks), and how many recordings of students doing a task to get and transcribe. And, how much is also related to the amount of time and energy a teacher/evaluator will need to use in order to collect the data, perhaps design a DCI, transcribe or note down the data, and make sense of the data. Even though richly detailed data in the form of recordings and transcriptions of student and teacher feedback sessions, or interviews with stakeholders, may be valued, it will take a lot of time to capture the recordings, listen to and transcribe them, or even just summarize the recordings and make sense of them. Classroom observations may take slightly less time. Depending on a teacher's/evaluator's note-taking skills and the clarity, in their own minds, of what they are looking for, capturing the data may take only as long as the class meeting itself. In the case of a teacher video-recording his or her own class, capturing the data may take only as long as watching the recording. In general, the more the data collection, the more frequent the data collection, and the more the detail sought, the more time and energy will be needed by a teacher/evaluator to use the data for a formative evaluation.

Table 6.6 gives types of data collection done or mentioned in the literature on formative evaluation, along with the DCIs that may need to be

TABLE 6.6 Data Collection Types, Data Collection Instruments and Protocols, and Resulting Data

Data collection type	Data collection instruments (DCIs) and basic protocol	Resulting data
Interviews Stufflebeam & Shinkfield, 2007 Sugarman, 2008	• Interview DCI (a list of questions to ask, aligned with EQs) • See example of an exploratory interview DCI in Table 6.4 • How many stakeholders to interview, how many times, and when in terms of the formative evaluation	• Data are transcribed or summarized spoken utterances • Data are rich in detail • Data focus on an individual or a few individuals • Data are a "snapshot" unless successive interviews done
Class observations Davies, Newcomer, & Soyadan, 2006 Gorsuch & Sokolowski, 2007 Stufflebeam, 2000 Stufflebeam & Shinkfield, 2007 Sugarman, 2008 Vandergrift, 2000	• Classroom observation DCI (a list of features to focus on, aligned with EQs) • Simple DCI may be sheets of paper on which times and EQ-relevant observations are noted • DCI can be a checklist • DCI can be detailed, pre-theorized grid (e.g., COLT protocol reported in Flyman-Mattsson, 1999) • Class to be recorded or not • If class to be recorded who is focus of camera or microphone • How many class observations, and successively or not	• Data are written descriptions of what is seen and heard • Data can be counts of teacher-student contacts, or minutes spent on specific activities • Data can be transcriptions of an individual's utterances if class is recorded • Data may be less detailed if descriptions of whole class are the data • Data may be more rich in detail if class is recorded • Even recorded, transcribed utterances may not be detailed for every single person in class • Data more broad than detailed • Data show processes and are more longitudinal

(continued)

TABLE 6.6 Data Collection Types, Data Collection Instruments and Protocols, and Resulting Data (continued)		
Data collection type	Data collection instruments (DCIs) and basic protocol	Resulting data
Students' written or spoken work Ellis, 1997	• Student work sample protocol (a list of all student written or spoken work potentially of interest, aligned with EQs) • Teacher/evaluator notes down any written work being planned for students over a one- or two-week period • Data can be free writing, writing in workbooks, diary entries, book reports • Teacher/evaluator notes down any spoken work that may arise over a one or two week period • Data can be recordings of spoken diaries, passages read aloud, group work • Teacher/evaluator makes plans to collect written work or record spoken work • Teacher/evaluator decides which group or groups to record in large class situations	• Data are written texts, or transcribed or summarized spoken language • Data are rich in detail • With written or spoken work, whole class can be focused on BUT recorded spoken work will take time and energy to transcribe or summarize • Data are "snapshots," as many aspects of second language development will not show up in only one- or two-weeks' time
Document collection Black & Wiliam, 1998 Davies, Newcomer, & Soydan, 2006 Ellis, 1997 Sugarman, 2008	• Document collection protocol (a list of all documents potentially of interest aligned with the EQs) • Data can be lesson plans, textbooks (or photocopies of relevant pages), class handouts, teacher logs, student homework, quizzes, tests, workbooks, video and audio clips used in instruction, syllabuses, power points, or descriptions of learning software used • Teacher/evaluator decides whether to collect documents once or over a one or two week period	• Data are written texts of varying length • Data has varying levels of detail (textbook pages without seeing actual use in class are decontextualized and reveal less detail; while teacher logs may have much detail) • Data do not focus on people per se but add interpretive power to classroom observations or interviews • Some teachers/evaluators conduct interviews with stakeholders with documents in hand ("How do you use this particular exercise?") • Data are more snapshots

(continued)

TABLE 6.6   Data Collection Types, Data Collection Instruments and Protocols, and Resulting Data (continued)

Data collection type	Data collection instruments (DCIs) and basic protocol	Resulting data
Student self-assessment Arnold, 2009 Black, 2009 Black & Wiliam, 1998 Ellis, 1997 Vandergrift, 2000	• Student self-assessment protocol (a list of whether, how, and how often students do written or spoken self-assessments) • Teacher/evaluator notes what questions, if any, students are asked to respond to for self-assessments • Teacher/evaluator notes whether students respond in their 1st or 2nd language • Data can be students writing in a journal or filling out a self-assessment worksheet • Data can be students recording themselves in a language lab or at home • Teacher/evaluator decides whether to collect data once or over a one or two week period (see Arnold, 2009) • Teacher/evaluator decides which individuals' self-assessments to collect in a large class situation	• Data are written texts of varying length, or transcriptions or summaries of spoken language • A self-assessment worksheet may not have much detail • Written or spoken self-assessments may contain much detail depending on how much students write or speak, how articulate they are, whether they are writing or speaking in the L1 or L2s, and on the questions they are asked to respond to • Data can focus on whole class or on individual students • Data can be snapshots of individuals but if collected over two weeks' or even three weeks' time may reveal longitudinal information (see Gorsuch & Taguchi, 2010)
Tests and quizzes Ayala & Brandon, 2008 Black, 2009 Cronbach, 1963 Ellis, 1997 Sugarman, 2008	• Test and quiz collection protocol (a list of tests or quizzes which may take place during the data collection period) • Teacher/evaluator needs to explain how the test or quiz items (questions) are relevant to the formative evaluation EQs (if an EQ focuses on vocabulary instruction why collect students' scores on grammar quizzes?) • Teacher/evaluator needs to explain how the test or quiz items are relevant to the course outcomes (if course outcomes relate to second language speaking fluency, why collect multiple choice reading test scores?) • Teacher/evaluator should note whether students' scores on only selected, EQ or outcomes-relevant test or quiz items are recorded	• Data are numbers or scores on EQ-relevant test or quiz items or subsections • Data are not detailed • Data can focus on whole class or on individuals • Data are snapshots

(continued)

TABLE 6.6 Data Collection Types, Data Collection Instruments and Protocols, and Resulting Data (continued)

Data collection type	Data collection instruments (DCIs) and basic protocol	Resulting data
Feedback to students Black, 2009 Black & Wiliam, 1998 Leung, 2007 Vandergrift, 2000	• Student feedback protocol (a description of whether and what feedback processes take place in the course) • Data may be written by teacher on students' written or spoken work in the form of corrections or grades or comments • Data may be from teacher orally during class or in tutoring sessions (oral feedback would be recorded, and either transcribed or summarized) • Data may be from students to other students either in writing or orally • Teacher/evaluator needs to decide whether to collect data once or over a one or two week period • Teacher/evaluator needs to decide whether to collect feedback on as many students who got feedback or from a few individuals	• Data are written documents or texts, or transcribed or summarized spoken language • Data may also be counts of feedback of different lengths or levels of detail or different kinds (sentence level corrections versus comments on discourse elements of students' writing or speaking) • Data may have different levels of detail depending on whether the data are written or spoken • Data may have different levels of detail depending on level of detail provided by teacher or students • Data can focus on whole class or on individuals • Data are snapshots (repeated collection might suggest whether teacher or students are consistent in the type and length of feedback they give)
Questionnaire Ellis, 1997 Gorsuch & Sokolowski, 2007 Stufflebeam, 2000 Sugarman, 2008	• Questionnaire DCI (a list of questions, aligned with EQs) • Can be paper and ink, or electronic • Teacher/evaluator needs to decide length of questionnaire (more than 20 items may reduce "return rate") • Teacher/evaluator needs to decide types of items to use (open ended, ranking, rating scale from 1 to 5), or what combination of item types to use • Teacher/evaluator needs to explain how each item is related to EQs and curriculum areas being focused on • Teacher/evaluator needs to decide to administer questionnaire once, or more than once over a period of at least three weeks	• Data are ranking or rating scale scores, or written texts for open-ended items • Data may have different levels of detail depending on questionnaire item type • Data focus on whole class or large groups • Data are snapshots • Some questionnaires may be administered more than once if teacher/administrator wants to discern patterns of change in attitude or other non-language trait

created and basic information for a data collection protocol that will need to be decided upon and sketched out.

The information in Table 6.6 may seem overwhelming, but it is a reference. It is not prescriptive. In other words, teachers/evaluators can pick and choose data collection types in accordance with their data collection plan (Table 6.5), the depth or breadth of classroom processes they wish to capture, and the amount of time and energy they are willing to use. The bare outlines of our five data collection protocols for ESL 5310 can be seen in Table 6.5. It is apparent we chose to do: (a) one interview of the teacher, one interview of two students, and one interview of two TAs; (b) two class observations; (c) document collections of all materials used by instructors, TAs, and students, including three to five lesson plans; (d) two to three office hour observations; and (e) a survey of all six TAs and 14 students. We wanted a mixture of detailed data and snapshot data (interviews and survey), data focused on processes (two or three successive classroom and office hour observations), and data providing rich contextual details (document collection). We have provided two data collection protocols here as examples. We also use the examples to explain some fundamentals of the data collection process. These fundamentals would be part of a more detailed data collection protocol.

DISCUSSION QUESTION 12

Do you seem to prefer any one type of data collection type? Why do you think so? Is it because you have more experience with this data collection type? Does it seem somehow more "proper"? How so?

Collecting Data for a Formative Evaluation

Now that the data collection plans are in place, it remains to collect the data using data collection protocols and data collection instruments.

Two Data Collection Protocols

We will illustrate two data collection protocols here, one for the interviews with two students, and one for the two classroom observations we planned. Note how, in Table 6.7, the protocol for the student interviews is in fact a data collection instrument with some added notes about the data collection process that underscores some fundamental procedures for data collection. These fundamental procedures have to do with how to get needed data while protecting the rights of the stakeholders and also establishing the validity, or accuracy, of the data.

TABLE 6.7 Data Collection Protocol for Student Interviews

ESL 5310 Student Interview (data collection instrument)
EQ1: *What materials do instructors, TAs, and students use in and out of class? How do they use them, and how often?*
In-class What materials do you use in class? What other materials? Do you use either the Performance Test or the Listening Test in class? What do you do with the materials? Tell me more. How often do you use the materials?
Out-of-class How often do you visit an instructor during office hours? How do you choose an instructor or TA to visit? What do you wish to accomplish during your visit? What materials do you take with you? Do you take your textbook with you? Why or why not? What do you do during office hour visits? Do you use the language learning lab? How often? What materials do you use in the language learning lab? Aside from visiting an instructor or TA during office hours and using the language learning lab, what do you do on your own to do well in ESL 5310? What materials do you use? How do you use them? How often do you use them?
EQ2: *How well do the materials support the outcomes in and out of class? Is there content validity? Are stakeholders satisfied with the materials in light of course outcomes?*
Stated course outcomes: 1. Able to speak unrehearsed English proficiently. 2. Able to give a class presentation on a prepared topic in your discipline and respond to questions. 3. Able to hear and understand English.
In-class What do you think it means to speak English well? Do you think the textbook or other materials helps you speak English well? How so? Do you think the textbook helps you learn how to give a presentation? How so? Do other materials used in class help you learn how to give a presentation? How so? Do the materials help you choose and develop a topic in your discipline? Do the class materials help you speak fluently in presentations? How so? Do the class materials help you do well with understanding questions during presentations? How so? Do the class materials help you do well with answering questions during presentations? How so? Do the class materials help you hear and understand English? How so?
Out-of-class Do the materials you use in office hours with an instructor or TA help you speak English well? How so? What about materials in the Language Learning Lab? What about materials you use on your own?

(continued)

TABLE 6.7   Data Collection Protocol for Student Interviews (cont.)
Do the materials you use in office hours with an instructor or TA <u>help you learn how to give a presentation?</u> How so? What about materials in the Language Learning Lab? What about materials you use on your own? Do the materials you use in office hours with an instructor or TA <u>help you learn how to understand questions during a presentation?</u> How so? What about materials in the Language Learning Lab? What about materials you use on your own? Do the materials you use in office hours with an instructor or TA <u>help you learn how to answer questions during a presentation?</u> How so? What about materials in the language learning lab? What about materials you use on your own? Do the materials you use in office hours with an instructor or TA <u>help you hear and understand English?</u> How so? What about materials in the language learning lab? What about materials you use on your own?
Protocol Interview two students once each by randomly selecting from among regular attendees on the student list. Contact by e-mail asking for interview and providing the actual interview questions. Assure students their identities will never be revealed and that their participation is purely voluntary. If selected students do not answer after two e-mails, choose another two students. Record interviews after showing students how to turn off the recorder for off-the-record comments. Roughly transcribe interviews, send transcriptions and recordings to students for review and comment. Use details from interviews to design contextualized items for the planned student survey of all 14 students.

The interview data collection instrument for ESL 5310 formative evaluation was designed in terms of the EQs by differentiating between EQ1 and EQ2, and in-class and out-of-class materials use. As noted in the data collection protocol, two students were asked for an interview by email and provided with the data collection instrument. In the email, and again in person, they were assured their participation was wholly voluntary and that their identities would remain confidential. One student did not respond after two emails and so another student was randomly chosen from among the students who were actively attending class. The interviews were held face to face at a time and place of the student's convenience, and were recorded. The students were shown how to turn off the recorder if they wanted to say anything off the record. After the interview was over, the recordings were transcribed, which took about two hours for each interview. The transcription was broad in the sense that we wanted to represent what the respondents said. At the same time, we did not play the recording over and over to get all of the "ehs" and "ums" and other details unnecessary to understanding the speaker's intended meaning. This was not a detailed, highly conventionalized transcription that someone in, say, conversation analysis would need for their own brand of research.

Within three days, the transcriptions and the recordings themselves were sent to each respective student for comment based on the overall themes of, "Is this what you intended to say?" and "Is there anything you wish to add?" Both students responded by email that the transcriptions largely represented what they wanted to say and that they had nothing to add. One student thanked the teacher/evaluator for the recording, saying he would listen to it for his own purposes of spoken English development.

Some fundamentals of data collection become apparent here. Of course, we want to collect the needed data in a timely fashion. At the same time, teachers/evaluators have to protect the rights and dignity of the stakeholders, who may feel that their participation might change their grade (if they are students). Some stakeholders do not wish to be put in the position of saying something unflattering or unexpected about the teacher or a colleague or a classmate. Thus, for our interview, students were only contacted twice to solicit an interview. Those who did not wish to participate were allowed to do so without having to say so. Students were also promised anonymity and were given some sense of social control during the interview by giving them the recorder and control over the stop button. Finally, they were shown the transcript made up of their own words that they could confirm or disconfirm. Even at this point, students could say, "I don't want my words to be used further," and the teacher/evaluator would have accepted that. Many universities have procedures for protecting the rights of research participants and this forms the basis for some of the fundamentals named here. (See http://www.baylor.edu/research/irb/index .php?id=20752 for a relevant website at Baylor University.) Mainly they are based on commonsense notions of fair play and a desire to maintain smooth, respectful relations in the classroom. A second fundamental consideration is establishing the validity, or accuracy, of the data. This was done with the interview by designing the interview data collection instrument in terms of each EQ and adding specific questions according to the materials specified in the data collection plan (Table 6.5). A second part of the data collection protocol aimed at validation was showing the transcript to each student and asked whether the transcription was accurate and conveyed what they intended to say.

Table 6.8 outlines the data collection protocol for the two classroom observations for ESL 5310.

TABLE 6.8   Data Collection Protocol for Two Classroom Observations

Protocol

Main focus of data collection (bold): **EQ1: What materials do instructors, TAs, and students use in and out of class? How do they use them, and how often?**

What to look for: Any use of materials specified in the data collection plan such as the textbook, textbook audio and video DVD, SPEAK-like questions, repeated reading materials, other instructor- or student-selected materials. Observation notes will be written by hand and will be time coded to portray how long instructor/TA/students do particular activities with materials. Teacher/evaluator will sit in back a back corner.

Because this course has rotating lead TAs, select two successive class meetings where the same lead TA is "leading" both classes to observe use and possible re-use of materials, and any other processes that might take more than one class meeting to complete.

Randomly select in terms of the lead TA who is teaching. Ask permission to attach a lapel recorder to the lead TA with the promise the recording and resulting transcript will be confidential, and will be made available to the lead TA alone for professional development or personal purposes. If the lead TA for the two planned observations is unwilling or seems reluctant, the lead TA for the next two successive classes will be contacted.

Record the class in terms of the lapel microphone attached to the lead TA. This will capture added detail for the observation notes already being taken, and may capture feedback or other EQ-relevant verbal interactions the lead TA may have with individual students or in small group work. It is not assumed the student or students will be perfectly clearly heard on the recording.

Again, as noted in the protocol, the lead TA for the next two successive class meetings was contacted to ask permission to attach a microphone to her lapel and make the recording, transcript, and classroom observation notes available to her. She was promised confidentiality. She said she was willing, even after being assured she was under no obligation whatsoever to participate. The two classes were observed and the handwritten notes were typed into a word processing document, which took only 15 minutes for each observation note set. The audio files were listened to in conjunction with the notes where the teacher gave directions for using materials, or answered students' questions about the materials, or interacted with small student groups while using the materials. They were transcribed in the broad fashion described earlier and embedded in the observation notes. This second stage took longer, about 90 minutes for each audio file. Transcription, even broad transcription, is richly detailed, but time-consuming. The observation notes and the recordings were sent to the lead TA and she was asked to confirm whether she understood the notes to be accurate according to her recollection. As a professional courtesy, the teacher/evaluator offered to answer any questions the TA had, or to discuss any part of the observation for professional or personal development reasons. The rights and dignity of the lead TA were respected by promising confidentiality and by being repeatedly assured she could withdraw at any time and without reason. It was made clear to her these were her recorded words and actions, which she had ultimate control over. The accuracy of the data were ensured by using the EQ to guide the taking of the notes, and by having a second real-time data source upon which to check the notes: the audio recording.

Collecting data using questionnaires, document collection, collection of feedback to students, or any other data collection type (see Table 6.6) should arise from a simple, practical data collection protocol that maps out how the data will be collected, what questions will be asked, of whom, and how many times. The protocol should address the two fundamental considerations previously outlined: That of how the rights and dignity of the stakeholders will be protected, and how the data can be established as being accurate and valid.

DISCUSSION QUESTION 13

If you were to interview a colleague, classmate, or student today, can you think of any challenges to collecting this data? What could you plan to do or say in your data collection protocol that would help you meet these challenges?

Analyzing the Data, Answering the EQs, and Composing Decision Points

Any data analysis, such as tabulating responses on items on a questionnaire, or identifying themes in an interview, needs to answer the evaluation questions (EQs) and supply the basis for decision points.

Answering the EQs: An Example From Student Interviews

Here is a case in point based on our formative evaluation of a German foreign language class. In your data analysis, you are likely to come up with themes such as "vocabulary takes a back seat," "vocabulary not recycled," or "students expected to study by memorizing list" based on transcripts such as these (S = student; E = evaluator):

E: What do you do in class to learn vocabulary?

S: It's usually in the same style as learning grammar. We'll just have vocabulary words.

E: It's like a list?

S: Yeah. And then we'll assignments and whatnot to use them right after we learn them. Vocabulary is the weak point in that class. I'm not quite sure why but we have trouble with vocabulary. Grammar is something we work on a lot and then vocabulary is just a side dish. It's just like here is some vocabulary as well to throw in with that assignment. Sometimes they'll go hand in hand where we have some grammar and then some vocabulary on the side you can just toss into your salad.

E: Do you sense that the vocabulary is being recycled from chapter to chapter?

S: No. It's a new set every time, and a lot of the time we'll learn that vocabulary and we never see it again. After a couple of months we'll come back up on it, and it's like what is this? I know I learned this but didn't use it enough to cement it.

* * *

E: What do they do in class to help you learn vocabulary? Are you supposed to study the list ahead of time?

S: We are supposed to look at them ahead of time but it's one of those things where you really don't want to study it because you know there's a lot of things you're never going to see again and you could be spending time studying the structure of grammar and those things you are going to be using continuously. I think not enough emphasis is being placed on the vocabulary in studying.

E: So it really doesn't get taught explicitly in class?

S: It does. We'll spend a little time on vocabulary but we won't spend as much time using it.

E: What do you do in class to use vocabulary?

S: It's along the same lines as with grammar. We'll have the terms and we'll use them in a sentence and that's about it. We're expecting to learn the vocabulary and memorize it, because there are quizzes over the vocabulary. We're given the word either in English or German and we have to translate it over. The teacher will say, "Make sure you learn your vocabulary" or it will be on the homework that we should learn our vocabulary and then next class we'll have a quiz. It's a pop quiz, but it's foreseeable.

How, then, to put to use these themes with reference to the EQs? Here are two suggestions: (a) review the relevant EQs, and (b) pose direct answers to the EQs as a paragraph from each relevant data source. Here are the relevant EQs with answers from just the one data source: interviews with three students. Note we also make space under each EQ for additional data sources we developed for the German course formative evaluation:

EQ1: *What activities are done in the classroom that involve explicit vocabulary instruction?*

Student interviews suggest vocabulary is presented to students as lists in the book. Quizzes involve seeing English or German words and then translating them over into the other language. Student interviews suggest that students believe the teacher sees vocabulary as a "side dish" with much more attention being paid to grammar. Some vocabulary in the book is not reviewed or recycled in later chapters, and also some vocabulary presented in the PowerPoint presentations are never heard or seen again, not even within the same lesson. There is an impression that vocabulary is taught but then not used. It seems to be expected that students do most of their work out of class memorizing lists. One student recalled a vocabulary activity where the teacher and a teaching assistant read a dialog out loud and students could then ask about words they didn't know.

Classroom observation

Student questionnaire

EQ2: *What activities do learners do outside of class in which they are self-instructing vocabulary?*

Student interviews revealed the following: use a translation application, look over the list in the book and memorize, tries to use new words three times, be selective about which words to learn with more effort (more likely to be used in chapter), write out German vocabulary from the list and describe them in English, quiz oneself using the list, use German Wikipedia to find words of interest, write down German words and English translations (also helps with spelling), and use a translation application to find words not in the list (in order to read a German website or listen to German music).

Classroom observation

Student questionnaire

Answering the EQs: An Example From Classroom Observations

Here is an example from classroom observations we did for our formative evaluation of ESL 5310. We outlined these classroom observations earlier in the chapter. Here is a portion of the observation notes with recorded utterances embedded in the notes:

> 3:38—Lead teacher (LT) begins, greets class. Instructs students to stand up and pairs them up according to their birth month. Directs students (Ss) to DVD 4.10 and 4.11. Ss are to keep books closed. Ss will watch "before" and "after" DVD files of a Korean stats international teaching assistant (ITA). LT assigns a teaching assistant (TA) to each group so each group has two students and one TA.

> 3:41—LT tells Ss to do exercises associated with the DVD files. Talks and tells students to focus on her their ability to comprehend her if she is their TA. "You're going to work on exercises and opinions and so on." LT plays the two DVD files.

> LT joins one pair of students. One male student says to another, "It sounds like she [the ITA in the DVD file] is continually asking questions." One male student asks LT: "These tones are not correct, right?" LT answers: "They should be correct," but then changes track saying, "These show what she is saying," clarifying that while the arrows describe what the TA is saying in the DVD file, she should not use the rising tones because they don't make sense. "She shouldn't use so many rising tones, right?" "She should use more falling tones and more interaction with students like she does in the second DVD file."

> LT redirects two Ss to discuss their opinions with each other. The same male student says, "Then we should study this one [second DVD file] so we can see the correct tones." LT answers: "Right, but you can also discuss why these choices she makes are not completely correct. Some of them are confusing, they are not sure whether she is asking a question or not."

Themes arising from this classroom observation data may include: recordings from textbook used in class to generate discussion in small groups, some students engage the material differently than other students and may "take over" a discussion (not necessarily in a positive direction), and not all students participate in the discussion. An examination of the second classroom observation transcript revealed the textbook and recording were not used nor referred to, although some main concepts such as tone choices were brought up again, and students worked in small groups with other materials. Thus, the paragraphed answer to the relevant EQ was:

> **EQ1:** *What materials do instructors, TAs, and students use in and out of class? How do they use them, and how often?*

Textbook and audio file use in the classroom observations: The audio and video files were used once. The recording was played only once. These materials may not be reviewed in subsequent classes. The free practices (which are associated with many of the audio files) may not be used as much as the controlled practice, I suspect because the TAs fear quibbling with students over the "correctness" of the audio scripts or the point of the lesson. TAs may not know how to deal with students who really do not or cannot hear a rising tone.

Textbook and audio file use in student interviews:

Textbook and audio file use in office hour observations:

Textbook and audio file use in TA interviews:

Textbook and audio file use in student questionnaires:

Performance test use in the classroom observations:

Performance test use in the student interviews:

Etc.

As with the example from the German course, note how additional spaces are prepared for answers to the EQs from different materials (textbook and audio files, performance test, SPEAK-like questions, etc.; see Table 6.5) from different data sources and stakeholders (classroom observations, student interviews, etc.).

Composing Decision Points

As noted at the beginning of this chapter, decision points are suggestions for teachers/evaluators resulting from a formative evaluation. Decision points have direct value to teachers/evaluators in both principle and practice. This kind of help is important to us personally and also at a public level. As Brown (1989) reminds us, evaluation is systematic, which suggests that in doing a formative evaluation we do not blindly or randomly make up improvements to our courses. In other words, we act on specialized knowledge and awareness (principles) that we develop while doing a formative evaluation. At a public level, decision points show to stakeholders and the world at large that we think and act using principles and forethought as opposed to impressionistic, fleeting desires, or feelings of insecurity.

Decision points also have practical value on several levels. First, we can choose from among the decision points which ones to act upon. In other words, we choose to do the decision points we can do with what time and energy we have. Alternatively, we can choose which decision points are the most urgent to do. Second, decision points can be used to help us avoid making drastic changes in a course that may not have a good result for anyone. A common remark heard at meetings is, "We need a new textbook." Sometimes this is true, but getting a new textbook is not an answer in itself. Well-composed decision points for materials or teaching practices in the classroom may: (a) reveal that current materials are not being used effectively, and (b) provide specific suggestions on using the materials more effectively. In essence, decision points become a teacher's/evaluator's own agenda, making them less susceptible to the agendas of others being imposed on him or her.

Well-composed decision points have three elements: (a) Decision points are composed as choices, (b) decision points should be related to the formative evaluation at hand, and (c) decision points should be written with enough detail to be understood by others. Concerning element letter a, decision points are best composed and presented as choices. They should begin with words such as "consider" or "think about." Decision points using this type of language can be put into list form for discussion with others or for self-review. A teacher/evaluator may end up with 10 or more decision points on a list, representing a rich and principled resource for course improvement to be used at the teacher's discretion.

For element letter b, decision points should be related to the results of a formative evaluation. Many decision points emerge as teachers/evaluators read through their data and use the data to answer their EQs (evaluation questions). Other decision points emerge while reviewing the results of a formative evaluation. See Table 6.9 for a partial decision point digest one teacher/evaluator made for the ESL 5310 course while reading through data, answering EQs, and reviewing the results of the formative evaluation. These types of decision points can be traced back to the EQs, and to the stakeholders and curriculum areas identified in a data collection plan (Table 6.5). We can be somewhat assured that we then have a principled basis for a decision point. Oftentimes, teachers think of great ideas while doing a formative evaluation, but that are not related to the formative evaluation.

TABLE 6.9 Partial Decision Point "Digest" for ESL 5310
Decision Points for Textbook and Audio Files
1. Consider printing out teachers' manual for TAs, using explanations and answer keys as a knowledge source.
2. Consider emphasizing mirroring section from textbook (pp. 167–173) throughout the course as homework assignments to be checked during office hours or class.
3. Consider creating a handout for students of listening and speaking tasks suitable for homework or independent use/office hours from the textbook and audio/video disk.
4. Consider using textbook pair work activities during office hours.
5. Consider dealing with errors students think they found in the textbook audio scripts using this process: • First, ask S to say the audio script the way he or she thinks she hears it. Use at least two thought groups on each side—do not have the student reproduce just the one word or thought group. • Second, ask S to say the audio script they way he or she thinks it is represented in the audio script. • Third, ask the S if the meaning is different between the two versions. • Fourth, play the audio script. • Fifth, again ask S to say the audio script the way he or she thinks she hears it. • Sixth, again ask S to say the audio script the way he or she thinks it is represented in the audio script. • Seventh, point out that level and falling tones are sometimes hard to distinguish. Falling tones are still lower in comparison to level tones. • Alternate seventh, ask student to say the three or four thought groups with all rising tones or all falling tones or all prominence or no prominence. Help create contrasts for students to hear.
6. Consider returning to and reusing explanations of discourse intonation (DI) in the book, and use the explanations to connect DI features to intended meaning when giving feedback or whenever a DI question comes up.
7. Consider giving periodic direct instruction of transcription conventions in the textbook to both TAs and students. TAs can also deepen their understanding by teaching it to students.
8. Consider when students express doubt that DI is not perfectly consistently used (as most grammar in a language is not), recasting use of DI in terms of appropriateness, not correctness. Refocus on how the instance of DI use changes the meaning of the intended message.
9. Consider not supplying answers to students during discussion activities based in the textbook. If a student or group of students is simply not hearing a falling tone or does not agree that prominence should be used on that particular syllable or word, do this process: • Student says three or four thought groups around the feature in question in the way how he or she hears it or thinks it should be done. • Press student to comment on what this says about intended meaning. • Student says the same language using different DI (how it appears in the audio script or in another way of the student's choosing). • Press student to comment on and contrast (if appropriate) intended meaning.

(continued)

TABLE 6.9   Partial Decision Point "Digest" for ESL 5310 (cont.)
10. Consider while in small groups if questions arise about the audio script or transcription conventions or the recording, TA takes note of them. During the whole group discussion TA urges student to bring the question up.
11. Consider capitalizing more on student-to-student feedback on textbook activities. Routinely have Student A "do" his or her part again, and Student B to reconfirm his or her answers or feedback.
12. Consider spending 30 seconds more on giving instructions on textbook activities while referring directly to activity features, and the DI feature being focused on.

Thus there is little conceptual groundwork for the idea. For instance, while studying vocabulary teaching in the German language course, one evaluator thought of quite grand ideas about using more authentic literature in class for students' cultural enrichment. Upon reflection, however, the idea had little basis in what had been learned about the course in the formative evaluation and could be dismissed in the immediate present as something to be explored in a future formative evaluation. These "creative extras" should be noted down of course, but then should be stored away for further thought and future action.

Concerning letter c, decision points should be written with enough detail that another person can understand it, someone who is outside the formative evaluation. Thinking of this another way, the decision point needs enough detail so that in a month's or a year's time, the teacher/evaluator can understand what he or she intended. Here is an example from the German course formative evaluation of a decision point that lacks detail: "Consider recycling vocabulary more." Here is the same decision point written with more sufficient detail: "Consider recycling vocabulary more, particularly in PowerPoint presentations already being used, which students can be allowed to access online in pdf form." A teacher/evaluator reading this a year from now will know what was intended. Table 6.9 shows examples of decision points.

APPLICATION TASKS: Using an Interview to Write EQs and Assessing a Published Formative Evaluation

First task idea: Choose a course, preferably one being taught by a colleague, to write provisional EQs for. Assuming the course does not have a course logic model, use the exploratory interview items (Table 6.4) to interview your colleague. Add items as necessary to reflect the local situation, or to follow-up on interesting points your colleague comes up with. Then follow all four remaining steps: (a) review the interview at least twice and keep a running memo of reactions to the responses; (b) use the memo to review and introspect, and identify areas of emerging interest; (c) prioritize and choose one or two curriculum areas to focus on; and (d) write evaluation questions for the formative evaluation. Show your colleague your EQs to get his or her comments.

Second task idea: Retrieve a published second language course evaluation and fill out the data collection plan (see appendix for this chapter and also Table 6.5) according to the information given in the article. Remember, it must be an actual evaluation, not an article about evaluation (see Chapter 10). Evaluate the plan. What is missing? Or has the evaluator taken on too much for a formative evaluation? Note: Many articles are evaluations where the data are not used while the course in going on, but rather to show the worth of a course after the fact. If the author wanted to do a formative evaluation that needs to be more nimble, lean, and timely, how could he or she use a data collection plan to prioritize what data to collect and from whom? Which cells need to be eliminated or revised?

APPENDIX Formative Evaluation Data Collection Plan								
Stakeholders →								
Teacher								
Students								
Supervisor								
Administrator								
Others?								
Curriculum ↑	Instruction	Materials	Schedule	Participants' roles and responsibilities	Tests	Facilities	Course transparency (syllabuses, descriptions of assignments)	

References

Arnold, N. (2009). Online extensive reading for advanced foreign language learners: An evaluation study. *Foreign Language Annals, 42*(2), 340–366.

Ayala, C. C., & Brandon, P. R. (2008). Building evaluation recommendations for improvement: Insights from student formative assessments. In N. L. Smith & P. R. Brandon (Eds.), *Fundamental issues in evaluation* (pp. 159–176). New York, NY: Guilford Press.

Black, P. (2009). Formative assessment issues across the curriculum: The theory and the practice. *TESOL Quarterly, 43*(3), 519–524.

Black, P., & Wiliam, D. (1998). Inside the black box: Raising standards though classroom assessment. *The Phi Delta Kappan, 80*(2), 139–148.

Brown, J. D. (1989). Language program evaluation: A synthesis of existing possibilities. In R. K. Johnson (Ed.), *The second language curriculum* (pp. 222–241). Cambridge, England: Cambridge University Press.

Cronbach, L. J. (1963). Course improvement through evaluation. *Teacher's College Record, 64,* 672–83.

Davies, P., Newcomer, K., & Soydan, H. (2006). Government as structural context for evaluation. In I. F. Shaw, J. C. Green, & M. M. Mark (Eds.), *Handbook of evaluation: Policies, programs and practices* (pp. 163–183). Thousand Oaks, CA: Sage.

Ellis, R. (1997). *SLA research and language teaching.* Oxford, England: Oxford University Press.

Flyman-Mattsson, A. (1999). Students' communicative behavior in a foreign language classroom. *Lund University Department of Linguistics Working Papers, 47,* 39–57. Retrieved February 16, 2014, from http://lup.lub.lu.se/luur/download?func=downloadFile&recordOId=528691&fileOId=624445

Gorsuch, G. & Sokolowski, J. (2007). International teaching assistants and summative and formative student evaluation. *The Journal of Faculty Development, 21*(2), 117–136.

Gorsuch, G. J., & Taguchi, E. (2010). Developing reading fluency and comprehension using repeated reading: Evidence from longitudinal student reports. *Language Teaching Research, 14*(1), 27–59.

Isaac, S., & Michael, W. (1997). *Handbook in research and evaluation* (3rd ed.). San Diego, CA: Educational and Industrial Testing Services.

Kiely, R., & Rea-Dickins, P. (2005). *Program evaluation in language education.* Houndsmills, England: Palgrave MacMillan.

LaRocco, M. J. (2012). Chinese international teaching assistants and the essence of intercultural competence in university contexts. In G. Gorsuch (Ed.), *Working theories for teaching assistant development* (pp. 609–653). Stillwater, OK: New Forums Press.

Leung, C. (2007). Dynamic assessment: Assessment *for* and *as* teaching? *Language Assessment Quarterly, 4*(3), 257–278.

Richards, J.C. (2001). *Curriculum development in language teaching.* Cambridge, England: Cambridge University Press.

Stufflebeam, D. L. (2000). Foundational models for 21st century program evaluation. In D. L. Stufflebeam, G. F. Madaus, & T. Kellaghan (Eds.), *Evaluation models: Viewpoints on educational and human services evaluation* (pp. 33–83). Norwell, MA: Kluwer.

Stufflebeam, D., & Shinkfield, A. (2007). *Evaluation theory, models, and applications.* San Francisco, CA: Jossey-Bass.

Sugarman, J. (2008). *Evaluation of the dual language program in the North Shore School District 112, Highland Park, IL.* Washington, DC: Center for Applied Linguistics.

Teachers of English to Speakers of Other Languages. (2010). *Position statement on the acquisition of academic proficiency in English at the postsecondary level.* Alexandria, VA: Author. Retrieved from http://www.tesol.org/docs/pdf/13489.pdf?sfvrsn=0

Vandergrift, L. (2000). Setting students up for success: Formative evaluation and FLES. *Foreign Language Annals, 33*, 290–303.

Wiliam, D. (2011). *Embedded formative assessment.* Bloomington, IN: Solution Tree Press.

7

Curriculum and Assessment, and Instrument Validation

Tests and Quizzes

Murphy's law: If anything can go wrong, it will.
Corollary 6: Whenever you set out to do something, something else must be done first.
—Block (1980)

In this chapter we outline a model for validation of *data collection instruments*[1] used in course evaluation, specifically tests and quizzes. We use the model to describe practical strategies for increasing the clarity with which tests and quizzes are related to the course outcomes, to the course curriculum, and to stakeholders. These strategies together build up a portfolio of *validation evidence* that can be used while reporting the results of an evaluation. We offer advice on how to report validation evidence for each validation strategy. Finally, we offer chronological steps for validation of a test or quiz.

This is the fifth chapter in which the stakeholders, outcomes, assessment, and curriculum evaluation model (SOAC) is applied to second

---

1. For all terms in *italics*, see Glossary.

Evaluating Second Language Courses, pages 133–164
Copyright © 2016 by Information Age Publishing
133

and foreign language classrooms. The purpose of this chapter is to complete the next-to-last step in the evaluation process, namely looking carefully at the data collection instruments we wish to use to evaluate our course, such as tests or lists of interview questions. This "careful looking" is called *validation*. Validation is a process whereby a data collection instrument is designed, piloted, revised, and used, with much forethought and afterthought as to what is being measured. Validation should produce validation evidence, which could be a description of what is being measured along with sample test items, or recounting interviewees' reactions to written transcriptions of interviews they participated in. The point is to confirm or disconfirm that a data collection instrument functions as intended, and captures some predetermined second or foreign language knowledge or skill, teacher attitude, or student perception—whatever is being investigated to answer *evaluation questions* (EQs). This chapter, along with Chapter 8 on observations, interviews, and questionnaires, contributes to our ability to address questions raised in the "Reading and Assessing Publications of Course or Program Evaluation" template given in Table 10.1 in Chapter 10. Knowing more about validation enables us to assess the credibility of evaluation reports written by others, and enhances the clarity and credibility of our own evaluation projects.

In this and the next chapter, we deal with the how-to of data collection instrument validation, which is rarely treated in the evaluation literature. We agree with Block (1980) in the quotation at the beginning of the chapter: whenever we try to do something, we find something else that must be done first. In the context of course evaluation, that something, we argue, is validation. Validation is foundational in that we cannot hope to pose EQs, collect and analyze data, and then evaluate a course on the basis of the data, simply because we hope our data collection instruments are capturing the information we intend to capture. We need to base our hopes and good intentions on something more concrete. In this chapter we deal with tests and quizzes as data collection instruments. A test will be broadly defined as an assessment instrument that functions to assess what students have learned (Alderson, 1986, p. 6). These could be end-of-chapter quizzes, mid-term exams, final exams, students' spoken or written work, or student self-assessments (see Chapter 6, Table 6.6). In Chapter 8, we will focus on classroom observations, interviews, and questionnaires, which are three common data collection types in evaluation.

DISCUSSION QUESTION 1

Have you ever written a quiz or a test? What was the quiz or test about? How did you go about writing it? Did it "work"? How do you know?

DISCUSSION QUESTION 2

As a second language learner, have you ever taken a quiz or test that you felt was truly unfair? What about a test that you felt was fair, even if you did not like taking the test? What makes you think a quiz or test is fair or unfair?

DISCUSSION QUESTION 3

Have you ever heard of validation or test validity in the context of second language classes or programs? What do the terms mean to you? What would you like to know about them?

Instrument Validation and Evaluation

One way to look at this part of course evaluation is to focus on the relationship of assessment in the SOAC model to course objectives, the course curriculum, and stakeholders. See Figure 7.1. To review, the *evaluand*, the element in the middle, refers to the course or that part of the course we are evaluating; and *assessment* is concerned with measurement of whatever it is we are investigating in order to evaluate a course. Our focus in this chapter is on measurement, or assessment, of student learning with data collection instruments such as tests and quizzes. *Outcomes* are the goals or objectives of a course, and finally, *curriculum* refers to how the course (the textbook, the teaching, etc.) supports learners to attain the course outcomes. *Stakeholders* are everyone who has an interest in the course, including teachers, learners, parents, administrators, and others.

Assessment and Outcomes

The arrow between assessment and outcomes has to do with reckoning with the course outcomes. When we introduced the SOAC model in

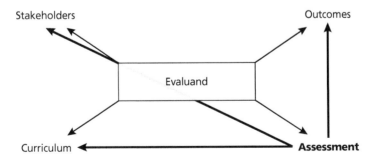

Figure 7.1 The SOAC model showing the relationship of assessment to outcomes, curriculum, and stakeholders.

Chapter 2, we noted that when we state outcomes for a course, we then must find the most appropriate, clear, and credible way to measure learner activity to investigate whether course outcomes are met. This relationship represents *summative evaluation*, which we will discuss in Chapter 9. We mentioned a study by Adair-Hauck, Willingham-McLain, and Youngs (2000) where one course outcome was that college-level foreign language learners should be able to write with reasonable grammatical accuracy in French. The learners were given three successive writing tests that presumably measured learners' increasing grammatical accuracy in written French: not beauty of expression, and not length, but grammatical accuracy. Validation of these tests would begin with a careful description of what is being measured.

What is being measured is called a *construct*. A construct is a learner ability we intend to measure based on theory or well-established notions of second language learning. For course evaluation, we want the construct of a quiz or test to match the constructs that are found in a course outcome. Introspection, and/or a *course logic* study (see Chapter 5) would uncover the constructs that are embedded in course outcomes, based on whatever well-established notions of second language learning that are held by the teacher/evaluator (see Chapter 5, Tables 5.1 and 5.2 for examples under the "Functions," and "Functions and Activities" headings). It is easy to see how important this aspect of validation is. If we cannot establish through validation that our tests and quizzes are measuring students' learning with direct reference to the course outcomes, then we cannot claim that the course is accomplishing what it is supposed to accomplish.

Assessment and Curriculum

The arrow between assessment and curriculum suggests that any data collection instruments used in the evaluation must have a real and practical relationship to the curriculum. If learners are spending a lot of time memorizing second language grammar rules using materials and classroom activities, but which do not recycle or emphasize vocabulary, a test or quiz on vocabulary may not have what is called *content validity*. That is, the test, which might ask students to write definitions or read a passage with selected vocabulary and then answer questions about it, has no real relationship with the curriculum as it is practiced by teachers and experienced by students. The test may do a very good job measuring vocabulary knowledge, meaning one can argue for *construct validity* of the test. And the test may actually align with a course outcome on vocabulary. Nonetheless, the previous description suggests the test lacks content validity. Content validity refers to the extent to which a test or quiz reflects the content presented and is practiced in class, but not only in a surface topical sense, such as giving and getting directions, or reading narrative passages from folk tales, etc. There also has to be a match in the sense that learners are doing things with the second language on a test that are similar to what they do in class or with homework. Thus, the idea of a construct can be invoked in discussions of content validity.

To illustrate: In reviewing the end-of-course test for a well-known pronunciation textbook, Gorsuch (2001) found that topically the test more or less reflected what was in the textbook. However, she found that on one major section of the test, students had to read both parts of a lengthy dialog with long utterances out loud, which was something never done in the textbook or in class. Rather, the teacher and learners focused on short pair work activities. It can be argued that because the test task was different from what learners had done up to that point, that the test might not allow the students to demonstrate their new knowledge. Said another way, learners' knowledge grew in one way as a result of the curriculum, but the test might not detect that. The construct of using specific pronunciation features in short, semiscripted pair work activities may be different than the construct of using those same features in a lengthy, unrehearsed dialog with unknown vocabulary. To sum up: If tests or quizzes are used to measure student learning for the purpose of an evaluation, and if those tests have a limited relationship with what the curriculum actually has students doing, we may see changes in their learning, but we cannot claim that the curriculum of the course is responsible for the changes.

DISCUSSION QUESTION 4

Thinking about a test or quiz you gave as a teacher, or took as a student, do you feel it was adequately related to your course outcomes? Why or why not? Were there issues with the course outcomes not being stated, or some other lack of clarity of the course outcomes?

DISCUSSION QUESTION 5

Thinking about a test or quiz you gave as a teacher, or took as a student, do you feel it was adequately related to the working curriculum of the course? Why or why not? What was it about the test or quiz that seemed different from, or the same, to what you experienced in the course as a teacher or learner?

Assessment and Stakeholders

The connection between assessment and stakeholders may not seem immediately evident. After all, it is learners who take tests and quizzes, not parents, teachers, or administrators. Yet learners' achievement on the assessments (tests and quizzes) matter to stakeholders, apart from functioning as a way to assign worth to the course outcomes and course curriculum. Learners care about how they are tested and what they experience as test candidates. Learners, and their families, also care about how well learners do on tests or quizzes, which may determine whether they pass a course or whether they graduate. Foreign language learners are not confident about tests that they do not believe a course curriculum prepares them for (Gorsuch, 2009). The relationship between assessments and stakeholders will be further discussed in conjunction with a test validity model detailed later in the chapter.

DISCUSSION QUESTION 6

Can you think of additional ways stakeholders may care about the assessments used in a course? What interest would administrators have? What interest may parents have? What interest may the teacher/evaluator have, apart from how well a test or quiz functions to estimate learners' movement toward course outcomes?

Validity and Instrument Validation

Validity and instrument validation have long been a key concern for test makers (Spolsky, 1968, p. 94). For most of the 20th century, validity was understood as measuring what you thought you were measuring. For example, if you designed a speaking test and you offered evidence that your test was indeed measuring speaking, your test was considered valid. During the last few years, some new understandings of validity have emerged and been accepted. See Table 7.1 for a partial listing.

First, we cannot say that a test itself is valid or invalid. A test can be well designed, which can certainly be used as an initial and important argument for validity. Whether a test is valid rests more on the students' scores on

TABLE 7.1 Emerging Understandings About Instrument Validity and Validation

1. A test is not in itself valid. Interpretations made from students' test scores from a test given at a particular time is what is valid, or not.
2. A test is never truly validated. One can only argue for the validity of a test, and continue to collect validation evidence each time the instrument is used.
3. Validity has one primary category, that of construct validity.
4. If validation evidence is not offered in a report, we are not required to accept the interpretation of the scores given by the author or authors.

the test and the interpretation we assign to the scores (Cronbach, 1990, p. 145). One part of this new understanding is that validation and validation evidence are attached to particular test scores, administered on a certain date to certain students. In that sense, validation is particular and not universal. Another part of this new understanding requires that we search out the appropriateness of our interpretations of students' scores. If we wish to show a change in learners' French second language spoken fluency, it makes sense to capture their speaking at the beginning of a study abroad course and then again at the end of a course (e.g., Freed, 1995). We cannot give the test only once, at the end of a course, and assert an interpretation that the course was a "success" because students were more "fluent." They may have been fluent to begin with.

Second, it is now believed that a test is never considered fully validated. One can and should offer validation evidence, but there is no set threshold and no complete argument that says "the interpretations made from scores on this test we think is measuring such and such a construct are v...a...l ...i...d." The process of validation is never-ending and is never finished. The validation strategies we suggest in this chapter may be done over a semester or over a period of years.

Third, in the past validity was thought to have multiple components, meaning that there were different kinds of validity. An example was used previously: *content validity*. For a time, content validity was thought to be something distinct from what was called construct validity. Brown (2005) noted: "In order to investigate content validity, testers must decide whether the test is a representative sample of the content the test was designed to measure" (p. 221). Implied in this statement was the idea that a second language test of, say, Tagalog listening ability, could have distinct subtests matching the various areas of listening that students had worked on in classes, such as "distinguishing minimal pairs...listening for facts...listening for main ideas" (Brown, 2005, p. 221). This conception of validity is useful for teachers/evaluators who want their tests and quizzes to comprehensively sample what students have been working on (the working curriculum).

However, validity is now considered a single entity by some, where the key category is the construct. This conception of construct validity has a basis in learning as part of psychology and learners' cognition: "Since these constructs occur inside the brain, they must be observed indirectly" (Brown, 2005, p. 227). Thus the existence of a construct—the knowledge, skill, or ability we think we are measuring—can only be inferred from learners' responses to test items. It is helpful to think in terms of what learners do with the second language in class. Are they reading short passages repeatedly, finding definitions for unknown words, searching out other examples of the same words (perhaps verbs) in different forms in other passages, and then rewriting passages in their own words (Swaffar & Arens, 2005)? The question then is how we design quizzes or tests that ask students to do the same kinds of things, perhaps with a new passage, and then using scores from the tests to infer that learners can identify patterns in the second language (one construct), can accurately estimate word meaning (another construct), and have some knowledge of the passage meaning (a third construct). Stated another way, *constructs* are the predetermined, prethought-out ability, knowledge, or skills we think we are measuring.

We argue that while construct validity is a primary concern when using tests and quizzes to evaluate a course, content validity as classically defined continues to have tremendous utility for teachers/evaluators. From these examples given on the vocabulary quiz and the pronunciation textbook test, it is clear that construct validity and content validity, in application, have a good deal of overlap. Yet the basis of concern that motivated each example came from course curricula, in other words the activities, materials, and instruction that learners experience in a course. If a test is to be used to evaluate a course, it has to be related to the course curriculum as much as it is related to the constructs embedded in the course outcomes (Figure 7.1).

Fourth and finally, if test validation evidence is not offered in a report, we are not required to accept the score interpretation (Bachman, 1990, p. 243; Weir, 2005, p. 11), such as "the students increased their listening comprehension significantly, so the new curriculum was successful." This means we should not accept test results from tests or quizzes that lack supporting validation evidence.

DISCUSSION QUESTION 7

Which of these four new understandings of validity seem easiest to comprehend? Which of them do you have questions about? What are the questions?

A Validity Model

We offer a validity model adapted to the concerns of course evaluators. We use the model (Figure 7.2) to describe practical strategies for using tests and quizzes that are clearly related to the course outcomes and course curriculum, and to suggest ways to generate validation evidence.

Although the new understanding of test validity and validation described in the previous section came from multiple sources, the most complete description was formulated in Messick (1989) and helpfully summarized in

	interpretation	use
evidence	A. score interpretation	B. test usefulness
consequences	C. stakeholder values	D. social consequences

Figure 7.2 A test validity model adapted for course evaluators.

Kunnan (1998). Figure 7.2 has four considerations arranged vertically and horizontally, including evidence, consequences, interpretation, and use. Each of these interact conceptually to suggest actions on the part of language testers, and by extension, course evaluators. They appear as quadrants in 2×2 fashion. It is from these four quadrants (A, B, C, and D) that validation strategies emerge.

We suggest two considerations while examining this model. First, Kunnan (1998) examined published test validation studies and concluded that as a field we are most experienced with score interpretation (Quadrant A), and least experienced with the other three quadrants, especially examining the social consequences of our tests (Quadrant D). This indicates where we were as language test users in terms of our awareness of how to validate tests and quizzes, at least in 1998. This may explain why evaluation reports provide test validation evidence in such variable ways and degrees of detail (see the RAP template analyses in Chapter 10). Second, as conceptually significant as the model in Figure 7.2 is, it does not tell us exactly what to do or suggest an order in which to do it. This might not be surprising, because there is no agreed-upon type of validation evidence a classroom teacher/ test maker/test user, much less a course evaluator, is required to provide. There is no agreed upon order in which to present validation evidence, nor which type should be a priority.

Given our concerns expressed in Chapter 6 that course teachers/evaluators have limited time and energy, we offer a suggestion from Hambleton (2012) that the amount of validation evidence teachers should provide depends in part on how important the test is. By "important" we could mean how significant a test or set of quizzes is to investigating the part of a course we are evaluating. For instance, in a Japanese foreign language course where accurate oral language production based on dialogs is named as a primary outcome, quizzes that call for students to demonstrate their speaking skill in scripted role-plays may be considered important. These quizzes might be a logical focus for validation efforts. Quizzes or a test for the same course that capture learners' knowledge of the target language culture may not seem a logical focus for validation, particularly if this is one of the less clear or well thought-out parts of the course. By important we could also mean tests or quizzes that are salient in learners' eyes for whatever reason. Here is a second example: In a study of learners' confidence to do various things using a foreign language, Gorsuch (2009) found that learners felt least confident of their ability to do well in a Spanish oral test administered in a language learning lab. She formulated two explanations for their strikingly low levels of confidence, either (a) learners were not getting enough practice doing similar tasks in class, or (b) teachers were not explicitly drawing learners' attention to classroom tasks that supported their ability to do well in oral tests. The oral test would be a prime candidate for validation efforts, given learners' strong feelings about the test, and the explanations offered for learners' low confidence.

DISCUSSION QUESTION 8

In a second language course you recently took or taught can you think of any one test or quiz in a course that seemed more important than others? What made them more important? Because you were told they "counted" for more, or for other reasons?

We now list and discuss validation strategies for gathering empirical data within each quadrant of the model in Figure 7.2. Later we present them in chronological steps so that a teacher/evaluator can create a validation action plan.

Validation Strategies Suggested by Quadrant A (Score Interpretation)

Test Reliability

Validation evidence suggested by Quadrant A includes the now-traditional and most often-used types of validity evidence such as construct and content validity. One indirect strategy for validating a test in this tradition is to calculate test reliability. While calculating test reliability is beyond the scope of this book, there are detailed and practical descriptions of estimating test reliability for many types of tests found in Brown (2005), and also Fulcher (2010). *Reliability* indicates the level to which a test can be trusted to consistently measure a construct, such the ability to write coherent paragraphs in the second language. For such a writing test to be reliable, a teacher/evaluator would need to show, for example, that the same grading criteria are used on all learners' tests, and used in the same way each time the test is given, and used in the same way by different raters. But someone who can show that a test captures some knowledge or skill consistently still has to argue for what knowledge or skill is being captured. That is why reliability calculation might be termed an indirect validation method.

Construct Validation

A test or quiz *construct* is the theoretical model of the ability, knowledge, or skill the test is measuring. For instance, if you give an end-of-chapter quiz on vocabulary, then vocabulary learning is the construct. Any evidence you can provide that you are measuring the construct is construct validation. In addition to estimating test *reliability,* here are three construct validation strategies: defining the construct, differential group study, and intervention study. These strategies might be termed more direct in that they involve stating what the intended construct is and then demonstrating the existence of the construct.

Defining the Construct

A good first move would be to define the construct. Second language vocabulary learning is an example. To define this, one could consult literature on the subject and try to determine what the field currently and commonly says second language vocabulary learning is. For many second language teachers, vocabulary learning means students have studied a list of words in isolation, have committed them to memory, and can define them briefly and in a surface way using their first language. This would amount to those teachers' statement of the construct. Whether this treatment of vocabulary is adequate to support a stated course outcome about vocabulary learning is something worth considering, and is an issue that can be addressed using a *course logic study* (Chapter 5).

A perspective more based in second language learning theory, however, would point to considering "how many words [learners] know (breadth of knowledge) and how well they know those words (depth of knowledge)" (Loewen & Reinders, 2011, p. 110). Depth of knowledge suggests that the construct of vocabulary learning has to do with using the vocabulary. This is also reflected in a more learner- and teacher-practice view expressed by a foreign language learning website author: "Learning long lists of unrelated words is boring, difficult and doesn't help you much when you come across those words in a different context" and "A great way to build up your vocabulary is to have a go at reading books.... When reading, try to guess the meanings of any words you don't know" (Ager, 2014). This website was located in less than a minute using the search term "vocabulary learning."

This would change a statement of construct to something like: "Vocabulary learning is defined as learners' ability to recognize known words in a second language reading passage, and use the words and some guesswork to construct meaning." A statement of construct such as this could never fit a test in which students memorized isolated words and then briefly defined them using the first language. Such is the power of defining a construct using one's own words, and a reading of current and commonly held notions of second language learning. If a teacher/evaluator showed colleagues his or her construct definition, and then queried them as to its clarity or meaningfulness, the evaluator might then gain additional perspectives on the construct, and get ideas on how best to design or tweak a test or quiz to capture it. Validation evidence would be notes on the construct definition process and colleagues' reactions to the written construct, as well as any suggestions they made on revising the construct statement and test items to match the construct.

Differential-Group Study and Intervention Study

To generate data for construct validation of a test or quiz, Brown (1988, p. 103) describes two additional strategies: a differential-group study and an intervention study. A differential-group study requires you to find two groups, one of which you can argue has the construct ability (i.e., a group of second-year students) and a group that you argue does not have the construct (a first-year group at the beginning of the year). The test or quizzes are given to both groups of students. We then compare the scores of the two groups, and to the extent they are different we claim the difference is due to the second-year students "having the construct," assuming the second-year students have the higher scores. Thus we can claim that the test or quizzes are measuring "something" (the construct) because it shows the second-year group "has" it and the first-year group does not.

An intervention study uses the same logic, but with this method, the test is administered to a group at the beginning of the course, and then again at the end of the course. The intervention is the course that takes place during the interval. At the beginning of the course, the learners do not "have" the construct. If all goes well, and the test is actually capturing the construct we intend, learners will have higher scores at the end-of-course administration because they have the construct. For a detailed report using this method to validate a foreign language pronunciation test, see Gorsuch (2001). Validation evidence using either of these strategies would be comparisons of the two groups' mean (average) test scores, as in: Group 1 students' mean score = 79.96 (out of 100 points), Group 2 students' mean score = 31.12 (out of 100 points), with a mean difference of

48.84 points. This reflects a differential group study approach. Or, pretest mean score = 31.12 and posttest mean score = 79.96 with a gain of 48.84 points. This second example reflects an intervention study approach.

Content Validation

Described earlier in this chapter, content validation works to establish the extent to which a test or quiz reflects the content presented and practiced in class. This approach is based the assumption that your test or quizzes are a representative sample of the content area you are testing. The content area is often called the domain by test developers (see domain theory). For example, if a test is a final exam and learners are told that the test will cover the entire semester, then the semester curriculum is the domain that ought to be tested. Thus, if a textbook and instruction based on the textbook comprised the main part of the curriculum, and Chapters A, B, C, and D were covered, then that is the domain for the final exam. The idea of a representative sample comes down to a human judgment that a test covers a specified domain adequately. Collecting these judgments begins with the test user, who reviews the test and the four textbook chapters, making comparisons between test items, topics, and activities in the textbook. The textbook may focus on listening comprehension of basic academic lectures on history and science through a process of previewing vocabulary, topic activation, listening to a lecture multiple times, taking notes, and then reviewing notes. Do the test items match these topics and processes? Does the test focus only on listening to a single lecture on literary criticism once, without taking notes, and then answering the questions about the lecture? We might conclude that the test is not sampling the domain adequately. The validation evidence from this internal comparison would be notes to the effect that only a fraction of the test domain is being sampled in the test. Needless to say, this is not strong validation evidence. Assuming the test matches the domain better than this example suggests with a similar listening text to the book and similar processes of listening to and comprehending a lecture, a test user might then proceed to showing his or her test or quiz to colleagues and asking them to make a comparison between the test and the textbook chapters. Validation evidence then would include notes about colleagues' reactions to the test or quiz items and textbook chapter comparisons.

DISCUSSION QUESTION 9

Which of the strategies described from Quadrant A seem appealing to you? Why? Does one seem easier to do, or does one seem more effective as an argument for validity?

Validation Strategies Suggested by Quadrant B (Test Usefulness)

For Quadrant B, Kunnan (1998) considers test-taker characteristics such as how different learners use different test-taking strategies, which may advantage them or disadvantage them on particular kinds of tests. This quadrant also includes considerations of how differences in learners' academic background, second language background, age, and gender may affect how well they do on tests. Thus test "usefulness" in this context refers to whether test users/teachers/evaluators can use a test or quizzes with learners across the board, using the same tests and the same scoring procedures for all learners. Ginther and Stevens (1998, p. 174), for example, compared different learner groups on a Spanish language test, finding that Mexican English bilingual speakers, native Mexican Spanish speakers, and White English-speaking Spanish speakers answered test items differently. Their answers suggested that the test scores reflected some learners' experiences in second language classes (listening, reading, and writing), but other learners' experiences using Spanish outside the classroom (speaking). If one is trying to use such a test to evaluate a course that primarily provides in-class learning experiences, then some learners' scores on this test will be high regardless of what went on in classes. Although Ginther and Stevens (1998) use their test for placement purposes, some implications for course evaluation emerge. They discuss a strategy of leaving out the speaking test scores for the Mexican English bilingual and native Mexican Spanish speakers, and judging only their listening, reading, and writing subtest scores. For evaluation purposes this would more reflect the in-class experiences of these learners, who still have things to learn within those language skill areas, and which the course presumably addresses. Validation evidence here would amount to noting that group differences were found and that a differential scoring strategy was used.

Test-Taker Bias

But learners' second language background is only one among many learner characteristics that may affect performance on tests and quizzes, and thus "muddy up" the interpretations we can make with scores. How do we take these into account and guide our validation efforts? Following Weir's thinking on test-taker group bias (2005), we offer a test-taker bias validation strategy stated as basic categories. *Test-taker bias* is used in a testing-technical sense here and means a characteristic of some persons in a group that might affect their test scores, especially if it is unidentified and not taken into account. Test-taker bias validation evidence would amount to an account that a teacher/evaluator has identified relevant sources of bias and has taken steps to deal with them in their tests and quizzes. Table 7.2 lists possible sources of test-taker bias under one of three categories: character-istics that are judged difficult to control, characteristics that might be less difficult to control, and easier-to-control characteristics that can and should be controlled for. Our placement of sources of bias is intuitive, thus we sug-gest that these lists are descriptive rather than prescriptive. This means that teachers/evaluators have to consider their own situation and make their own lists for the purpose of planning a course evaluation.

We doubt it is useful or possible to present a detailed strategy for all sources of test-taker bias, but a general approach might be (a) acknowl-edge those characteristics in Category A, (b) develop a policy to deal with the characteristics in Category B, and (c) deal proactively with category C. In Category A ("Difficult to control") validation evidence might be a written account of second language background group differences, such as what Sohn and Shin (2007) do for a test of Korean. They found that a large number of heritage speakers of Korean enrolled in Korean classes and lacked literacy skills in the language, much like true beginners. In con-trast, some of the heritage speakers excelled in speaking. As the Korean courses had outcomes for all four skills of speaking, listening, reading, and writing, these before-course and before-test group differences could affect whether or not a course curriculum appeared to be supporting learners to attainment of the outcomes.

In a few cases, a teacher/evaluator might be able to go beyond a simple account of test-taker differences and change their testing practices. For in-stance, a teacher/evaluator may note that a number of his or her students

TABLE 7.2 Possible Sources of Test-Taker Bias and Their Relative Difficulty to Control

A. Difficult to control	B. Less difficult to control	C. Easier to control
Age	Absent for test	Test familiarity
Gender	Late for test	Test preparation
Cognitive style	Sickness	Test environment
Native language		Physical disability
Second language background		
Country of origin		
Room conditions		
Family condition		
Educational background		
Weather		
Individual interests		

are returnees to formal education and as a result are substantially older than other students in the class (age). If the course outcomes include the ability to write a comparative essay, the teacher/evaluator may change the topics students are allowed to write on that would accommodate all learners' life experiences or current interests. Thus both younger and older students would be equally advantaged in that they could choose topics familiar to them to write about. In other cases, we have even less control over the gender composition of our classes, or differential groups who respond differently according to the weather on the day we give a key test. Thus a simple accounting may be the best validation strategy available.

For Category B ("Less difficult to control"), having policies sketched out beforehand will help generate validation evidence. If a teacher/evaluator is concerned about students' lateness to or absence from tests, he or she needs to think through what accommodations will or will not be done, such as offering the same test as a make-up. But what if the student is a day or more late and has had opportunities to ask classmates about the test or quiz? This may advantage the student in question, and disadvantage the other students because they had less time to prepare. If the situation actually arises, any validation evidence would include the policy and what was done, such as removing the late student's score from the evaluation.

Finally, for Category C ("Easier to control"), steps need to be taken to ensure learners are familiar with the test and are prepared for it. In the case of test environment, it may be that the test must be given in a different location than the normal classroom or under new conditions, such as a computer-administered test given in a language lab. The teacher/evaluator must then arrange for a practice test in the new location and then report this as validation evidence.

Validation Strategies Suggested by Quadrant C (Stakeholder Values)

Kunnan's caption for this quadrant is value implications (1998). Test validation, in Kunnan's eyes, needs to take into account feedback on the test from learners, teachers, specialists in "college and university subject matter" (p. 6), and other stakeholders. For teachers/evaluators this is clearly applicable to the idea of *stakeholders* and stakeholders' values. Using the SOAC model (Figure 7.1), this relationship can be seen in the arrow between assessments (tests and quizzes) and stakeholders. For example, a teacher/evaluator may value regular quizzes where learners handwrite a summary in the second language of a narrative text read in class during·

the week. This shows growth of second language writing ability in a specific genre, and shows whether learners are using vocabulary used in the texts. Such a test can be done quickly in class. The learners may have a different point of view: They would like to reread the texts before writing, they prefer a compare-and-contrast type of genre, and they want to compose their work on a word processing program rather than writing by hand. Based on feedback sought from the learners, the teacher/evaluator may tweak the weekly quizzes, allow for rereading of the texts, and have the quizzes in the computer lab. This would be reported as validation evidence. He or she may also make note of whether additional class sessions on writing summaries were offered, in the event that summary writing is believed to have greater alignment with a course outcome that stipulates learners should increase their ability to synthesize ideas in order to appreciate their own culture and other cultures (Swaffar & Arens, 2005). Teachers/evaluators may make a decision not to be so accommodative, but then be prepared to discuss this as validation evidence.

In Chapter 3 we discussed a graduate-level lab instructor preparation course where the students valued getting through the course as soon as possible, and getting whatever single "score" they needed to qualify to be science lab instructors. This meant passing a teaching simulation test, among other things. During our formative evaluation of the course (Chapter 6), we learned from course teaching assistants (TAs) and the learners themselves that the preferred method of passing the teaching simulation test was to choose one topic, develop a short presentation, and then give that same presentation again and again each time a presentation test was assigned, and during TAs' office hours. The learners' values included memorizing a single long presentation.

The TAs' values ran counter to this. They felt insulted that learners thought they could learn to communicate by memorizing a single presentation, without much care for the learners' future students, whose needs to learn chemistry or physics could not be met by a memorized presentation on one topic. Instructors in the course had yet another set of values that focused on course outcomes. A short-term outcome was improved ITA pronunciation and interpersonal communication, which was thought to lead to a long-term outcome: ITAs capable of extended discourse in academic and professional settings (see Chapter 5, Table 5.2). Putting energy into a single memorized presentation to be given again and again was not congruent with the course logic, nor with the course curriculum. A decision was made, in conjunction with course TAs, that each teaching simulation test the learners gave had to be on a different topic than the presentation given before. Further, the learners would be provided with more guided preparation activities for the test, with more attention paid to different communicative tasks, such as describing a process for one test and describing relationships between a "family" of related concepts for another test. Validation evidence here would be an account of the contrasting stakeholder values and a justification, based on an examination of the course outcomes, for designing a test or quiz in a particular way.

DISCUSSION QUESTION 10

Has a teacher ever asked you, as a second language learner, your opinions about a test? What was your feedback? As a teacher, have you ever asked for feedback from students or other stakeholders on a test?

DISCUSSION QUESTION 11

What accommodations do you think a second language teacher could try to make to take into account learners' feedback? Can learners' feedback be completely accommodated? Why or why not?

Validation Strategies Suggested by Quadrant D (Social Consequences)

We now discuss the fourth and final quadrant of our model (Figure 7.2), which is the intersection of test consequences and test use. We focus our discussion on *test washback*, which refers to the effect of a test on teaching and learning in classrooms at a local, regional, or even national level. In the SOAC model (Figure 7.1), this relationship is captured by the arrow between assessments and stakeholders. Some tests are thought to generate widespread, systematic changes in teaching and learning, such as the GRE (Educational Testing Service, 2014), which is offered in the United States and in more than 35 other countries on a continuous basis. The social consequence part comes when prospective graduate students, many of whom use English as a foreign language, consume time, energy, and money on courses and materials for test preparation. Other stakeholders, such as students' families, and test-preparation schools and publishers, are also potentially affected. Because we are interested only in tests that are made by teachers/evaluators, we focus at the most local level possible: the course. It is likely that teachers "teach to a test" written by others or some external body (see for example, Nishino, 2008), and it is worth studying the extent to which an external test is congruent with course outcomes and the curriculum (see Figure 7.1). But here we focus on strategies to validate tests and quizzes written by the teacher/evaluator.

DISCUSSION QUESTION 12

Can you think of social consequences for a test other than a student spending money on courses and materials to pass the test? Are these social consequences positive, or negative?

DISCUSSION QUESTION 13

Do you think a language classroom is a social place? What social consequences, both positive and negative, might result from using a particular test or series of quizzes?

How Test Washback is Defined and Studied

How test washback is defined and studied in the second language learning field varies. One seminal conception of test washback comes from Alderson and Wall (1993, p. 115) who note, "The notion that testing influences teaching is commonplace in the educational and applied linguistics literature" (see also Wall & Alderson, 1996). Wall (1997) uses her own term, "test impact," to describe the effect of a test on a larger context (stakeholders, schools, and societies), such as the previous example given with the GRE. In contrast, Wall defines test washback as the effect of a test at a very local level, that of learning and teaching in a classroom. In this book, we use test washback to refer to the effect of a test at any level of organization that could be courses, programs, schools, and societies. We posit that if the influence of the test can be shown to support course outcomes, then the test washback is positive. If the influence does not support course outcomes, then test washback is negative. The use of the terms "positive" or "negative" is not a value judgment, that some test is good or bad for learners. Rather, the two terms refer to whether there is evidence that a given test has some effect on what learners and teachers think or do in response to a test or series of quizzes that we intended and designed to be aligned with the outcomes of a course.

An Example of Positive Washback

Here is an example of positive washback. A teacher of Japanese decided to use a series of weekly "pair interview" quizzes where two learners were supposed to read a short text together and ask and answer questions about unknown vocabulary. She felt that students did not pay attention to each other when they spoke Japanese, and this bothered her. She thought learners could be better resources for each other than they realized, and that if she required students to work together for short periods for mutual benefit, they might become more willing to use Japanese with each other and listen to each other more in class. She held the quizzes once a week in class for 10 minutes. Learners were to construct a list of words from the text that week that they had looked up together and talked about. She also asked learners to estimate how much Japanese and how much of the L1 they had used to talk about the text together and make lists from. To her surprise, learners reported a steady number of new words they learned, even with different partners from week to week. The learners also reported using 50% Japanese and 50% of their L1s. She noted that at nonquiz times in class, students sometimes corrected each other, or supplied a missing word when a struggling classmate needed help.

How Test Washback for Courses Is Not Studied

That a test might have an effect on what teachers teach and what students learn strikes many teachers/evaluators as obvious. One often hears of a test that causes teachers to "teach to the test." This claim would be an example of test washback. However, Alderson and Wall (1993) note that in test washback studies there is much assertion on the part of the evaluator, but little actual validation evidence offered (see for example Prodromou, 1995). Alderson and Wall (1993) call for empirical data to be provided to investigate test washback, and the extent to which it does or does not occur.

A meta-analysis by Cheng (2008, p. 349) underscores how few test washback studies are actually done in which teaching and learning in courses and classrooms are focused on. Most test washback studies are conducted by testing experts working to validate large-scale high stakes tests, rather than by classroom teachers. This is because in many cases high-stakes tests are intentional attempts to change teaching on a broad scale (Shohamy, 2001). In these cases, test washback studies are important to confirm the extent to which the intention of the test administrators was accomplished. However, relatively few test washback studies have been conducted by classroom teachers using tests developed specifically for their classes. Cheng (2008) extensively reviewed test washback citing 62 references. In a close examination of these references, only four dealt with classrooms. The promise of test washback studies conducted by teachers/evaluators working with their own tests is to enlarge the investigation and understanding of test washback for the entire second language learning field.

Doing a Test Washback Study

To collect validation evidence for a test assuming the presence of test washback, we start with developing what we call a causal model. Once a teacher/evaluator is clear on how he or she thinks test washback may cause changes in teaching and learning in a course, he or she can take further steps to collect data to add to a portfolio of validation evidence.

Creating a Causal Model

Creating a causal model that could be shown to others for comment is a key piece of validation evidence. Saif (2006, p. 5) comes very close to this with his conceptual framework for washback, which we have adapted in Figure 7.3. Whereas Saif labels his three sequential stages as needs, means, and consequences, we focus more on how a teacher/evaluator can use this model to think through and talk to others about the ways tests or quizzes may cause changes in teaching and learning. We also think that simply describing the design of a test does not constitute a full causal model, even though such a description can be an important conceptual basis for a washback study (Saif, 2006, p. 5). Rather, a teacher/evaluator needs to hypothesize ahead of time the logical, curriculum-based outgrowths of test design the teacher plans to make manifest in the materials he or she develops or chooses, or the instruction he or she plans. We do not see choice of materials or instruction as straightforward, can-be-presumed-upon consequences of test design, but rather a missed opportunity to fully develop possible causes for potential changes in teachers' teaching and students' learning in terms of a course *curriculum* (see Chapter 2 on the SOAC model). Thus "needs" in Saif's 2006

Course context	Causes based on test or quiz design	Applied causes	Test/Quiz washback
Name course outcomes	Describe the test construct (What skill or knowledge does the test capture?	Search for congruence between materials and teaching, and tests and quizzes.	Describe changes in learning and/or teaching.
	Provide sample test items or tasks.	Describe plans for designing materials, including plans for intensity and frequency of use.	Are changes positive (supporting course outcomes)?
	Describe frequency and "weight" of test.		Are changes negative (not supporting course outcomes)?
	Provide a plan of how test or quiz scores are reported to learners (a numerical score, written feedback, verbal feedback).	Describe plan for selection of existing materials, including plans for intensity and frequency of use.	
		Describe plans for teaching methods or strategies, including plans for intensity and frequency of use.	

Figure 7.3 A causal model for test washback in classrooms.

model become "Course context" or the outcomes of a course. "Means" becomes "Causes based on test or quiz design," and "consequences" becomes "Applied causes." We have added a fourth column calling for a description of hypothesized washback, either positive or negative, that a teacher/evaluator can present to expert others for comment. The comments of others on the causal model, and the teacher's/evaluator's adjustments due to the comments, may become validation evidence. See Figure 7.3.

Naming the Course Outcomes

Naming the course outcomes (course context) allows a teacher/evaluator to describe the reasons for the design of a test, much as we might for collecting validation evidence based on Quadrant A (score interpretation). A first- or second-year Spanish foreign language course may be based on outcomes to improve learners' speaking and listening skills in specified study abroad settings (asking for and getting directions, asking for help taking a bus, buying study supplies at a local store). A teacher/evaluator may then argue, with or without success, that role-play tests he or she has written captures learners' speaking and listening skills in such situations.

Causes Based on Test or Quiz Design

Assuming colleagues agree that the statement of test construct and sample tasks comprise a test design that will likely capture learners' achievement of course outcomes (causes based on test or quiz design), a teacher/evaluator then needs to provide additional information that speaks to the test design-specific impact of the test results. How often are the role-play tests given? Only once? Two or more times? What is their "weight" in terms of how a learner's course performance is judged? Are the role-plays the main means of awarding a course grade, or are they minor players among other types of tests, such as that big, end-of-semester grammar and vocabulary test that so often seems to creep in, regardless of the course outcomes? A test that is given frequently may have more impact on learners' course-specific efforts than tests offered only once (e.g., Brown, Roediger, & McDaniel, 2014). A test or series of quizzes that are given more public weight in terms of learners' course grades may have more potential impact on teachers' and learners' course-focused activities (see Table 7.3, Number 12 in this chapter). As another example, note the German learners' attitudes toward vocabulary quizzes given in Chapter 6. Because the vocabulary quizzes were given infrequently, and had little weight, one learner reported doing nothing more than memorizing, and then forgetting, the specified vocabulary. The influence of the quizzes was minimal in terms of changing how the learner went about his business of learning.

Further, in what form are the test results given to learners: as written feedback or oral feedback? What is the level of detail of the feedback? This might be: "Your fluency and comprehensibility on the 'getting help taking the bus' task was adequate, but we sensed you had trouble understanding your partner's suggestions about a different route you could take.... Can you think of what you can say when you don't understand?" versus "You passed." Greater detail may provide more impact to learners' plans based on the feedback they receive. Is a numerical score given? If so, do learners have working descriptive knowledge of what a numerical score means?

Applied Causes

Finally, in Figure 7.3 a teacher/evaluator needs to provide information on his or her intentions concerning design and choice of materials, and plans for teaching that may be considered strongly connected to the test (applied causes). Here we are particularly concerned with not only the congruence of the materials, instruction, and the test design, but also the frequency and intensity of the test-inspired materials and/or instruction. For the overseas study role-play tasks previously mentioned, the teacher/evaluator may mention designing, selecting vocabulary lists, or grammar prompts that he or she thinks builds up to doing a role-play. He or she may also mention multiple video or audio recordings of authentic transactional encounters in Spanish with recursive, short tasks for learners to do as they listen. How the materials will be used instructionally would also be described. With the audio or video recordings, will learners listen to them repeatedly or just once? Will learners then do some practice role-plays based on the materials? How often will the test-supportive materials be used? How often will test-supportive teaching be done? Will the teacher/evaluator mention to the students the relationship of the materials and instruction to the test? How often? The teacher/evaluator's articulation of a causal model, and colleagues' comments on the model, is one form of validation evidence.

Test/Quiz Washback

A teacher/evaluator needs to provide plans for showing evidence that a test has resulted in washback. The teacher/evaluator working with the role-play tests in Spanish may argue that learners' increasing scores on the test over time will constitute evidence of washback. Here the value of having this four-part causal model for test washback (Figure 7.3) shows its worth. The part of the model on "Causes based on test or quiz design" already stipulates that a teacher/evaluator assess the degree to which sample tasks and a stated construct will likely capture learners' achievement of course outcomes (course context). If the role-play tests are accepted as likely capturing learners' speaking and listening skills in overseas study type situations, then a teacher/evaluator's plans to use increases in test scores as validation evidence for positive washback are well founded.

Additional Suggestions and Steps for a Test Washback Study

Fulcher and Davidson (2007, p. 228), taking a somewhat different orientation to test washback than Saif (2006), ask (a) how could we measure test washback; (b) after the introduction of a new test, what data might be collected to show test washback; and (c) why might collecting baseline data before using a new test be helpful? Here, "baseline data" means data on learner knowledge or skills in the form of tests, samples, or interviews, before a test washback study begins or a new test is introduced. To demonstrate test washback, then, a teacher/evaluator or the learners have to change between one point in time and another point in time. We reorder Fulcher and Davidson's (2007) questions and suggest: (a) gather baseline data, (b) come up with a plan to answer the question of how to measure washback, and (c) develop a plan of what data to collect. The baseline data, taken with plans to collect data, and the data collected after using the new test, would together comprise validation evidence.

We have further suggestions along these lines, which suggests a way of thinking about test washback as a field experiment. One is to decide beforehand which hypothesis to test. This will help a teacher/evaluator to decide what baseline data to collect and what subsequent data to collect after a new test is used. Alderson and Wall (1993) give 15 research hypotheses (Table 7.3).

We further suggest a teacher/evaluator commit to a research design beforehand, probably a case study design or an experimental design. Based on the hypothesis chosen to explore, the teacher/evaluator needs to create specific evaluation questions, such as "Will the Spanish study abroad role-play tests change how learners study and prepare?" or "Will the Spanish study abroad role-play tests lead me to devoting more time to role-play preparation and practice in class?" The teacher/evaluator needs to decide on data collection instruments to use. If studying the effects of test washback on teaching, classroom observations, and interviews might be appropriate. If studying the effects of test washback on learning, then classroom observations, tests, and their scores might be appropriate.

___

Examples of Test Washback Studies

Here we provide examples from published washback studies. Andrews, Fullilove, and Wong (2002) worked with a high-stakes English test given to

TABLE 7.3   Hypotheses That Can Be Used to Design a Test Washback Study
1. A test will influence teaching.
2. A test will influence learning.
3. A test will influence what teachers teach.
4. A test will influence how teachers teach.
5. A test will influence what learners learn.
6. A test will influence how learners learn.
7. A test will influence the rate and sequence of teaching.
8. A test will influence the rate and sequence of learning.
9. A test will influence the degree and depth of teaching.
10. A test will influence the degree and depth of learning.
11. A test will influence attitudes to the content, method, etc. of teaching and learning.
12. Tests that have important consequences will have washback.
13. Tests that do not have important consequences will have no washback.
14. Tests will have washback on all learners and teachers.
15. Tests will have washback effects for some learners and some teachers, but not for others.

Chinese high school students in Hong Kong, where the scores were used to determine entrance into university. Thus the test had strong social consequences. Changing the test might bring about improvements in learners' spoken English abilities, which up to then, had been widely seen as an area to improve at a national level. The hypothesis they selected was Number 2 in Table 7.3 ("A test will influence learning"). Two evaluation questions were constructed. This was a new test, so baseline data was collected on the old test to the extent it measured oral ability. No research design was mentioned in this study. Since it was decided that observation data was important to collect, Andrews et al. (2002) videotaped and rated the oral performances of students under the conditions of the new test and compared those ratings to ratings taken from the old test. Increased ratings from the new test were taken as evidence of positive test washback.

As part of a test washback study on a high-stakes performance test for international teaching assistants (ITAs), Saif (2006) conducted a needs analysis. He wanted to compare past teaching practice with present teaching practice under conditions of the new performance test, and thus asked hypothesis Number 4 in Table 7.3 ("A test will influence how teachers teach"). He tested this hypothesis by consulting graduate advisors, administrators, undergraduate students, and ITAs themselves. To obtain data on subjective needs (wants and expectations), he used open-ended interviews; and for objective needs (language proficiency), he used a questionnaire.

His argument was that if he could contrast past and present teaching practices, and show that under the present conditions of the new test that stakeholders' needs were being met, then he could claim test positive washback.

Finally, Burrows (2004) conducted a test washback study on a not-well-described classroom test using three data collection instruments: questionnaires of 215 teachers, interviews with 30 teachers, and observations of four teachers. As with Saif (2006), the purpose of the study was to investigate possible causal relationships between past teaching, present teaching, and a test.

Summary of Test and Quiz Validation Evidence

See Table 7.4 for a summary of the test or quiz validation evidence for use in a course evaluation.

In an evaluation report, validation evidence would appear in the data collection instruments section (see Chapter 4, Table 4.1). See also Chapter 10, example RAPs 1 and 3, Items 12–15 for examples of how validation evidence is stated. The amount of validation evidence that is reported varies, as we mentioned earlier. We suggest a strategy for building a portfolio of validation evidence, which is, in essence, allowing the SOAC model to take the driver's seat. At the beginning of this chapter, we discussed the SOAC model in Figure 7.1, and identified the assessment component as tests and quizzes. We related assessment to the course outcome component, arguing that we had to align tests and quizzes closely to the course outcomes so that we could establish that the course was accomplishing what it was supposed to accomplish, and that the tests would accurately reflect that. We then related assessment to the curriculum component, arguing that the tests and quizzes had to reflect the curriculum, otherwise, a teacher/evaluator could not claim that the curriculum of the course was responsible for changes in learners. Without these two logical connections, tests and quizzes may not be of real or apparent use to a teacher/evaluator for the purpose of course evaluation.

The validation strategies in all four quadrants can serve to establish the clarity of the relationships between the tests and quizzes of the course, and the outcomes and curriculum of the course. In Quadrant A, the content validation strategy is of direct use to demonstrate a relationship between the course curriculum, and tests and quizzes. In Quadrant C, notes on feedback from learners and then descriptions of a teacher/evaluator's response to the feedback in terms of test design, can demonstrate the teacher/evaluator has expended substantial thought on the relationship between a test and the course outcomes. As Kunnan (1998) noted, as a field we are most familiar with strategies described in Quadrant A, and likely teachers/

TABLE 7.4 Test or Quiz Validation Evidence for Course Evaluation	
Quadrant A. Score interpretation Construct validation (Defining the construct): – Notes on the construct definition process. – Colleagues' reactions to the written construct. – Suggestions from colleagues on revising the construct statement. – Suggestions from colleagues to better match test items to the construct. Construct validation (Differential group study and intervention study): – Comparisons of the two groups' mean (average) test scores. Content validation: – Notes from an internal comparison between the test items and the test domain (predetermined chapters from a textbook, for instance). – Notes about colleagues' reactions to the test or quiz items and test domain comparisons.	**Quadrant B. Usefulness** A general approach to group differences in classes: – Notes that a teacher/evaluator has identified relevant sources of bias. – Notes that the teacher/evaluator has taken pre-thought-out steps to deal with them in their tests and quizzes, such as creating an absent-for or late-to-test policy. Differences in second language background: – Notes that group differences were found and that a differential scoring strategy was used. Ensuring learners are familiar with the test or quiz: – Notes recounting that the teacher/evaluator arranged for a practice test.
Quadrant C. Stakeholder values Notes on feedback sought from the learners, and teacher's/evaluator's response to it with reference to the course outcomes. Notes on contrasting stakeholder values observed over time, and a justification, based on an examination of the course outcomes, for designing or revising a test or quiz in a particular way.	**Quadrant D. Social consequences** Develop a causal model for test washback. Notes on colleagues' reactions and comments to the model. Notes on collecting baseline data, using a new test, collecting subsequent data, and then comparing.

Note: Adapted from Kunnan (1998).

evaluators should plan to use them as kind of a default position. The strategies given in the other three quadrants, however, are equally useful and may set apart an evaluation report as unique.

DISCUSSION QUESTION 14

In your own words, how would you explain the relationships between assessment and outcomes, and assessment and curriculum?

DISCUSSION QUESTION 15

Imagine a colleague or someone interviewing you for a job is listening to you explain validation evidence for a test you used in an evaluation.

Which of the strategies above seems to be easiest for you to explain, or the most convincing?

Chronological Steps for Validating a Test or Quiz

Having discussed some categories of validation for tests and quizzes (Figure 7.2 and Table 7.3), we now offer a possible chronological order of doing validation. On one hand all ordering is arbitrary, but on the other hand a teacher/ evaluator has to begin somewhere. We have arranged the steps roughly into description, before-test administration, and after-test administration.

Instrument Identification and Description

Step 1: Identify the Test Instrument

Obviously you know the test, but assuming that sooner or later you will be reporting your validation as part of your course evaluation, it is necessary to identify your instrument to others. Things that you could report include the number of items, the name of the course in which you use the test, and where the instrument is used in the course (mid-term, final, weekly as an end of chapter review). You can also report where the course fits into the program, and the source of the test. In other words did you make it, buy it, or find it? Do you consider it to be important to know whether learners have the achieved course outcomes, or is the test or quiz a smaller piece of a larger puzzle? Is there any previously existing validation evidence? Finally, what is the name of the test?

Step 2: State the Instrument Purpose and How It Will Be Used

One way to do this would be to connect the instrument purpose and use to course objectives by explaining how the test (or subtests) are connected to various course outcomes.

Before-Test Administration

Step 3: Describe the Construct

By describe, we mean identify and define your construct. There are many examples in this chapter, and also in Chapter 5 on course logic.

Step 4: List Item Formats and Identify Your Scoring Strategy

Tell why you chose the item formats you did and how they are appropriate to your purpose. Examples of item formats are multiple choice, short answer, essay, presentations, role-plays, and recalls after reading a story. For second language reading or listening tests, explain why learners had to write or say their answers in the first or second language.

Step 5: Pilot the Instrument

Not all teachers/evaluators will feel they have time for this, but it should be considered. Piloting an instrument can tell us much about which items on the test or quiz worked well in allowing students to demonstrate their abilities and knowledge. Try to find a group of learners who are similar to the learners you plan to use the test or quiz with.

Step 6: Identify Sources of Test-Taker Bias and Create Responses to Them

The responses may be changes in the design of the test or changes in scoring procedures.

After-Test Administration

Step 7: Pull Together Construct or Content Validation Evidence

See Table 7.3, considering at least three or more strategies to report. Consider strategies not fully explained in this chapter, including estimating test reliability or item analyses (Brown, 2005; Fulcher, 2010).

Step 8: Determine *Cut-Scores*

Cut-scores are little discussed in our field. Many teachers/evaluators determine a 70%-correct level on a test or quiz as they believe this demonstrates learning or mastery beyond the level of learners simply guessing. But for alternatives see Brown (1995) and Griffee and Gevara (2011).

Step 9: Demonstrate Consequential Validation (Quadrant D)

APPLICATION TASKS: Looking for Validation Evidence in a Test Manual, Examining End-of Chapter Quizzes, and Planning a Test or Quiz Validation Project

First task idea: Even though we do not focus on commercially made tests that schools sometimes buy for assessment of learners and evaluation of programs, it is useful to carefully read the test manuals for the validation evidence they describe. Find a test and get access to a manual for the test. Most commercially available tests have websites with sample items and links to their test administrator manuals. Examples are:

- TOEFL Junior Test (https://www.ets.org/toefl_junior)
- Oral Proficiency Interview (http://www.languagetesting.com/oral-proficiency-interview-opi)
- Michigan English Language Assessment Battery (http://www.cambridgemichigan.org/resources/melab)
- Foreign Language Achievement Testing Service (http://flats.byu.edu/langlist.php?x=8)
- Wikipedia offers a list of language proficiency tests sources for 28 languages (http://en.wikipedia.org/wiki/List_of_language_proficiency_tests)

You can also find validation evidence in some major second language textbooks, if they provide tests. Read through the validation evidence they provide and list them under the four quadrants for Figure 7.2 and/or Table 7.3.

Second task idea: Find a major second language textbook and look for any end-of-chapter quizzes or review exercises they may provide. Compare a quiz with the content and activities of the chapter or chapters the quiz covers. Does the quiz have content or construct validity? Write up a short report and present it to colleagues or classmates.

Third task idea: Think of a test or quiz you are using now for a course you are teaching. What are the first three or four steps you can take to validate the test? Write up a short report and present it to colleagues or classmates for their feedback and further suggestions from them on what steps should follow.

References

Adair-Hauck, B., Willingham-McLain, L., & Youngs, B. (2000). Evaluating the integration of technology and second language learning. *CALICO, 17*(2), 269–306. Retrieved from https://calico.org/memberBrowse.php?action=article&id=509

Ager, S. (2014). *Omniglot*. Retrieved from http://www.omniglot.com/language/vocab.htm

Alderson, J. C. (1986). The nature of the beast. In A. Wangsotorn, A. Maurice, K. Prapphal & B. Kenny (Eds.), *Trends in language programme evaluation* (pp. 5–24). Bangkok, Thailand: Chulalongkorn University.

Alderson, J. C., & Wall, D. (1993). Does washback exist? *Applied Linguistics, 14*(2), 115–129.

Andrews, S., Fullilove, J., & Wong, Y. (2002). Targeting washback: A case study. *System, 30*, 207–223.

Bachman, L. F. (1990). *Fundamental considerations in language testing.* Oxford, England: Oxford University Press.

Block, A. (1980). *Murphy's law and other reasons why things go wrong.* Los Angeles, CA: Price Stern Sloan.

Brown, J. D. (1988). *Understanding research in second language learning.* Cambridge, England: Cambridge University Press.

Brown, J. D. (1995). Language program evaluation: Decisions, problems and solutions. *Annual Review of Applied Linguistics, 15,* 227–248.

Brown, J. D. (2005). *Testing in language programs.* New York, NY: McGraw Hill.

Brown, P., Roediger, H., & McDaniel, M. (2014). *Make it stick: The science of successful learning.* Cambridge, MA: Belknap Press.

Burrows, C. (2004). Washback in classroom-based assessment: A study of the washback effect in the Australian adult migrant English program. In L. Cheng, Y. Watanabe, & A. Curtis (Eds.), *Washback in language testing: Research and methods* (pp. 113–128). Mahwah, NJ: Erlbaum.

Cheng, L. (2008). Washback, impact and consequences. In E. Shohamy & N. H. Hornberger (Eds.), *Language testing and assessment* (pp. 349–364). New York, NY: Springer.

Cronbach, L. J. (1990). *Essentials of psychological testing* (5th ed.). New York, NY: Harper Collins.

Educational Testing Service. (2014). *GRE.* Retrieved from http://www.ets.org/gre

Freed, B. (1995). What makes us think that students who study abroad become fluent? In B. Freed (Ed.), *Second language acquisition in a study abroad context* (pp. 123–148). Amsterdam, the Netherlands: John Benjamins.

Fulcher, G. (2010). *Practical language testing.* London, England: Hodder Education.

Fulcher, G., & Davidson, F. (2007). *Language testing and assessment: An advanced resource book.* New York, NY: Routledge.

Ginther, A., & Stevens, J. (1998). Language background, ethnicity, and the internal construct validity of the advanced placement Spanish language examination. In A. J. Kunnan (Ed.), *Validation in language assessment* (pp. 1–16). Mahwah, NJ: Erlbaum.

Gorsuch, G. (2001). Testing textbook theories and tests: The case of suprasegmentals in a pronunciation textbook in an EFL setting. *System, 29*(1), 119–136.

Gorsuch, G. (2009). Investigating second language learner self-efficacy and future expectancy of second language use for high-stakes program evaluation. *Foreign Language Annals, 42*(3), 505–540.

Griffee, D.T. & Gevara, J.R. (2011). Standard setting in the post-modern era for an ITA performance test. *Texas Papers in Foreign Language Education, 2,* 3–16. Retrieved from http://studentorgs.utexas.edu/flesa/TPFLE_New/Issues/Summer%202011/2.%20Griffee%20and%20Gevera.pdf

Hambleton, R. K. (2012). Measurement and validity. In J. Arthur, M. Waring, R. Coe & L. Hedges (Eds.), *Research methods and methodologies in education* (pp. 241–247). Los Angeles, CA: Sage.

Kunnan, A. J. (1998). Approaches to validation in language assessment. In A. J. Kunnan (Ed.), *Validation in language assessment* (pp. 1–16). Mahwah, NJ: Erlbaum.

Loewen, S., & Reinders, H. (2011). *Key concepts in second language acquisition.* Houndmills, England: Palgrave MacMillan.

Messick, S. (1989). Validity. In R. L. Linn (Ed.), *Educational measurement* (3rd ed.; pp. 13–103). New York, NY: Macmillan.

Nishino, T. (2008). Japanese secondary school teachers' beliefs and practices regarding communicative language teaching: An exploratory study. *JALT Journal, 30*(1), 27–50.

Prodromou, L. (1995). The backwash effect: From testing to teaching. *ELTJ, 49*(1), 13–25.

Saif, S. (2006). Aiming for positive washback: A case study of international teaching assistants. *Language Testing, 23,* 1–34.

Shohamy, E. (2001). *The power of tests: A critical perspective on the uses of language tests.* New York, NY: Pearson Education.

Sohn, S.O., & Shin, S.K. (2007). True beginners, false beginners and fake beginners: Placement strategies for Korean heritage speakers. *Foreign Language Annals, 40*(3), 407–418.

Spolsky, B. (1968). Language testing: The problem of validation. *TESOL Quarterly, 2,* 88–94.

Swaffar, J., & Arens, K. (2005). *Remapping the foreign language curriculum: An approach through multiple literacies.* New York, NY: The Modern Language Association of America.

Wall, D. (1997). Impact and washback in language testing. In C. Clapham & D. Corson (Eds.), *Encyclopedia of language and education* (Vol. 7): *Language testing and assessment* (pp. 291–302). Norwell, MA: Kluwer.

Wall, D., & Alderson, J. C. (1996). Examining washback: The Sri Lankan impact study. In A. Cumming & R. Berwick (Eds.), *Validation in language testing* (pp. 194–221). Clevedon, England: Multilingual Matters.

Weir, C. J. (2005). *Language testing and validation: An evidence-based approach.* New York, NY: Palgrave Macmillan.

8

Curriculum and Assessment, and Data Collection Validation

Classroom Observations, Interviews, and Questionnaires

She hath prosperous art
When she will play with reason and discourse,
And well she can persuade.

—William Shakespeare, *Measure for Measure*

Other men are lenses through which we read our own minds.

—Ralph Waldo Emerson, 19th century American poet

In this chapter we outline practical strategies for validating *data collection instruments* and interpretations of data resulting from classroom observations, interviews, and questionnaires. The main goal is to increase the clarity with which classroom observations, interviews, and questionnaires are aligned with both the course outcomes and the course *curriculum*. Stakeholders are involved in that they may read and benefit from evaluation reports. Expert others (also stakeholders) are key to the validation strategies outlined in this chapter. Together, these strategies build up a portfolio of validation evidence

---

1. For all terms in *italics*, see Glossary.

Evaluating Second Language Courses, pages 165–194
Copyright © 2016 by Information Age Publishing
165

that can be used when reporting the results of an evaluation. We pay special attention to data triangulation in this chapter, as well as piloting data collection instruments.

This is the sixth chapter in which the stakeholders, outcomes, assessment, and curriculum evaluation model (SOAC) is applied to second and foreign language classrooms (see Figure 7.1, p. 135). As with Chapter 7, the purpose of this chapter is to complete the next-to-last step in the evaluation process, namely looking carefully at the data collection instruments and *data collection protocols* (working plans) we use to evaluate a course. We focus here on classroom observations, interviews, and questionnaires, which have great utility in course evaluation. Observations, interviews, and questionnaires are also commonly used in evaluation. The careful looking we describe means *validation*. To review, validation is a process whereby data collection instruments are designed, used, and the resulting data interpreted with much forethought and afterthought as to what is being measured. Validation should produce *validation evidence*, which could be a description of what is being measured along with sample questionnaire items, or recounting interviewees' reactions to written transcriptions of interviews they participated in. The point is to develop an argument that a data collection instrument captures some classroom process, teacher priority, or student perception—whatever is being investigated to answer *evaluation questions* (EQs). This chapter, along with Chapter 7 on tests and quizzes, contributes to our ability to address questions raised in the Reading and Assessing Evaluation Publications template given in Table 10.1 of Chapter 10. Knowing more about validation enables us to assess the credibility of evaluation reports written by others, as well as enhance the clarity and credibility of our own evaluation projects.

Many validation strategies involve asking "expert others" for reasoned judgments about a data collection instrument (Brown, 2001; Burns, 1999; Chaudron, 1991). These include colleagues, students, or supervisors. The quotes from both Shakespeare and Emerson reflect this interplay. It is with the help of knowledgeable others that we can add to the transparency of an *evaluation*. The quotes also suggest interplay between teachers/evaluators and yet another stakeholder group: the readers of evaluation reports. As we noted in Chapter 7, validation of tests, questionnaires, and other data collection instruments, are rarely treated in evaluation reports. At the same time, most readers can sense how clear or credible a report seems to be. We argue that when teachers/evaluators offer validation evidence on the way they plan, collect, and then interpret data, their reports or presentations will have more clarity and credibility. Of course many teachers/evaluators would, for their own sakes, want to establish that their data collection instruments are functioning well. They may never intend for their evaluation to be publicized. No one wants to waste their time on a data collection instrument that does not tell them what they need to know about the effects of an experimental reading program, or a particular way of answering language learners' questions (e.g., Wong & Zhang Waring, 2010). Yet the idea of having others scrutinize an evaluation, or help out with an evaluation, brings perhaps greater focus to our work. We note that this chapter is about developing *validation evidence*, and is not primarily about how to design observations, interviews, or questionnaires. There are many sources on these topics that we list at the end of the chapter under Suggested Reading. We also include examples of these *data collection instruments* aligned with specific evaluation questions (EQs) in Chapter 6, on formative evaluation.

DISCUSSION QUESTION 1

If you could ask someone to observe your teaching for your own reasons, what would you like to know? What could you ask the person to look for?

DISCUSSION QUESTION 2

Have you ever been interviewed as a learner or a teacher? What sorts of questions were you asked? What do you think the interviewer wanted to know?

DISCUSSION QUESTION 3

If you wrote a questionnaire, how would you feel about showing it to a colleague or even your boss before you administered it? Would you have any concerns?

Constructs, Validation, and Evaluation Revisited

As with tests and quizzes (Chapter 7), a key element of observation, interview, and questionnaire validation is the *construct*. A construct is the prethought-out model of the process, the attitude, or the perception, that we hope a data collection instrument is measuring. Collecting validation evidence adds to any argument we can make about the *construct validity* of an observation, interview, or questionnaire we design, or adapt. If we wish to investigate whether a United Kingdom-based language teacher training course changes how teachers do their jobs back home in China (Li & Edwards, 2013), then we need to provide validation evidence that an interview, perhaps paired with an observation, captures the construct. Using two or three different data collection instruments to capture the same construct is *triangulation*, which is one form of validation evidence.

How do we determine what the construct is? Thinking through the *course logic* of a course is one way (Chapter 5). The U.K.-based teacher training course logic mentioned earlier might go something like this: If Chinese English teachers are given instruction in pedagogy and language learning, and are led through experiential learning tasks where they become language learners, thus improving their command of English (the course curriculum), then teachers will develop "not only a rich repertoire of practical pedagogical skills... but also a deeper understanding of the rationale behind such practices" (the course outcomes; Li & Edwards, 2013, p. 393). The constructs would then be: (a) changes in teaching practices, and (b) changes in thinking about teaching practices. These constructs would become the focus for the design, use, and interpretation of any observation, interview, or questionnaire in the evaluation.

Note that the constructs mentioned here are aligned with the teacher training course outcomes. This is an important consideration. The SOAC model (Figure 7.1, Chapter 7), suggests that if a data collection instrument does not capture the intended constructs, then course participants may have changed in the intended ways (they attained the course outcomes), but the *assessments* (questionnaires, etc.) will not show it. There are many reasons why a questionnaire or interview may lack construct validity, and thus might not capture the constructs of interest. For example, wrong, off-topic questions may be asked of the wrong people (stakeholders), suggesting a design issue or a problem with the data collection protocol. A data collection protocol is the working plan of how data will be collected, including consideration of which stakeholders data will be collected from.

At the same time, the questions asked in an interview or the events looked for in an observation, both examples of assessments, have to have some relationship with the course curriculum (Figure 7.1, Chapter 7). In other words, the data collection must have *content validity*. Otherwise, an evaluator/teacher could not claim the curriculum was responsible for learners reaching the outcomes of the course. Li and Edwards (2013) somewhat establish the connection between their assessments and their curriculum. They note that in interviews they asked former course participants about "direct and practical methodological aspects" of the course on their teaching (p. 395) and their "conceptual... change" (pp. 395–396). In observations, they looked for "classroom methodology... classroom interaction, activities, and techniques" which were hoped-for results of the teacher training curriculum (p. 396). In other words, the evaluators probed for the effects of the curriculum they believed the participants experienced.

DISCUSSION QUESTION 4

What is a construct you would like to measure for an evaluation? What process, attitude, ability, skill, or perception would you like to measure? What stakeholder group would you like to focus on?

DISCUSSION QUESTION 5

Can you think of any circumstance where you might want to collect data, or indeed, do an evaluation, without a construct? What function might such data have?

Developing Validation Evidence for Observations, Interviews, and Questionnaires

In Chapter 7, Figure 7.2, we used a test validity model adapted from Kunnan (1998) to suggest different ways of creating arguments for the validity of tests and quizzes. By itself, the model does not suggest a chronological order for building a portfolio of validation evidence. Here, we work with a three-part model that is roughly chronological and thus can be used by teachers/evaluators to consider validation strategies at the outset of their evaluation, and throughout the rest of the data collection and data interpretation process. The more validation evidence that can be offered from any or all steps of data collection, the clearer and more credible an evaluation will be. See Figure 8.1.

The rest of this chapter is taken up in describing the three components in turn (designing/planning, doing, and analyzing). Practical examples are given of what might constitute validation evidence at each stage of the model. After a description of each component, we then identify where examples of validation evidence in the evaluation literature can be found as they pertain to classroom observations, interviews, and questionnaires (see Tables 8.2, 8.3, and 8.4). Publications *about* evaluation, *of* evaluation, and

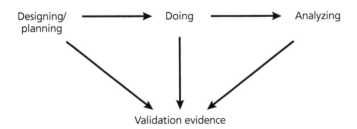

Figure 8.1 A chronological validation model.

of needs analysis are included, following the categorizations found in the Reading and Assessing Evaluation Publications templates in Chapter 10. If a suggested type of validation evidence is given, and many references follow it, it simply means that this form of evidence is often mentioned in the literature that was examined. If there are few or no references listed, it means that not many authors reported these types of validation evidence in the literature that was examined. This is a reflection of how variable is the attention paid to validation in the field. It is not a reflection of the usefulness or appropriateness of types of validation evidence. In the Designing/Planning section, we also discuss *piloting* data collection instruments and data collection protocols, and finally, data *triangulation*. Both of these strategies need to be planned early.

Designing/Planning Component

Designing and planning refers to establishing a data collection protocol, which is a working plan for data collection. A data collection protocol and any *memo* notes kept on its design and revision will together be a major source of validation evidence. For instance, after observing a class as a pilot project, a teacher/evaluator may want to audio record classes during data collection, because he or she could not keep up with the rich complexity of classroom events, taking only notes. This change in the data collection protocol, and the reason for it, can be mentioned as validation evidence. Data collection protocols often include an actual *data collection instrument*, such as a questionnaire or a list of questions for an interview. Thus a data collection protocol specifies how a data collection instrument is to be used.

Designing

The "designing" part of this component refers to a teacher/evaluator defining a construct, and then composing questions to ask in an interview or on a questionnaire, and categories to apply to a classroom observation. Thus, the activity of designing has much to do with a data collection instrument. As mentioned earlier, showing a data collection instrument to colleagues and discussing the items in terms of the constructs to be captured, is one form of validation evidence. A data collection instrument might also be adapted from another source, and then fitted to the construct a teacher/evaluator has articulated, as Mede (2012) does in her evaluation of an intensive English preparation program for an English-medium university in Turkey. The original source of her adapted questionnaire was from a colleague/evaluator teaching in the same program. Mede offers her adaptation of an instrument already shown to have relevance to her course curriculum as validation evidence.

Planning

The planning part of this component has to do with how the data collection instrument will be used to collect data, and which stakeholders the data will be collected from. In other words, planning has much to do with data collection protocols. In Chapter 6 on formative evaluation a data collection plan, or protocol, is presented with reference to the evaluation questions driving the evaluation (Chapter 6, Table 6.5). Memo notes on planning along these lines can be reported as validation evidence. For instance, the data collection plan indicates that the teacher will be interviewed once and then observed twice with respect to both EQ1 and EQ2, which deal with what materials are used, and whether the materials are sufficient to propel learners to the course outcomes. The plan is to observe classes twice, as the teacher/evaluator assumes that two lesson observations will provide more complete information than just one observation.

Additional details for planning can be motivated by the questions raised in Table 6.6 in Chapter 6 under the "Data collection instruments (DCIs) and basic protocol." For observations, these include decisions as to whether to record the class, whether to audiotape or video record, and who would be the focus of the microphone or camera. Validation evidence for the planning and design phase might be asking a colleague or supervisor to read through a data collection protocol and comment whether the plan seems appropriate, or suggest additional details that might be needed. The colleagues' comments, and the teacher/evaluator's decisions based on them would be validation evidence.

Piloting

Piloting a data collection instrument or a data collection protocol is one of the most useful things a teacher/evaluator can do. Piloting is a rehearsal for data collection done with the intent to improve a data collection instrument, or make needed adjustments to a data collection protocol. Notes on piloting, the results of the pilot, and revisions made in response to the piloting all constitute validation evidence. The reason we deal with piloting here is that piloting gives the most help at the designing and planning stage of data collection. A case in point: By administering a questionnaire to two foreign language department chairpersons and asking them to comment on each questionnaire item, Watanabe, Norris, and Gonzalez-Lloret (2009) identified items that were difficult for the respondents to answer. Without doing a pilot, these evaluators would have started out with a data collection instrument that was not as useful as it might be.

There are many reasons questionnaire items might not function well, such as items a respondent cannot answer because the wording is unclear (see Brown, 2001). In foreign language settings, the language of a questionnaire or interview may not be in the stakeholders' first language. This situation really requires a pilot to be done. Griffee (1999, p. 80) did a questionnaire pilot by going to young adult Japanese learners of English in a school cafeteria. He showed them the English-language questionnaire he wanted to use, and learned from the students that there were multiple words they did not understand in the items. By changing just a few words, the students could understand the items. In terms of piloting a data collection protocol, or the manner in which data are collected, an example was given about a teacher/evaluator deciding to audiotape classroom observations rather than just taking notes. If the teacher/evaluator proceeded with just taking notes, much information would be lost, making it harder to answer the evaluation questions.

Kiely and Rea-Dickins (2005) note that piloting is rarely treated in the evaluation literature, and we agree. We offer Table 8.1 that enumerates some basic guidelines for doing a pilot, along with sources from the evaluation literature.

TABLE 8.1   Guidelines for Piloting a Data Collection Instrument or Data Collection Protocol

What to do	Sources in the literature
Do observation, interview, or questionnaire with stakeholders much like the stakeholders focused on in the evaluation project.	Brown, 2001 Watanabe et al., 2009
Do observation, interview, or questionnaire under the same conditions that the data collection will be done.	Brown, 2001 Kiely & Rea-Dickins, 2005
Check for any comments a pilot respondent has written on a questionnaire, or unanswered questionnaire items.	Brown, 2001
Note any interview questions a pilot respondent finds difficult to answer.	
Ask pilot respondent to comment aloud on each item as they take a questionnaire.	Watanabe et al., 2009
Ask knowledgeable stakeholders for comments on early drafts of data collection instruments or data collection protocols.	Gorsuch, 2009
Provide an explanation for any changes to a data collection instrument or data collection protocol made as a result of a pilot.	Grau Sempere, Mohn, & Pieroni, 2009 Kiely & Rei-Dickins, 2005

DISCUSSION QUESTION 6

In a recent language class you taught or were a student in, did you experience an activity that was new to you, and did not go well? What happened? What might have been changed to improve the situation? Would a rehearsal (a pilot) have helped?

DISCUSSION QUESTION 7

Taking questionnaires online has become more common. Have you ever been unable to complete an online questionnaire because of some flaw in the questionnaire items, or some problem with the questionnaire software? What could have been done to improve the situation so the questionnaire designer can get the information he or she needs from respondents?

Triangulation

As mentioned earlier in the chapter, one validation strategy is to capture the constructs of interest by using two or three different data collection instruments. This is one kind of *triangulation* (Brown, 2001) and is often cited as validation evidence for a data collection instrument. The information under "Resulting data" in Table 6.6, Chapter 6 suggests some reasons why a triangulation strategy using different data collection instruments would be effective for generating validation evidence. Interviews, observations, and questionnaires, from among the many types of data collection listed in the table, seem to result in different kinds of data. Class observations can result in broad impressions rather than details, and if done successively, can capture longitudinal processes. Interviews are rich in detail but are one-time snapshots of a person's thoughts or memories. Questionnaires seem to result in broad or detailed information, depending on what the teacher/evaluator asks. So already it can be seen that the resulting data from each of the data collection types may complement each other. For instance, Chang (2014) used a questionnaire with 140 military cadets learning English in Taiwan, and then interviewd 10 of the same respondents, to answer two evaluation questions on *test washback*. The construct was "cadets' attitudes toward the ALCPT [a standardized language test] related to . . . its difficulty, time allotment, test format [and] their [resulting] behaviors . . . such as the quantity and quality of learning materials and learning methods" (Chang, 2014, p. 131). Chang administered the questionnaire first and then followed up with interviews with 10 volunteers "to assist the interpretation of the quantitative data" (p. 131). A decision to triangulate two or more data collection instruments can be noted in a data collection protocol and would constitute validation evidence.

DISCUSSION QUESTION 8

The example given of Chang (2014) suggests triangulation but also a kind of sequence of questionnaire first, interview second "to assist the interpretation of the quantitative data." Can you think of other sequences a teacher/evaluator might use, such as observation first, interview second; or interview first, questionnaire second? What might be the reasons for such sequences?

Applying the Designing/Planning Component to Observations, Interviews, and Questionnaires

To help organize the different examples of validation evidence previously given, and to offer additional examples from the literature, we developed Table 8.2.

TABLE 8.2 Generating Validation Evidence for Observations, Interviews, and Questionnaires at the Planning/Designing Stage

Observations	Interviews	Questionnaires

Provide a rationale for using classroom observation with reference to the *evaluation questions.*
About evaluation
  Bailey, 1977
  Burns, 1999
  Gebhard, 1999
  Turner, 2001
Of evaluation
  Sugarman, 2008
	Provide a rationale for doing interviews with reference to the *evaluation questions.*
	Of evaluation
	  Chang, 2014
	  Gu, 2003
	  Kiely, 2001
	  Slimani, 1992
	  Sugarman, 2008
		Provide a rationale for using questionnaires with reference to the *evaluation questions.*
		Of evaluation
		  Alhuqbani, 2013
		  Chang, 2014
		  Gorsuch, 2009
		  Katayama, 2007
		  Sugarman, 2008

Provide details on what is being focused on with reference to *evaluation questions* and reading of the relevant literature.
About evaluation
  Genesee & Upshur, 1996
 	
This can include:
Checklists
About evaluation
  Gebhard, 1999
  Genesee & Upshur, 1996
	Provide details on what is being focused on with reference to *evaluation questions* and reading of relevant literature.
	Of evaluation
	  Chang, 2014
	  Chapter 6 on formative evaluation
	  Dupuy & Willis Allen, 2012
	  Yang, 2009
		Provide details on what is being measured in each subsection of a questionnaire with reference to *evaluation questions* and reading of relevant literature.
		Of evaluation
		  Alhuqbani, 2013
		  Chang, 2014
		  Gorsuch, 2009
		  Katayama, 2007

(continued)

TABLE 8.2   Generating Validation Evidence for Observations, Interviews, and Questionnaires at the Planning/Designing Stage (cont.)

Observations	Interviews	Questionnaires

Categories of teacher or learner behavior
About evaluation
  Bailey, 1977
  Burns, 1999
  Chaudron, 1991
  Gebhard, 1999
Of evaluation
  Balleck, Kliebard, Hyman, & Smith, 1966
  Kiely, 2001
 	
Pre-theorized observation templates
About evaluation
  Galton, 1995
  Genesee & Upshur, 1996
Of evaluation
  Flyman-Mattsson, 1999
  Mitchell, 1992
 	
Time-coded observation sheet
About evaluation
  Bailey, 1977
Of evaluation
  Kiely, 2001
 	
Deliberately unfocused notes done initially with descriptions of later emerging themes which form the focus of subsequent observations
About evaluation
  Burns, 1999
  Chaudron, 1991
  Field notes taken in addition to recordings
Of evaluation
  Slimani, 1992
	This can include:
	Scripted interviews
	Of evaluation
	  Chang, 2014
	  Chapter 6 on formative evaluation
	
	Semi-structured interviews with scripted items plus open-ended items
	Of evaluation
	  Mede, 2012
	  Mitchell, 1992
	  Sugarman, 2008
	
	Providing actual interview items
	Of evaluation
	  Mitchell, 1992
	  Pfeiffer & Byrnes, 2009
		Kiely & Rea-Dickins, 2005
		Mede, 2012
		Pfeiffer & Byrnes, 2009

Demonstrate alignment between observation categories to course *curriculum.*
Of evaluation
  Kiely, 2001
  Li & Edwards, 2013
	Demonstrate alignment between interview items and the course *curriculum.*
	Of evaluation
	  Slimani, 1992
		Demonstrate alignment between questionnaire items and the course *curriculum.*
		Of evaluation
		  Dupuy, 1997
		  Gorsuch, 2009
		  Kiely & Rea-Dickins, 2005
		  Pfeiffer & Byrnes, 2009
		  Slimani, 1992

(continued)

TABLE 8.2 Generating Validation Evidence for Observations, Interviews, and Questionnaires at the Planning/Designing Stage (cont.)

Observations	Interviews	Questionnaires
Mention plans to *triangulate* observation data with other data collection types. **About evaluation** Burns, 1999 **Of evaluation** Li & Edwards, 2013 Miller, 1997	Mention plans and rationale for *triangulating* interview data with other data collection types. **Of evaluation** Chang, 2014 Gu, 2003 Li & Edwards, 2013 Slimani, 1992 Sugarman, 2008 *This can also include:* Mention plans and rationale for the order in which triangulated data collection instruments are used. **About evaluation** Lynch, 2003 **Of evaluation** Miller, 1997 Yang, 2009	Mention plans and rationale for *triangulating* questionnaire data with other data collection types. **Of evaluation** Chang, 2014 Slimani, 1992
Details on how many classes will be observed for how long. **About evaluation** Bailey, 1977 Genesee & Upshur, 1996 **Of evaluation** Slimani, 1992	Detail plans and rationale for who will be interviewed and how many times. **Of evaluation** Chang, 2014 Chapter 6 on formative evaluation Li & Edwards, 2013 Mede, 2013 Pawan & Thomalla, 2005 Slimani, 1992 Sugarman, 2008 Yang, 2009 *This can also include:* Describe plans on whether interviews will be "group focus" interviews or individual interviews. **Of evaluation** Li & Edwards, 2013 Pawan & Thomalla, 2005 Pfeiffer & Byrnes, 2009 Sugarman, 2008	Provide rationale for who will be surveyed (sampling plan). **About evaluation** Brown, 2001 *This can include:* Give rationale for administering questionnaire to a group more than once, over time. **Of evaluation** Mede, 2012 Slimani, 1992 Plans to monitor and report return rates of questionnaires (how many respondents answered). **Of evaluation** Gorsuch, 2009 Sugarman, 2008

(continued)

TABLE 8.2   Generating Validation Evidence for Observations, Interviews, and Questionnaires at the Planning/Designing Stage (cont.)

Observations	Interviews	Questionnaires

Plans and rationale for whether classes are recorded or not, and whether audiotaped or video recorded.
About evaluation
   Gebhard, 1999, p. 43
   Genesee & Upshur, 1996
	Plans for whether interview will be face-to face, over the phone or Skype, or via email or letter.
	Of evaluation
	   Yang, 2009
		Describe total number of items and subsections of a questionnaire.
		About evaluation
		   Brown, 2001
		Of evaluation
		   Alhuqbani, 2013
		   Arnold, 2009
		   Chang, 2014
		   Katayama, 2006
		   Sugarman, 2008
		
		This can also include:
		Provide actual items.
		Of evaluation
		   Arnold, 2009
		   Chang, 2014
		   Dupuy, 1997
		   Gorsuch, 2001
		   Katayama, 2007
		   Mede, 2012
		   Pfeiffer & Byrnes, 2009
		   Simpson & Mengi, 2014
		   Slimani, 1992
		   Sugarman, 2008
		   Tsou & Chen, 2014
		   Watanabe, Norris, &
		      Gonzalez-Lloret, 2009
		
		Description of questionnaire item formats (multiple choice, open-ended, etc.)
		About evaluation
		   Brown, 2001
		Of evaluation
		   Arnold, 2009
		   Dupuy, 1997
		   Pfeiffer & Byrnes, 2009
		
		If using multiple questionnaires, list all questionnaires with reference to *evaluation questions* and constructs being captured.
		Of evaluation
		   Tsou & Chen, 2014

(continued)

TABLE 8.2 Generating Validation Evidence for Observations, Interviews, and Questionnaires at the Planning/Designing Stage (cont.)

Observations	Interviews	Questionnaires
Describe whether the recordings will be transcribed. **About evaluation** Galton, 1995	Plans for whether interviews are recorded or not. **Of evaluation** Pfeiffer & Byrnes, 2009	Details on sources of adapted questionnaires. **Of evaluation** Alhuqbani, 2013 Dupuy, 1997 Katayama, 2007 Mede, 2012
Mention whether observing self or observing another teacher. **About evaluation** Burns, 1999	Details of any considerations regarding stakeholder privacy and rights, including interaction with a Human Subjects Review board at a school. **About evaluation** Kiely & Rea-Dickins, 2005	Details of any considerations regarding stakeholder privacy and rights, including interaction with a Human Subjects Review board at a school. **About evaluation** Kiely & Rea-Dickins, 2005 Rundblad, 2006 **Of evaluation** Chang, 2014
Descriptions of who is focused on in the observations with reference to the *evaluation questions*. **About evaluation** Burns, 1999 **Of evaluation** Li & Edwards, 2013 Mitchell, 1992	Plans and rationale for what language the interview will be conducted in. **Of evaluation** Chang, 2014 Li & Edwards, 2013 Mitchell, 1992 *This can include:* Description on process of translating interview questions and responses from one language to another.	Plans and rationale for what language the questionnaire will be in. **About evaluation** Brown, 2001 **Of evaluation** Chang, 2014 Katayama, 2007
Details of any considerations regarding stakeholder privacy and rights, including interaction with a Human Subjects Review board at a school. **About evaluation** Burns, 1999 Gebhard, 1999 Kiely & Rea-Dickins, 2005	Plans for transcribing interviewees' responses. Plans for sharing transcribed results with interviewee for checking and further comment. **Of evaluation** Chapter 6 on formative evaluation	Plans and rationale for method of questionnaire administration (face to face, by email, etc.). **About evaluation** Brown, 2001
Describe plans for doing pilot observations. **Of evaluation** Mitchell, 1992	Describe plans and rationale for doing pilot interviews. Notes on any changes to interview data collection protocol as a result of	Describe plans and rationale for doing a pilot questionnaire. Notes on any changes to questionnaire data collection protocol as a

(continued)

TABLE 8.2 Generating Validation Evidence for Observations, Interviews, and Questionnaires at the Planning/Designing Stage (cont.)		
Observations	**Interviews**	**Questionnaires**
	findings from a pilot. **Of evaluation** Sugarman, 2008	result of findings from a pilot. **About evaluation** Brown, 2001 Kiely & Rea-Dickins, 2005 **Of evaluation** Chang, 2014 **Of needs analysis** Watanabe et al., 2009
Descriptions of knowledgeable others' reactions to, or suggestions for, the observation data collection protocol.	Descriptions of knowledgeable others' reactions to, or suggestions for, the interview data collection protocol. **About evaluation** Genesee & Upshur, 1996	Descriptions of knowledgeable others' reactions to, or suggestions for, the questionnaire data collection protocol. **About evaluation** Genesee & Upshur, 1996 *This can include:* Others' reactions to sample items illustrating a stated construct (what is being measured). **About evaluation** Brown, 2001 **Of evaluation** Gorsuch, 2009
Notes on any changes made to data collection protocol plans or design.	Notes on any changes made to data collection protocol plans or design.	Notes on any changes made to data collection protocol plans or design.

This table is meant to be a resource and reference. The table is arranged vertically, although it can be seen that all three types of data collection have some general types of validation evidence in common, such as providing a rationale for using a particular data collection type with reference to the evaluation questions. All three types of data collection have better validation evidence if the teacher/evaluator can provide details on the construct being captured by the data collection protocols, detail what relevance the construct has to the evaluation questions, and describe what prior reading in the literature they have done on the construct.

Readers can consult the literature on how different authors word or propose their validation evidence. An example for observations is Kiely (2001, p. 247), who observed the vocabulary instruction in an ESL classroom by taking notes on activity categories of interest created by an examination of the materials used in the course. The activity categories of interest were, of course, constructs the author developed and wanted to capture. These included "Meta-EAP: A focus on knowledge and skills which relate specifically to developing EAP (English for Academic Purposes) skills—where learning might be considered directly transferable to the demands of studying other subjects through English" and "Direct language skills practice: a focus on language use and form more generally, where learning might be considered only indirectly transferable." Under this second general category, the author listed "S = speaking, R = reading, W = writing, V = vocabulary." The author computed teacher activity under these categories "as a proportion of the total classroom time" (Kiely, 2001, p. 247). Note also the congruence between the observation protocol and the course curriculum, in that the constructs were formed by an examination of the course materials.

DISCUSSION QUESTION 9

A re there any validation evidence examples in Table 8.1 that you are already familiar with? Are there any you are unfamiliar with? Which interests you? Why?

Doing Component

This component reflects what teachers/evaluators actually do with their data collection protocols as they interact with stakeholders in and out of the classroom. Doing is used deliberately because it best reflects the contingent activity that takes place during a period of data collection. By contingent we mean action taken in response to emerging, sometimes unforeseen, events. This could be as simple as a teacher/evaluator learning that stakeholders/learners talk a lot using the foreign language in the hallway before class while reviewing each other's homework. Seeing this, the teacher/evaluator might decide to stand unobtrusively in the hallway before class observations to hear more of such conversations. The teacher/evaluator may also decide to interview students to learn in what other ways they work together using the foreign language being learned. Either or both of these constitute changes to a data collection protocol. But contingent activity can also mean that a teacher/evaluator consults his or her data collection protocol and determines that some of the planned interviews have not yet taken place. He or she then attempts to arrange the needed interviews. To develop validation evidence for this fluid, intense period, the key is to keep a memo with notes of events or decisions or changes, if any, in a data collection protocol. Memos, as described in Chapter 6 on formative evaluation, are either handwritten and dated notes, or simply a word processing document with dated entries.

In the doing stage, classes are observed, and recordings and notes from the observations are transcribed or typed up. Questionnaires are given out and taken back, and stakeholder responses are entered into a spreadsheet or typed up if stakeholders are responding with words to open-ended questionnaire items. Electronic questionnaires are sent out, and returning results are examined, and then kept in readiness for immediate action or later analysis. Interviews are arranged for and take place. Recordings of interviews are transcribed or interview notes are typed up. Observation and interview recordings and/or notes are organized and set aside for later analysis.

Applying the Doing Component to Observations, Interviews, and Questionnaires

From Table 8.3, it may seem there are fewer kinds of validation evidence in the literature, particularly *of* evaluation. This may be because validation evidence in published reports is provided largely in the language of plans (will do) or as past action (did) in the data collection protocol sections of reports. In other words, the author's comments may not be stated in "doing" terms. For instance, Katayama (2007, p. 65) notes as past actions things done during data collection: "The questionnaire was anonymous and administered to 249 students who volunteered to participate and signed consent forms." Some may wonder what anonymity and consent forms have to do with validation at the Doing stage of data collection. One way to look at this is to consider whether trust between a teacher/evaluator and the person providing the data, is likely to result in true and complete information, or close to it. Certainly, the desire to gain trust from stakeholders has its clearest expression while doing data collection.

There tends to be more treatment of the rationales for different validation strategies in publications about evaluation, as in Burn's (1999) suggestion to keep track of how soon after an observation the recording of an observation is listened to. Teachers/evaluators may do this, but may not have the space in a published report *of* evaluation to mention it.

As with Table 8.2, Table 8.3 is meant to be a reference. The table is arranged vertically, although as can be seen, some types of validation evidence are shared by observations, interviews, and questionnaires alike, such as describing note taking on the locations, times, and circumstances of the data collection. For an example of how validation evidence is worded in a publication *of* evaluation, note Slimani (1992, p. 203): "As the number of learners was rather small, all thirteen could be interviewed in about one

TABLE 8.3   Generating Validation Evidence for Observations, Interviews, and Questionnaires at the Doing Stage

Observations	Interviews	Questionnaires

Describe how soon after the observation a recording is transcribed or listened to, or notes are written.
About evaluation
    Burns, 1999
	Reports of which stakeholders are interviewed and how many times.
	Of evaluation
	    Li & Edwards, 2013
		Outline whether the return rate of questionnaires is monitored.
		Of evaluation
		    Alhuqbani, 2013
		    Gorsuch, 2009
		
		This can include:
		Note any actions taken to increase return rate.
		About evaluation
		    Brown, 2001
		Of evaluation
		    Pfeiffer & Byrnes, 2009

Description of keeping notes, recordings dated and in order.
About evaluation
    Burns, 1999
    Genesee & Upshur, 1996
Of evaluation
    Kiely, 2001
 	
This can include:
Notes on frequency of note-taking
About evaluation
    Genesee & Upshur, 1996
 	
Description of whether checklists of teachers' or students' behavior are regularly recorded.
About evaluation
    Genesee & Upshur, 1996
	Reports on how long each interview takes.
	Of evaluation
	    Chang, 2014
	    Li & Edwards, 2013
	    Pfeiffer & Byrnes, 2009
	    Slimani, 1992
		Describe setting, circumstances in which questionnaires are administered.
		
		This can include:
		Location, time of group administrations.
		About evaluation
		    Brown, 2001
		Of evaluation
		    Alhuqbani, 2013
		    Kiely & Rea-Dickins, 2005
		
		Describe whether respondents are promised anonymity.
		About evaluation
		    Brown, 2001
		Of evaluation
		    Chang, 2104
		    Katayama, 2007
		
		Note whether respondents are told the purpose of the questionnaire in advance.
		About evaluation
		    Brown, 2001

Description of how notes are kept on observations that include locations, times, and other contextual features.
About evaluation
    Burns, 1999
    Galton, 1995
	Description of location, context of interviews.
	Of evaluation
	    Li & Edwards, 2013
	    Slimani, 1992
		Describe how questionnaire data are treated until the analysis phase.
		
		This can include:
		Process of entering quantitative or qualitative

(continued)

TABLE 8.3 Generating Validation Evidence for Observations, Interviews, and Questionnaires at the Doing Stage (continued)

Observations	Interviews	Questionnaires

Of evaluation
    Mitchell, 1992
	This can include:
	Noting the timing of the interview in relation to observations capturing the working course *curriculum*.
	Of evaluation
	    Slimani, 1992
	
	An account of instructions to interviewees.
	Of evaluation
	    Kiely & Rea-Dickins, 2005
		data into software program.
		About evaluations
		    Brown, 2001

Describe interaction, if any, between observer and teachers and students.
About evaluation
    Bailey, 1977
    Burns, 1999
    Gebhard, 1999
Of evaluation
    Slimani, 1992
	Describe interviewees' language preferences for the interview and what language or languages the interview was held in.
	Of evaluation
	    Mitchell, 1992
	    Slimani, 1992
		Report how the questionnaire data collection protocol is changed during data collection.
		
		This can include:
		Revising questionnaire data collection instrument in response to pilot questionnaire results.
		Of evaluation
		    Chang, 2014
		    Gorsuch, 2009
		    Pfeiffer & Byrnes, 2009
		    Sugarman, 2008
		
		Description of how well the planned questionnaire administration functions (such as electronic administration) and any actions taken if necessary.

Provide details on running memos to self-monitor observer bias.
About evaluation
    Burns, 1999
    Galton, 1995
    Gebhard, 1999
Of evaluation
    Li & Edwards, 2013
	Offer details on whether interview transcriptions are sent to interviewees for comment or confirmation.
	Of evaluation
	    Pawan & Thomalla, 2005
	    Chapter 6 on formative evaluation
		Describe of how the data are stored in a secure location.

Describe any explanations given to teacher and/or students on evaluation purpose.
Of evaluation
    Li & Edwards, 2013
	Note whether interviewees are informed of the evaluation purpose.
	Of evaluation
	    Chang, 2014	

(continued)

TABLE 8.3 Generating Validation Evidence for Observations, Interviews, and Questionnaires at the Doing Stage (continued)

Observations	Interviews	Questionnaires

Provide details on how privacy and dignity of teacher and/or students or other stakeholders is maintained during data collection.
Of evaluation
  Kiely, 2001
  Slimani, 1992
	Provide details on how privacy and dignity of teacher and/or students or other stakeholders was maintained during data collection.
	Of evaluation
	  Chang, 2014
	  Chapter 6 on formative evaluation
	  Li & Edwards, 2013
	  Mitchell, 1992	

Keeping notes on changes in observation data collection protocol due to emerging information or insights.
About evaluation
Genesee & Upshur, 1996
	Report changes in observation data collection protocol resulting from emerging themes or events.
	
	This can include:
	Describe whether additional interviewees are sought and why.
	Of evaluation
	  Pawan & Thomalla, 2005
	
	Noting when interviewees request a different interview format, such as group interviews, as opposed to individual interviews.
	Of evaluation
	  Pawan & Thomalla, 2005
	
	Noting when interviewees request a different interviewer.
	Of evaluation
	  Pfeiffer & Byrnes, 2009
	
	Noting when interviewees decline to be recorded.
	Of evaluation
	  Mitchell, 1992
	
	Describe follow-up questions beyond the planned interview items.
	Of evaluation
	  Mede, 2012
	  Slimani, 1992	

hour, on the same day, after the third lesson recording." She mentions a rationale for having the interviews within a certain time limit after a particular lesson: "the learners' responses had to relate to these precisely observed (in class) events" (p. 203). In this way the author also demonstrates alignment between her observations and the course curriculum.

DISCUSSION QUESTION 10

How would you compare validation strategies in Table 8.3 and Table 8.2? What seems to be in common? What seems different?

Analyzing Component

Analyzing refers to making sense of the data that has been collected with reference to the evaluation questions (EQs). The analyzing component of our chronological validation model (Figure 8.1), then, concerns developing validation evidence on the processes a teacher/evaluator uses to make sense of, or interpret, the data that were collected. The data need interpretation in order to answer evaluation questions and to formulate decision points, which are specific suggestions focused on the elements of the course that were investigated. See Chapter 6 on formative evaluation for examples of decision points. Thus, a teacher/evaluator needs to know how to demonstrate to himself or herself, and to others, that the information he or she has collected is valid, clear, true, and a reasonable basis for making decision points. As with the other two components of the validation model, memo notes on teacher/evaluator activity are a major source of validation evidence. Working on data analysis can in turns be solitary and then collaborative, and memos are effective for capturing processes occurring at both of these times. Much of what appears in Table 8.4 can be noted in a running memo.

Here is an example of how an evaluator provided a written summary of data themes from an interview with direct reference to evaluation questions (Yang, 2009, p. 85):

> I present and describe the findings about each of these four themes in detail, and explain any answers, insights, or understandings we gained about the focal evaluation questions...1. Intended/desired outcomes of presemester teacher induction: Achieved or not? The interview with the ELI Director and the Assistant Director revealed what they saw as the intended outcomes of pre-semester induction practices, as shown in Table 3.

TABLE 8.4   Generating Validation Evidence for Observations, Interviews, and Questionnaires at the Analyzing Stage

Observations	Interviews	Questionnaires

Description of how transcribed observations or observation notes are categorized.
About evaluation
  Burns, 1999
  Chaudron, 1991
  Galton, 1995
  Gebhard, 1999
Of evaluation
Kiely, 2001
 	
This can include:
Description of how data are categorized with reference to the *EQs*.
About evaluation
  Burns, 1999
Of evaluation
  Kiely, 2001
	Description of form the collected data takes.
	
	This can include:
	Description of method or level of detail of the transcript.
	Of evaluation
	  Chapter 6 on formative evaluation
	
	Whether transcripts or notes have been shared with interviewee for comment.
	Of evaluation
	  Chapter 6 on formative evaluation
	  Kiely & Rea-Dickins, 2005
	  Pawan & Thomalla, 2005
		Identify *statistical procedures* used for quantitative data.
		
		This can include:
		Provide statement as to why a particular analysis is used (*statistical clarity*).
		Of evaluation
		  Gorsuch, 2009
		
		Provide descriptive statistics for each item including mean, standard deviation, mode, etc.
		About evaluation
		  Brown, 2001
		Of evaluation
		  Gorsuch, 2009
		  Katayama, 2007
		  Mede, 2012
		  Tsou & Chen, 2014
		  Watanabe et al., 2009
		
		Provide frequency of responses and percentage data on categories within items ("strongly disagree = 29% of respondents," "disagree = 4 respondents, or 11% of respondents," "agree," "strongly agree," "yes," "no," etc.).
		Of evaluation
		  Alhuqbani, 2013
		  Chang, 2014
		  Katayama, 2007
		  Mede, 2012

If observation initially open-ended (no predetermined categories), describe emerging themes used later for analysis.
About evaluation
  Burns, 1999
	Outline of process used to code themes data into predetermined categories.
	Of evaluation
	  Chang, 2014
	  Kiely, 2001
	  Kiely & Rea-Dickins, 2005
	  Pawan & Thomalla, 2005
	  Yang, 2009
		Provide readily checkable interpretations for statistical analyses.
		
		This can include:
		Include prose reports of quantitative data.
		Of evaluation
		  Alhuqbani, 2013
		  Chang, 2014

(continued)

TABLE 8.4 Generating Validation Evidence for Observations, Interviews, and Questionnaires at the Analyzing Stage (continued)		
Observations	**Interviews**	**Questionnaires**
		Report descriptive statistics, etc., next to text of each questionnaire item. **Of evaluation** Chang, 2014 Gorsuch, 2009 Show interpretations of data to others. **About evaluation** Brown, 2001
Describe whether data categorizations have inter-observer reliability (one form of *peer review*). **About evaluation** Burns, 1999 Chaudron, 1991 Mitchell, 1992 *This can include:* Playing audiotape or video recording of an observation until two colleagues agree on categorizations for the data. **About observation** Galton, 1995 Comparing two colleagues' counts of categorized data. Colleague A: 10 instances of teacher feedback. Colleague B: 11 instances of teacher feedback. Calculating percentage agreement between two colleagues' categorizations (91% agreement).	Discussion of and reporting of interrater reliability of data into coded categories (one form of *peer review*). **Of evaluation** Chang, 2014 Li & Edwards, 2013 Pfeiffer & Byrnes, 2009	Provide post-statistical analysis. *This can include:* Report reliability coefficients on quantitative data (groups of items or the entire questionnaire). **About evaluation** Brown, 2001 **Of evaluation** Chang, 2014 Mede, 2012 Report *p-values* on appropriate statistical comparisons. Report *effect size* on appropriate statistical comparisons.
Provide examples from observation transcript or notes to illustrate categories or patterns or findings. **About evaluation** Burns, 1999	Provide examples from interview transcript or notes to illustrate categories or patterns or findings. **Of evaluation** Chang, 2014 Kiely & Rea-Dickins, 2005	Describe process by and reli-ability for which qualitative data are categorized. **About evaluation** Brown, 2001 **Of evaluation** Watanabe et al., 2009

(continued)

188 ■ *Evaluating Second Language Courses*

TABLE 8.4   Generating Validation Evidence for Observations, Interviews, and Questionnaires at the Analyzing Stage (continued)

Observations	Interviews	Questionnaires
Of evaluation Kiely, 2001 *This can include:* Describe showing the categories or patterns with the raw data examples to colleagues and getting their response.	Li & Edwards, 2013 Pawan & Thomalla, 2005 Pfeiffer & Byrnes, 2009	*This can include:* Description of an iterative (cyclical) process for interpretation. **About evaluation** Brown, 2001 Finding quotations from raw data to represent categories. **Of evaluation** Simpson & Mengi, 2014 Tsou & Chen, 2014 Watanabe et al., 2009 Provide interrater reliability on qualitative data categorization (answers written in words).
Outline results of comparing triangulated data for repeating patterns or themes. **About evaluation** Burns, 1999 **Of evaluation** Kiely, 2001 Li & Edwards, 2013 Slimani, 1992	Provide details on method of analysis. *This can include:* Explicit mention of evaluation theory and description of its effect on analysis. **Of evaluation** Pawan & Thomalla, 2005 Description of an iterative (repeating) analysis over time. **Of evaluation** Chang, 2014 Description of software used for thematic analysis. **Of evaluation** Li & Edwards, 2013	Report results of triangulation with other data collection instruments. **About evaluation** Brown, 2001 **Of evaluation** Chang, 2014
Providing a written account or summary of data themes with reference to the *EQs*. **About evaluation** Gebhard, 1999 **Of evaluation** Chapter 6 on formative evaluation	Provide a written account or summary of data themes with reference to the *EQs*. **Of evaluation** Chang, 2014 Chapter 6 on formative evaluation Kiely & Rea-Dickins, 2005 Yang, 2009	Compare results with previous studies using the same or similar instrument. **Of evaluation** Alhuqbani, 2013

TABLE 8.4 Generating Validation Evidence for Observations, Interviews, and Questionnaires at the Analyzing Stage (continued)

Observations	Interviews	Questionnaires
Report on colleagues' or others' responses to interpretations of data. **About evaluation** Burns, 1999 Chaudron, 1991 Galton, 1995 *This can include:* Formulating alternative interpretations and getting others' responses (one way to seek *negative evidence*).	Report on colleagues' or others' responses to interpretations of data. *This can include:* How stakeholders formulate interpretations. **Of evaluation** Pawan & Thomalla, 2005 Formulating alternative interpretations and getting others' responses (one way to seek *negative evidence*).	Provide discussion of reasons for and possible effects of low response rates. **Of evaluation** Gorsuch, 2009 Watanabe et al., 2009
Details on repeated cycles of data examination and analysis. **About evaluation** Burns, 1999 **Of evaluation** Kiely, 2001	Give account of how sponsors of the evaluation may have constrained evaluators. **Of evaluation** Mitchell, 1992 Pawan & Thomalla, 2005	Provide discussion on whether the questionnaire itself had an effect on respondents' behavior. **Of evaluation** Slimani, 1992
Note speculations on whether the context of data collection has an effect on the findings (one way of probing for *areas of uncertainty*). **About evaluation** Galton, 1995 Gebhard, 1999 **Of evaluation** Kiely, 2001 *This can include:* Noting whether classes observed are "ordinary" classes or especially prepared for the observation. **Of evaluation** Li & Edwards, 2013	Provide discussions of any constraints that may affect stakeholders' responses to interviews (one way of probing for *areas of uncertainty*). **Of evaluation** Li & Edwards, 2013 Pawan & Thomalla, 2005 Slimani, 1992 *This can include:* Report of systematic effects of language gap between evaluators and stakeholders. **Of evaluation** Mitchell, 1992	
	Provide description of how interviewees' comments were translated or interpreted into the language of the teacher/evaluator. **Of evaluation** Li & Edwards, 2013	

(continued)

TABLE 8.4 Generating Validation Evidence for Observations, Interviews, and Questionnaires at the Analyzing Stage (continued)		
Observations	Interviews	Questionnaires
	Report on whether triangulated data agree with findings of interview. **Of evaluation** Pfeiffer & Byrnes, 2009 Yang, 2009	

APPLICATION TASKS: Evaluating Validation Evidence in Reports, and Planning and Piloting an Observation

First task idea: Some of the evaluation articles discussed in this chapter are readily available online, including Alhuqbani (2013), Chang (2014), and Miller (1997). Other evaluation articles are readily available through interlibrary loan. Choose one publication *of* an evaluation where the author uses observations, interviews, or questionnaires, and evaluate the validation evidence against Tables 8.2, 8.3, and 8.4 in this chapter, or against the RAP matrix in Chapter 10. Appendix A is a good source for finding actual evaluation reports. What are one or two more pieces of validation evidence that would increase the clarity and credibility of the report?

Second task idea: We thank Gebhard (1999) for the idea of first practicing doing a classroom observation in a coffee shop or some other public place and taking observation notes. Plan to visit a public place for about 30 minutes where you can freely and unobtrusively observe human activity around you while taking notes. Ahead of time, write down some topics in your notebook you are interested in. This could be whether most people come by themselves, or come in groups; or how people pay for the things they buy; or whether and how people sitting near each other communicate (think: many people today sit at the same table but do not talk because they are busy texting someone). Take notes for about 30 minutes using the topics as focal points. Were the topics useful to fully understand what was happening? Or did you end up focusing on things other than behaviors under those topics? How might this experience change how you do a future observation?

Suggested Reading

For interview and questionnaire construction and validation:

Brown, J. D. (2001). *Using surveys in language programs*. Cambridge, England: Cambridge University Press.

For observation, interview, and questionnaire construction and validation and in-depth discussions on piloting, and also procedures for calculating *p-values* and *effect sizes*:

Griffee, D. T. (2012). *An introduction to second language research methods*. TESL-EJ Publications. Available: http://www.tesl-ej.org/pdf/ej60/sl_research_methods.pdf

For ideas on observation categories:

Gebhard, J. (1999). Seeing teaching differently through observation. In J. C. Richards (Ed.), *Language teaching awareness* (pp. 35–58). Cambridge, England: Cambridge University Press.

Kiely, R., & Rea-Dickins, P. (2005). *Program evaluation in language education*. Houndmills, England: Malgrave MacMillan.

References

Alhuqbani, M.N. (2013). Assessing the academic English needs of King Fahd Security College officers: Implications for the development of an EAP program. *The Journal of Teaching English for Specific and Academic Purposes, 1*(2), 143–167. Retrieved from http://espeap.junis.ni.ac.rs/index.php/espeap/article/view/40

Arnold, N. (2009). Online extensive reading for advanced foreign language learners: An evaluation study. *Foreign Language Annals, 42*(2), 340–366.

Bailey, L. (1977). Observing foreign language teaching. *Foreign Language Annals, 10*(6), 641–648.

Balleck, A., Kliebard, H., Hyman, R., & Smith, F. (1966). *The language of the classroom*. New York, NY: Teachers College Columbia University.

Brown, J. D. (2001). *Using surveys in language programs*. Cambridge, England: Cambridge University Press.

Burns, A. (1999). *Collaborative action research for English language teachers*. Cambridge, England: Cambridge University Press.

Chang, C.W. (2014). Washback effect on ALCPT on cadets in Taiwan: A case study. *The Journal of Teaching English for Specific and Academic Purposes, 2*(1), 125–140. Retrieved from http://espeap.junis.ni.ac.rs/index.php/espeap/article/view/71/42

Chaudron, C. (1991). Validation in second language classroom research: The role of observation. In R. Phillipson, E. Kellermann, L. Selinker, M. Sharwood Smith, & M. Swain (Eds.), *Foreign/second language pedagogy research:*

A commemorative volume for Claus Faerch (pp. 187–196). Philadelphia, PA: Multilingual Matters.

Dupuy, B. (1997). Voices from the classroom: Intermediate-level French students favor extensive reading over grammar and give their reasons. *Applied Language Learning, 8*(2), 285–293.

Dupuy, B., & Willis Allen, H. (2012). Appropriating conceptual and pedagogical tools of literacy: A qualitative study of two novice foreign language teaching assistants. In G. Gorsuch (Ed.), *Working theories for teaching assistant development* (pp. 275–315. Stillwater, OK: New Forums Press.

Flyman-Mattsson, A. (1999). Students' communicative behavior in a foreign language classroom. *Lund University Department of Linguistics Working Papers, 47,* 39–57. Retrieved February 16, 2014, from http://lup.lub.lu.se/luur/download?func=downloadFile&recordOId=528691&fileOId=624445

Galton, M. (1995). Classroom observation. In L. Anderson (Ed.), *International encyclopedia of teaching and teacher education* (2nd ed.; pp. 501–506). Cambridge, England: Cambridge University Press.

Gebhard, J. (1999). Seeing teaching differently through observation. In J. C. Richards (Ed.), *Language teaching awareness* (pp. 35–58). Cambridge, England: Cambridge University Press.

Genesee, F., & Upshur, J. (1996). *Classroom-based evaluation in second language education.* Cambridge, England: Cambridge University Press.

Gorsuch, G. (2009). Investigating second language learner self-efficacy and future expectancy of second language use for high-stakes program evaluation. *Foreign Language Annals, 42*(3), 505–540.

Grau Sempere, A., Mohn, M. C., & Pieroni, R. (2009). Improving educational effectiveness and promoting internal and external information-sharing through student learning outcomes assessment. In J. M. Norris, J. McE. Davis, C. Sinicrope, & Y. Watanabe (Eds.), *Toward useful program evaluation in college foreign language education* (pp. 139–162). Honolulu: University of Hawai'i, National Foreign Language Resource Center.

Griffee, D. T. (1999). *Course evaluation by quantitative and qualitative methods.* (Unpublished doctoral dissertation.) Temple University, Tokyo, Japan campus.

Gu, P. Y. (2003). Fine brush and freehand: The vocabulary learning art of two successful Chinese EFL learners. *TESOL Quarterly, 37*(1), 73–104.

Katayama, A. (2007). Students' perceptions of oral error correction. *Japanese Language and Literature, 41*(1), 61–92.

Kiely, R. (2001). Classroom evaluation: Values, interests and teacher development. *Language Teaching Research, 5*(3), 241–261.

Kiely, R., & Rea-Dickins, P. (2005). *Program evaluation in language education.* Houndmills, England: Malgrave MacMillan.

Kunnan, A. J. (1998). Approaches to validation in language assessment. In A. J. Kunnan (Ed.), *Validation in language assessment* (pp. 1–16). Mahwah, NJ: Erlbaum.

Li, D., & Edwards, V. (2013). The impact of overseas training on curriculum innovation and change in English language education in western China. *Language Teaching Research, 17*(4), 390–408.

Lynch, B. (2003). *Language assessment and programme evalution.* Edinburgh, Scotland: Edinburgh University Press.

Mede, E. (2012). *Design and evaluation of a language preparatory program at an English medium university in an EFL setting: A case study.* (Unpublished doctoral dissertation.) Yeditepe University, Istanbul, Turkey.

Miller, J. (1997). Case study in second language teaching. *Queensland Journal of Educational Research, 13*(1), 33–35. Retrieved from http://education. curtin.edu.au/iier/qjer/qjer13/miller1.html

Mitchell, R. (1992). The independent evaluation of bilingual primary education: A narrative account. In J. C. Alderson & A. Beretta (Eds.), *Evaluating second language education* (pp. 100–140). Cambridge, England: Cambridge University Press.

Pawan, F., & Thomalla, T. G. (2005). Making the invisible visible: A responsive evaluation study of ESL and Spanish language services for immigrants in a small rural county in Indiana. *TESOL Quarterly, 39*(4), 683–705.

Pfeiffer, P., & Byrnes, H. (2009). Curriculum, learning, and identity of majors: A case study of program outcomes evaluation. In J. Norris, J. Davis, C. Sinicrope, & Y. Watanabe (Eds.), *Toward useful program evaluation in college foreign language education* (pp. 183–207). Honolulu, HI: National Foreign Language Resource Center.

Rundblad, G. (2006). *Ethics is essential.* Retrieved from www.appliedlinguistics. org.uk

Simpson, A., & Mengi, E. (2014). The characteristics of an exemplary teacher: What are they? *The Journal of Teaching English for Specific and Academic Purposes, 2*(1), 89–99.

Slimani, A. (1992). Evaluation of classroom interaction. In J. C. Alderson & A. Beretta (Eds.), *Evaluation second language education* (pp. 197–221). Cambridge, England: Cambridge University Press.

Sugarman, J. (2008). *Evaluation of the dual language program in the North Shore School District 112, Highland Park, IL.* Washington, DC: Center for Applied Linguistics.

Tsou, W., & Chen, F. (2014). ESP program evaluation framework: Description and application to a Taiwanese university ESP program. *English for Specific Purposes, 33,* 39–53.

Turner, C. (2001). The need for impact studies of L2 performance testing and rating: Identifying areas of potential consequences at all levels of the testing cycle. *Studies in Language Testing, 11,* 138–149.

Watanabe, Y., Norris, J., & Gonzalez-Lloret, M. (2009). Identifying and responding to evaluation needs in college foreign language programs. In J. Norris, J. Davis, C. Sinicrope, & Y. Watanabe (Eds.), *Toward useful program evaluation in college foreign language education* (pp. 5–56). Honolulu, HI: National Foreign Language Resource Center.

Wong, J., & Zhang Waring, H. (2010). *Conversation analysis and second language pedagogy.* New Yor, NY: Routledge.

Yang, W. W. (2009). Evaluation of teacher induction practices in a U.S. university English language program: Towards useful evaluation. *Language Teaching Research, 13*(1), 77–98.

9

Outcomes and Assessment, and Summative Evaluation

> *There is no merit in persisting with syllabuses, materials and teachers,*
> *or with particular training, instructional strategies and activities—no matter*
> *how attached we may be to them, for emotional or theoretical reasons—if they*
> *do not produce the planned learner behaviors.*
>
> —Mackay, Wellesley, Tasman, and Bazergand (1998, p. 116)

> *Have regard for the end.*
>
> —Chilon, Spartan legislator and poet

Chapter 9 highlights the relationship of SOAC model components *outcomes* and *assessment*, where a teacher/evaluator determines whether learners met the outcomes set out at the beginning of the course, based on tests, questionnaires, interviews, and other course assessments. This is *summative evaluation*,[1] a summing up of the worth of a course to make policy changes for the future. A model of summative evaluation is given, with questions that can be applied to any summative evaluation project. In this chapter, the model is applied to

---

1. For all terms in *italics*, see Glossary.

Evaluating Second Language Courses, pages 195–209
Copyright © 2016 by Information Age Publishing
All rights of reproduction in any form reserved.

an exit interview or self-inventory that teachers/evaluators can use to generate decision points regarding a future course.

This is the seventh and final chapter in which the stakeholders, outcomes, assessment, and curriculum evaluation model (SOAC) is applied to second and foreign language courses. This chapter is on summative evaluation, which is the process of judging the worth of a course, after the course has been taught, for purposes of accountability. Thus the relationship between the outcomes of a course and the assessments designed for the course is highlighted. In summative evaluation, *data collection instruments* in the form of quizzes, tests, questionnaires, observations, and interviews are used to determine whether learners met the course outcomes set out at the beginning of the course. Assuming the data collection instruments have been validated and indeed measure what we intend them to measure (see Chapter 7 and Chapter 8), information from a summative evaluation can be invaluable in assigning worth to a course. Assigning worth for purposes of accountability, in the most productive sense, means creating policy decisions, or *decision points,* for future courses. The first quotation given at the beginning of this chapter refers to several directions these decision points can take, such as changing instruction, materials, and activities (see also Bachman, 1999 and Brown, 1989). The second quotation simply reminds us that all things come to an end, whether it is a job, a time living somewhere, or a course. There is worth in distilling what we learned teaching the course in ways that can positively influence the future, not just for the teacher/evaluator him or herself, but for others.

When summative evaluation is mentioned, many educators respond with dismay. It is true that evaluations done by external others may be done of us, of our programs, and of our courses, for reasons that do not seem to benefit us. As an example: At one American university, foreign language teachers are required to provide annual information on what percentage of learners got a B or higher in classes. Even with this most innocuous type of accountability, it is easy to see why answering decontextualized questions at this level of generality can be frustrating to teachers. In Chapter 1, we argued that evaluations may operate at different levels of concern (Chapter 1, Tables 1.1 and 1.2). What we have focused on in this book is at the classroom level and at the level of research concerns, the results of which may reach beyond the immediate classroom. But we have also recounted the work of Mitchell and her colleagues (1992), who operated at a national level as external evaluators focused on bilingual education in Scotland. They found that national-level administrators did not value the data used in the evaluation, yet the 1992 publication of this important work attests to the worth of the evaluation they did. The assessments they used, and their interpretations of data arising from the assessments, were of worth to the evaluators, to the teachers and schools they worked with, and to the many readers of their report. We argue that summative evaluation activity that teachers/evaluators do for their own purposes is always worthwhile. And for those external others who come along, teachers/evaluators will have information at hand to offer, if not in the form external evaluators may expect. See Appendix A for a bibliography of actual evaluation reports that address various levels of concern.

DISCUSSION QUESTION 1

What do you think or feel when a course ends? What accounts for your thoughts and feelings?

DISCUSSION QUESTION 2

As a teacher or learner, have you ever sat down at the end of a course and thought through what was accomplished? What might you list down as an accomplishment? What does the accomplishment have to do with your expectations or plans when you started the course?

DISCUSSION QUESTION 3

If someone offered to help you do a summative evaluation for a course, what would you evaluate? What would you like to be able to say about the worth of the course or course parts being evaluated?

To help with any summative evaluation project the readers of this book have in mind, a model of summative evaluation is given in this chapter, with questions that can be applied to any summative evaluation project. In this chapter, the model is applied to an exit interview or self-inventory that teachers/evaluators can use to generate decision points for a future course.

What is Summative Evaluation and Where Is It in the SOAC Model?

Summative evaluation is the relationship between assessment and outcomes. Assessment refers to data collection instruments (tests, questionnaires, interviews, observations, etc.) and data collection protocols used to answer the question of whether learner outcomes have come about (e.g., Did students' vocabulary knowledge improve?). Outcomes are statements of what ought to come about in terms of learner knowledge, ability, or attitude as a result of

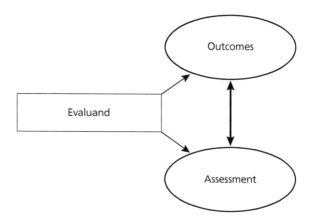

Figure 9.1   The SOAC model and summative evaluation.

participating in a course. Outcomes can be written for a course using an *outcome validation study* (Chapter 3), a *needs analysis* (Chapter 4), or by examining *course logic* (Chapter 5). In Chapter 4 we gave examples of learner outcomes, such as "raise [students'] confidence in their ability to read L2 texts" (Arnold, 2009, p. 348), which we adapted into a more specific form of outcome: "Learners will demonstrate increasing confidence to read L2 texts through self-reports of their reactions to a text and recounting the reading processes they use." Note how, in the adapted outcome, one assessment is already suggested: learner self-reports. This demonstrates the interdependence of assessments and outcomes. Assessments are used to decide whether learners met the outcomes, and the outcomes themselves suggest forms of assessment to use to do that. Summative evaluation is a reckoning: Did learners meet the outcomes? If so, what can we learn from that? If not, what can we learn from that? What is best left alone, and what ought to be changed and how? See Figure 9.1.

Why Summative Evaluations for Courses Are Not Often Done

This question poses an interesting contrast to our question in Chapter 6: Why do a *formative evaluation*? We argue that summative evaluations in a formal sense are not often done by teachers/evaluators. One reason is that for teachers/evaluators, a course never really ends. Teachers are often responsible for multiple, different courses, and of necessity their thinking is fluid and aimed at solving "problems" on many fronts given their own resources and experience. Even with substantial chronological breaks between the end of one set of courses and the beginning of another set, it is likely that during the break, teachers are still thinking and experiencing their past, present, and future students' learning as a seamless, and compelling, process. Woods (1996) effectively describes the tremendous cognitive investment language teachers make in ongoing planning and perceiving processes.

A second reason summative evaluation is rarely done by teachers is that this type of evaluation may seem to belong more to external others such as department chairs or accreditation agencies (Southern Association of Colleges and Schools, 2006). When some kind of program or school evaluation is requested, usually some departmental administrator creates a committee to address the issue of how to "translate" the business of teaching and learning into categories of information desired by the external evaluators. For an account of this see Gorsuch (2009). Thus there may be a buffer between teachers/evaluators and external evaluators. An accreditation report of an English language program in Kuwait shows a committee of authors who were program directors, coordinators, and two instructors among 20 listed in an organizational chart (Jacques, Combs, McMurray, Awwad, Loomis, & Suffi, 2009). One other buffer between teachers/evaluators and summative evaluation is that accreditation and formal accountability evaluations are done only periodically (see Gorsuch, 2009).

Finally, in the event teachers/evaluators leave one job for another job, they are likely busy thinking about the future, and not reflecting on the past. We argue that such "leavers" may have accumulated knowledge about courses at the institution that approach that of a summative evaluation. Yet this resource seems not to be tapped, if the literature is any indication, hence our project for this chapter on constructing and conducting exit interviews using a summative evaluation model as a basis.

DISCUSSION QUESTION 4

Have you ever done or participated in a summative evaluation for an external authority? What was your role?

DISCUSSION QUESTION 5

If you have not done a summative evaluation for an external authority, would there be a chance you could do so? Why would you wish to? What reservations might you have about doing a summative evaluation?

DISCUSSION QUESTION 6

What do you think about the idea of talking to a teacher who is leaving your school? What kinds of questions would you ask such a person? How would you treat their answers? Can you think of any difficulties you might have getting the teacher to talk to you? How would you deal with such difficulties, if any?

Summative Evaluation and Formative Evaluation Compared

Whether summative evaluation or formative evaluation, the processes of doing an evaluation project are the same. Because our Chapter 6 on formative evaluation and Chapters 7 and 8 on *instrument validation* are detailed, we refer back to the chapters as resources for writing *evaluation questions*, planning *data collection protocols*, keeping all-important memos on ongoing evaluation and *instrument validation* activities, answering *evaluation questions*, and composing *decision points*. And, we refer back to specific tables or figures in these chapters, even as we define similarities and differences between summative and formative evaluation.

Similarities and Differences Between Summative Evaluation and Formative Evaluation

First, both summative evaluation and formative evaluation can be done by teachers. Even though we previously made an argument that summative evaluation may seem to belong to administrators or outside others, there is much value in teachers/evaluators doing summative evaluation for their own purposes. This leads to a second similarity: Both types of evaluation have the purpose of evaluating curriculum practices (Chapter 6, Table 6.5) and creating decision points (Chapter 6, Table 6.9). Finally, both summative and formative evaluations make use of the same kinds of evaluation questions, data collection instruments, data collection protocols (Chapter 6, Tables 6.6 and 6.7), and instrument validation strategies (Chapters 7 and 8).

There are also differences between formative and summative evaluation. See Table 9.1 for a summary.

A Summative Evaluation Model

Because this book is about *course evaluation* and directed at teachers/evaluators, it seemed important for us to create a summative evaluation model that focused on the concerns of language educators working in various roles, including that of teacher. As we discussed before, summative evaluation seems to belong to department or college administrators. While their points of view about what evidence best indicates learners have met course

TABLE 9.1   Differences Between Formative Evaluation and Summative Evaluation

1. Summative evaluation occurs after a course is over, while formative evaluation occurs during a course. (Bachman, 1989; Scriven, 1967)
2. Summative evaluation can be broad in scope with multiple areas of focus including instruction, materials, and schedule together (see Chapter 6, Table 6.5), whereas formative evaluation is usually limited to single areas such as specific instructional practices and how they affect learners. (Ayala & Brandon, 2008; Vandergrift, 2000)
3. Summative evaluation may allow more time and more reflection because the course is not underway, while formative evaluation is of necessity "lean, nimble, and focused" because it takes place while the course is underway.
4. Summative evaluation likely does not occur to teachers naturally, for the reasons we gave earlier: Courses never really seem to end from teachers' points of view, and summative evaluations are more often associated with rare, externally motivated evaluations. On the other hand formative evaluation occurs naturally in the sense that teachers cannot help but think about their course and what is happening in it while they are teaching. This is true even if such reflection is unsystematic and non-accountable, meaning no written record is kept.
5. Summative evaluation is more used for more macro-level decision points (*Should we try this new textbook? Should we keep using this vocabulary app on students' cell phones?*) whereas formative evaluation is more used for micro-level decision points (*Did students think the handouts were useful? Do they want me to correct them in class?*).
6. Decision points arising from a summative evaluation may be longer in coming and may take longer to implement, while decision points from a formative evaluation are likely to arise more quickly for during-course decisions.

outcomes are undoubtedly informative, we argue that the points of view of teachers are equally important. And, in our experience, teachers become administrators, and administrators become teachers.

To create a summative evaluation model, we believed we needed to capture multiple points of view. To create questions and categories that accomplished this, we did interviews of various stakeholders in university foreign language programs. These included department chairpersons, language section coordinators, and teachers in college-level foreign languages. Using an iterative, longitudinal data analysis procedure, we found strikingly similar comments from stakeholders that amounted to categories in a summative evaluation model. These categories suggest what ought to be reported in a summative evaluation, and what kind of evidence ought to be brought together to demonstrate learners' achievements against the outcomes of a course.

Table 9.2 is a summative evaluation model that has 16 course evaluation categories with suggested questions for each category. The questions appear in the form of an exit interview for teachers who are leaving a school. The categories and questions can be used as an interview, or as an

TABLE 9.2 Summative Evaluation Model With Categories and Questions	
Categories	Questions
Note: Categories and questions related more directly to outcomes and assessments in the SOAC model (Figure 9.1) are highlighted in italics.	
1. **Information about yourself** Responses to these questions can serve as a summative evaluation report introduction, or a description of course stakeholders.	• How long you have been teaching? • List your academic credentials and relevant past experience. • How long you have been teaching this particular course, for example from month/year to month/year?
2. **Course status** Responses to these questions can serve as a course description in a summative evaluation report.	• What was the level of the course (first year, second, undergraduate, graduate)? • Did you originate the course or was it already established in the curriculum? • Did you elect to teach the course or was it assigned to you? • Was it part of your specialty?
3. *Course goals and objectives* Responses to these questions can serve as a course description in a summative evaluation report.	• *According to the syllabus, what were the course goals, objectives, or learning outcomes?* • *Did you participate in the creation of the goals or were they given to you?* • *Did you refer to them during your tenure as you planned the course?* • *Did you have any additional personal goals for this course?*
4. **Student profile** Responses to these questions can serve as a description of course stakeholders in a summative evaluation report.	• Was this a required class or an elective? • Were the students majors, minors, or non-majors? • What do you believe were the students' motivation to take this class? • What was your course enrollment over the time you taught? • Did you have attendance problems? If so, what was the result? • Did you have any problems with students? If so, what were the problems? • Where were your students from? • During the time you taught this course, did you notice any changes in the kinds of students in the course? • *Did you have any feedback or communication about the course from your students after they graduated or moved on? What did they say?* • *Do you believe any of the topics raised in the questions above required changes made to the stated course outcomes? What changes should have been made, and why?*
5. **Curriculum implementation/ lesson plans** Responses to these questions	• What time of day did you teach? What effect might that have had? What was the condition of the students (rested, tired, hungry)?

(continued)

TABLE 9.2 Summative Evaluation Model With Categories and Questions (continued)	
Categories	Questions
can serve as a course description in a summative evaluation report.	• What was a typical class like? What did you usually do first, second, etc.? For example, did you lecture part of the time and then do exercises? How did you usually end the class?
	• *Did you assign any course projects? How were they related to the curriculum and the outcomes?*
	• How were you creative in teaching this class? Did you try anything new?
	• How would you describe your teaching methodology? Did you use communicative language teaching or a more grammatical approach? What were the difficulties?
	• *What were the course outcomes? For example, if you taught using communicative language theory, did that cause confusion for the students? Did the students seem to enjoy it? Was there resistance?*
	• *Did you do any cultural activities in class, how did students respond? Did you see any difference in attitude as a result of assigning these activities?*
	• *If you maintained a teaching diary, what are some examples you recorded?*
6. *Assessment* Responses to these questions can serve as a data collection and analysis description, and a results description in a summative evaluation report.	• *What tests were administered (weekly quizzes, midterm, final, other)?*
	• *How long have you been using it/them?*
	• *Where did your tests come from? Did you make them or were they given to you?*
	• *Did you collect any evidence that your tests were working?*
	• *At what point in the semester did you give them?*
	• *Are other teachers using the same tests?*
	• *Did you notice any pattern in the test score results over the years?*
	• *Do you know if your students evaluated the course? What were the results?*
	• *Can you provide any of your quizzes and exams?*
7. **Course textbook** Responses to these questions can serve as a course description, and a results description in a summative evaluation report.	• Over the time you taught this course, about how many textbooks did you use?
	• Who chose the textbook?
	• What was the process by which the textbook was chosen?
	• Did you teach most chapters of the textbook or did you select only a few? How did you decide?
	• *Did you ever ask your students their opinion of the textbook? If so, what was their response?*
	• What were the strong points of the textbook? What were the weak points?

(continued)

TABLE 9.2 Summative Evaluation Model With Categories and Questions (continued)

Categories	Questions
8. **Other materials used on a regular basis** (lecture outlines, notes, PowerPoint presentations, videos, handouts) Responses to these questions can serve as a course description, and a results description in a summative evaluation report.	• *What material worked best?* • Attach any materials you would like to share in the Appendix. • Was there an external event such as a film series or conference while you were teaching? Was there any effect on your class? • Did any of your students do a study-abroad program? Did you experience any problems with students after they returned, for example were they out of sync with students who did not go? Were you able to use the experience of those who went in your teaching?
9. **Your classroom** Responses to these questions can serve as a course description, and a results description in a summative evaluation report.	• Was your classroom of sufficient size? • Did you put anything on the walls that helped your teaching? • Were the desks, tables, chairs helpful in your teaching? • What did you not have, but would have liked to have had in your room?
10. **Office hours** Responses to these questions can serve as a course description in a summative evaluation report.	• Did you have an office? If not, where did you stay between classes? • Did you maintain regular office hours? • If you did, about how many students visited your office each semester? • What was the main reason for their visits? • How were you able to meet those reasons? • Would you recommend any changes in our office hours procedures? • How would you rate staff support?
11. *Grades* Responses to these questions can serve as a results description in a summative evaluation report.	• *In a typical semester, what was your pass/fail grade ratio for this course?* • *What grades did students expect? Was there an assumption on the part of students that they would expect an A or B?* • *Did you fail any of your students?* • *If you failed a student, what caused you to do so?*
12. **Supervision and training** Responses to these questions can serve as a stakeholder or course description, and a results description in a summative evaluation report.	• When you first began teaching, was there an orientation? • If there were an orientation, did you consider it effective? • Did you have regular coordination meetings? • Where was the meeting location and time? • How would you describe your relationship to the course coordinator? • Were any of your classes observed? Did you receive feedback?

(continued)

TABLE 9.2 Summative Evaluation Model With Categories and Questions (continued)	
Categories	Questions
	• What did you do that your supervisor was not aware of, maybe you tried it only a few times. Did it work? • Overall, do you think the training you received was adequate? • Can you give an example of a situation were you not adequately prepared for? • Were you involved in any research alone or with a mentor? • To what extent did MA or advanced courses of training influence your teaching? • How did material from previous teacher colleagues including syllabuses, materials, and tests influence your teaching?
13. **Collegiality** Responses to these questions can serve as a stakeholder description in a summative evaluation report.	• How were you treated by others in the program the course was in? Can you give an example? • How did you communicate with your colleagues (email, wikis, file sharing)?
14. **Your next location** Responses to these questions can serve as description of policy recommendations (decision points) in a summative evaluation report.	• Do you feel prepared to create and/or participate in a program similar to this one? • What prepared you to contribute to the creation of curriculum at your next school? • How has your attitude changed from the time you started teaching this course to now?
15. **Suggestions and warnings** Responses to these questions can serve as description of policy recommendations (decision points) in a summative evaluation report.	• What recommendations do you have to change the course? • What suggestions would you like to make to those remaining in the program?
16. **Appendices** Responses to these questions can serve as a course description in a summative evaluation report.	1. *Course syllabus* 2. Teaching or lesson plan 3. *Tests* 4. Materials and handouts

introspective self-inventory. The questions, however, can be used to guide data collection for a summative evaluation report, and do not have to be used as an exit interview. For instance, for Category 7 on the course materials, the questions "Did you ever ask your students their opinion of the textbook? If so, what was their response?" may be used to plan data collection in the form of student questionnaires, or observations in successive class meetings. Responses to the questions can also be used to describe a course, and describing evaluation results when writing a summative evaluation report.

Since summative course evaluation may take place in a variety of teaching situations, we suggest that a teacher/evaluator address only the questions that fit the situation. Categories and questions related more directly to outcomes and assessments (Figure 9.1) are highlighted in italics. We also include information with each category that will help readers construct a summative evaluation report, if needed.

The categories and questions are wide-ranging. Some may not seem directly related to learner outcomes. Yet it becomes apparent that the teachers, section coordinators, and department chairpersons who we talked to, find that the structures that support student learning can be taken in account in summative evaluation, such as facilities, training, grading policies, and collegiality. In Table 9.2, we posed the questions in the past tense, reflecting two assumptions: First, if a summative evaluation is done once a course is over, teachers/evaluators would be posing any of the questions in Table 9.2 as retrospective; and second, we argue the questions can serve as the basis for an exit interview for teachers. With some forethought, the exit interview can also be done with students who are moving on, for valuable insights from this stakeholder group. Information from, and even mention of, such exit interviews almost never appears in the literature.

DISCUSSION QUESTION 7

Which of the categories in Table 9.2 seems most relevant to summative evaluation, as you understand it at this point? Which categories or questions seem least relevant?

An Exit Interview Project

We are suggesting an exit interview data collection protocol as a project for readers of this book. After reviewing data collection protocols, we finish with an example of an exit interview protocol designed for graduate students/teachers who are finishing their graduate program and thus are departing as foreign language teachers. In some settings, graduate students seeking degrees in Spanish, German, or Arabic are supported as instructors in undergraduate foreign language courses. By the time an average MA or doctoral-level student completes his or her degree, he or she may have taught foreign language courses from 1–4 years, during which time he or she has accumulated experience and developed points of view.

To review, a data collection protocol is a working plan for specific kinds of data collection. A protocol may include an actual data collection instrument, such as a questionnaire or a quiz, or a list of questions for an interview. A data collection protocol might also be listing what documents to collect, for example lesson plans, class handouts, photocopied pages of textbooks, etc. See the section in Chapter 6 on data collection protocols. Note that in Table 9.2 under the category Appendices that documents such as a course syllabuses and tests are suggested as documents that can be collected. Table 9.2 in and of itself is not a complete data collection protocol, even though questions from the table can be chosen to assemble a data collection instrument as an interview or self-inventory. What is still missing is a statement of the purpose for the interview, a plan for what will be asked, and a plan for who to interview, when, and how many times.

An Exit Interview Data Collection Protocol for Teachers in a Spanish Program

The purpose of the exit interview is to track graduate students/instructors upon their graduation from a Spanish literature and linguistics graduate degree. They were supported as Spanish instructors for undergraduate first- and second-year courses. The purpose of tracking the departing teachers is to learn to what extent they believed the undergraduate learners met the outcomes of the courses they enrolled in, in particular the final fourth semester course most students take to complete a foreign language requirement. A second learning outcome, although unstated, is to develop the graduate students/instructors into competent Spanish instructors with the ability to succeed professionally in other settings. Thus a second purpose for the exit interviews is to learn from departing graduate students/ teachers the extent to which they believe they were supported to meet the outcome. The responses from the interviewees are considered an *assessment* of an undergraduate language course, and also of the training program.

Questions for the interview are to be selected from the categories and questions appearing in the summative evaluation model in Table 9.2. The questions were determined by reviewing the undergraduate second-year course goals, which included "learners will be able to ask and answer basic questions in Spanish," and "learners will demonstrate an appreciation of the cultures of Spanish-speaking regions," among others. Thus questions will be selected from Categories 1, 2, 3, 4, 5, 6, 7, and 11, which together would create a coherent context for the course outcomes and assessments based on stakeholders' responses. Questions from Categories 12, 14, and 15 will be asked because they deal directly with training the stakeholders received in order to be teachers, and with suggestions and concerns they have from accumulated experience in the program.

Those who are to be interviewed are at least 5 out of 10 departing Spanish instructors, who are graduating from their graduate Spanish program. Because they will be interviewed three times over the period of a year, the instructors will need to agree to provide their contact information, such as an email address. There will be three interviews: one that will be done in the month of graduation/departure, a second interview that will be done six months after graduation/departure, and a final interview that will take place 12 months after graduation/departure. Interviews will be conducted face-to-face, by Skype, or telephone. Departing students/teachers will be provided with a list of questions prior to the interview.

> ### APPLICATION TASKS: Planning and Conducting an Exit Interview for Students in a Foreign Language Course, and Evaluating a Report of a Summative Evaluation

First task idea: As we noted previously, the model presented in Table 9.2 can be used to design exit interviews for learners in a language course. Create an interview protocol for a group of learners about to finish a course. What categories in Table 9.2 provide questions appropriate for soon-departing students, given the course outcomes? What questions need to be changed? And what additional questions need to be asked that do not appear in Table 9.2? Show your data collection protocol to a colleague and then pilot the interview with an actual student. Keep a memo on changes you wish to make to the data collection protocol. Present your pilot results to colleagues or to a supervisor, and/or collect more data.

Second task idea: Find a chapter in a book or a journal article you believe describes a summative evaluation (see Appendix A for many examples). Note what makes you believe the report is a summative evaluation. Do the authors say it's a summative evaluation? What is said that makes you believe the report is being done after the fact, and for purposes of accountability? Finally evaluate the publication using Rap #1 (Reading and assessing publications *of* an evaluation) in Chapter 10, Table 10.1. Is there anything in the publication that will help you design, conduct, and write up your own summative evaluation of a course?

References

Arnold, N. (2009). Online extensive reading for advanced foreign language learners: An evaluation study. *Foreign Language Annals, 12*(2), 340–366.

Ayala, C. C., & Brandon, P. R. (2008). Building evaluation recommendations for improvement: Insights from student formative assessments. In N. L. Smith & P. R. Brandon (Eds.), *Fundamental issues in evaluation* (pp. 159–176). New York, NY: Guilford Press.

Bachman, L. F. (1989). The development and use of criterion-referenced tests of language ability in language program evaluation. In R. K. Johnson (Ed.), *The second language curriculum* (pp. 242–258). Cambridge, England: Cambridge University Press.

Brown, J. D. (1989). Language program evaluation: A synthesis of existing possibilities. In R.K. Johnson (Ed.), *The second language curriculum* (pp. 222–241). Cambridge, England: Cambridge University Press.

Gorsuch, G. J. (2009). Investigating second language learner self-efficacy and future expectancy of second language use for high stakes program evaluation. *Foreign Language Annals, 42*(2), 505–540.

Jacques, S., Combs, M., McMurray, M., Awwad, R., Loomis, R., & Suffi, K. (2009). *Self-study report for commission on English language programs accreditation.* Retrieved from http://www.auk.edu.kw/iep/accreditation/accr_ss_report_intro.pdf

Mackay, R., Wellesley, D., Tasman, D., & Bazergan, E. (1998). Using institutional self-evaluation to promote the quality of language and communication training programs. In P. Rea-Dickins & K. Germaine (Eds.), *Managing evaluation and innovation in language teaching: Building bridges* (pp. 111–131). London, England: Longman.

Mitchell, R. (1992). The independent evaluation of bilingual primary education: A narrative account. In J. C. Alderson & A. Beretta (Eds.), *Evaluating second language education* (pp. 100–140). Cambridge, England: Cambridge University Press.

Scriven, M. (1967). The methodology of evaluation. In R. W. Tyler,, R. M. Gagne, & M. Scriven (Eds.), *Perspectives of curriculum evaluation* (pp. 39–83). Chicago: Rand McNally.

Southern Association of Colleges and Schools. (2006). *Southern Association of Colleges and Schools.* Retrieved from http://www.sacscoc.org/

Vandergrift, L. (2000). Setting students up for success: formative evaluation and FLES. *Foreign Language Annals, 33,* 290–303.

Woods, D. (1996). *Teacher cognition in language teaching.* Cambridge, England: Cambridge University Press.

10

Reading and Assessing Evaluation Publications

Memory is a child walking along a seashore. You can never tell what small pebble it will pick up and store with its treasured things.

—Attributed to Pierce Harris
American clergyman and journalist

Course evaluations can often end up on a pile of good intentions that are not realized, mainly because of lack of planning but also because teachers/evaluators are busy. One strategy for adequately planning an evaluation is to read evaluation publications and reports, and build up knowledge and ideas about evaluation. This chapter offers RAP (reading and assessing evaluation publications) templates that are used to analyze evaluation reports so as to appreciate the points most relevant to planning and carrying out an evaluation. Four types of evaluation publications are posited: (a) publications *of* an evaluation, (b) publications *about* evaluation, (c) publications *of* a needs analysis, and (d) publications *about* need analysis. Four RAP templates are offered, one for each type of publication.

---

1. For all terms in *italics*, see Glossary.

Evaluating Second Language Courses, pages 211–241

O ne challenge to do course evaluation lies in the tendency to be unsure about the purpose for the project at an early stage. Educators
are busy people, and unless we can settle on a course evaluation purpose
and a workable plan, we get swept up in the details of our regular teaching
and then fail to do the evaluation. What can help? One strategy is reading
the evaluation literature and storing up knowledge and memories of other
evaluators' ideas and experiences that come to us through their publications. Sometimes, as the writer Pierce Harris tells us, our memory will cast
up what we need to know at a time when we need it. In other words, doing
some reading of evaluation studies and publications over time will help our
course evaluation efforts and planning.

This chapter presents templates for *reading and assessing evaluation publications*[1] (RAP) that are useful for understanding the evaluation literature
and discovering the knowledge we need. Each set of RAP questions reflects
criteria that are needed to analyze and understand the evaluation literature. One concern for many teachers wanting to do a course evaluation is
that they are not as familiar with the evaluation literature as they are with
the pedagogical or research literature. This lack of familiarity means that
they may miss important points because they are not aware of them, and as
a result are not looking for them. In addition, if several teachers/evaluators
are reading what can be complex and unfamiliar evaluation articles, discussions on doing a course evaluation may be difficult.

DISCUSSION QUESTION 1

H ave you read any publications you would like to tell your colleagues
about? What would be important for them to know? How would you
organize what you wish to say?

To deal with these problems, four RAP templates are presented. Each is
designed for a different type of article common in the evaluation literature.

1. Reading and assessing publications *of* an evaluation.
2. Reading and assessing publications *about* evaluation.
3. Reading and assessing publications *of* a needs analysis.
4. Reading and assessing publications *about* needs analysis.

In Numbers 1 and 2, we mean both course evaluation and *program
evaluation.* Our experience is that articles about second language program evaluation are more common than articles about second language
course evaluation, which is one reason we wrote this book. Program evaluation is a process by which we collect information and assign a judgment
of worth to several related courses that comprise a program, while course

evaluation focuses on a single course or parts of a course. Regardless of the difference in focus, reading publications of or about evaluation can be of value to teachers/evaluators planning to do an evaluation. We will briefly describe each RAP and then provide templates for them. Finally, we will do a more in-depth treatment of the first type of RAP by explaining the RAP criteria and then applying the RAP to two evaluation articles: one using primarily quantitative data (numbers) and the other using primarily qualitative data (words).

Brief Descriptions of Four Types of RAPs

First is the RAP *of* an evaluation. This type of article, often published in a journal or a book of collected articles, describes how an evaluator went about the evaluation and what the results were. An example of this type of article is Bruning, Flowerday, and Trayer (1999) in which they evaluated how educators developed and disseminated a statewide foreign language standards framework. The RAP asks readers to answer questions (criteria) appropriate to understanding this type of evaluation publication. Since some of these criteria can be applied to both evaluation and research articles, an asterisk (*) indicates that the criterion is considered necessary and unique for evaluation. This RAP ends with reflective questions on the strengths or the weaknesses of the evaluation portrayed in the article, and queries readers on what they learned about course evaluation from reading the article.

Second is the RAP *about* evaluation. Articles about evaluation are usually found in books of collected articles such as Alderson and Beretta (1992) or in books such as Brown (1989). Rather than reporting an actual evaluation, Brown (1989) presents directions for conducting a program evaluation. This second RAP template includes criteria on whether the term *evaluation* is defined and also criteria that probe the key points of the publication. There are criteria for claims made for evaluation in the publication, and a reflective question on what the reader learned about course evaluation. A final criterion suggests the reader look over the article's reference list to see if any of the citations might be of interest.

Third is the RAP *of* a needs analysis. Recall from Chapter 1 that a key distinguishing feature of evaluation is the presence of a *needs analysis*, which is the formal process of collecting data on learner needs. Articles of needs analyses are found in journals and books of collected articles such as Long (2005a). In this book we find 11 articles all purporting to describe a needs analysis, such as one done exploring the second language needs of nonnative English speaking chambermaids at a hotel (Jasso-Aguilar, 2005). It is easy to see how a needs analysis is an essential component of evaluation. In order to create a second language course and then evaluate the course, we need to understand what the learners (chambermaids in this case) need to use the second language for. At any rate, this RAP asks if the needs analysis portrayed in the article was done to develop a course and if resulting course objectives were discussed. It also asks about course *stakeholders* and purpose, what *data collection instruments* were used, and whether *validation evidence* was offered for the data collection instruments and *data collection protocols*. In other words, was the data collection shown to provide relevant and credible data? This RAP also includes criteria that ask how the data were analyzed and then how needs were derived from them. This RAP concludes with reflective questions about the strengths and weaknesses of the needs analysis, and what the reader learned about needs analysis.

Fourth is the RAP *about* needs analysis. As with articles about evaluation, articles about needs analysis are typically found in textbooks or books of collected articles, such as Richards (2001). In Richards, needs analysis appears as a chapter in a textbook on curriculum design and revitalization. The RAP about needs analysis asks if the term needs analysis was defined, what the key points of the article are, what claims are being made, and what the reader learned about needs analysis.

DISCUSSION QUESTION 2

Can you think of any publications you heard about or read that might fit into one of the four types of RAPs? How would you go about retrieving this publication if you wanted to read or reread it and use the RAPs that follow to assess it?

In all reading and assessing publications (RAP) templates, the question of what the reader learned about course evaluation or needs analysis is important because we think knowledge is accumulated. If we wish to do course evaluation, we need to know and assess current practices that are relevant to the process. Here are the four templates. Specialized terms appear in italics and can be found in the glossary for this book. An asterisk (*) indicates that the criterion is considered necessary and unique for course or program evaluation publications, as opposed to articles on or about research in general. We intend these templates to be photocopied and completed by those who are reading evaluation articles or book chapters.

TABLE 10.1 **RAP 1: Reading and Assessing Publications *of* an Evaluation**	
Publication citation (authors, year, journal name, etc.)	
Short summary of publication	
Basic Description	
1. Were course or program *goals* or *outcomes* discussed or analyzed?	
*2. Was a *needs analysis* provided, discussed, or even mentioned?	
3. What was the duration of the course or program? What was the duration of the evaluation?	
4. Were course or program participants described?	
5. Were types of instruction in the course or program identified?	
6. Was it clear whether all or part of the course or program was evaluated?	
Purpose of the Evaluation	
*7. Were *stakeholders* identified?	
8. Were the *evaluation purpose* and *evaluation questions* (EQs) stated?	
*9. Was an *evaluation model* or theory used or mentioned?	
10. Was a *research design* identified and used?	
11. Was this a field study or a lab study?	
Data Collection and Analysis	
12. Were *data collection instruments* (DCIs) identified and described?	
13. Were DCIs provided?	
14. For each DCI was *reliability* discussed?	
15. For each DCI was *validation evidence* provided?	
16. If courses or programs were compared, were the DCIs *program-fair?*	

(continued)

TABLE 10.1 RAP 1: Reading and Assessing Publications *of an* Evaluation (continued)	
Quantitative Data Collection and Analysis	
17a. Was each *statistical procedure* identified?	
18a. Were *statistical assumptions* stated and addressed?	
19a. Was there *statistical clarity*?	
20a. Was a *p-value* given? At what level was it set?	
21a. Was an indicator of practical significance such as *effect size* reported?	
Qualitative Data Collection and Analysis	
17b. Could you follow the sequences of how the data were collected and analyzed?	
18b. Was the author's role and status within the site explicitly described?	
19b. Were any forms of *peer review* used?	
20b. Were *areas of uncertainty* identified?	
21b. Was *negative evidence* sought, found, and reported?	
Evaluation Results	
*22. Were the *evaluation questions* (EQs) answered in a clear way?	
*23. Were policy and/or pedagogical recommendations given?	
Strengths	
Weaknesses	
Citations in the reference list of the publication. Were any articles or other publications in the reference list of interest to you? List here. Use the list to request or retrieve the publications.	
Bottom line: What did you learn about evaluation?	

* Indicates that the criterion is considered necessary and unique for course or program evaluation.

TABLE 10.2 RAP 2: Reading and Assessing Publications *About* Evaluation	
Publication citation (authors, year, journal name, etc.)	
Was *evaluation* defined?	

Synthesis
 A short synthesis of the publication
 Key points
   1.
   2.
   3.
   4.
   5.	

Evaluation Methodology
 What points do the author(s)
 claim are essential for doing an
 evaluation?
   1.
   2.
   3.
   4.
   5.	

Citations in the Reference List of the Publication Were any articles or other publications in the reference list of interest to you? List here. Use the list to request or retrieve the publications.	
Bottom line: What did you learn about evaluation?	

TABLE 10.3 RAP 3: Reading and Assessing Publications of a Needs Analysis	
Publication citation (authors, year, journal name, etc.)	
Short summary of publication	
Course/Program Criteria	
1. Was the *needs analysis* (NA) analyzing an existing course or program?	
2. If "yes" were the course or program *goals* or *outcomes* identified?	
3. If course or program *goals* or *outcomes* were identified, was a *goal validation* study done?	
4. If an existing course or program was not the focus, what was the focus of the NA?	
Stakeholders	
5. Were *stakeholders* identified?	
6. Did the author identify aspects of the social, political, or educational environment that might inform or illuminate *stakeholder* problems/needs? (Examples: growing need for interpreters, institutional mandate to increase enrollments, government policy to increase second language communication skills of citizens)	
Purpose and *Evaluation Questions*	
7. Was the purpose of the NA stated?	
8. Were *evaluation questions* (EQs) stated?	
Needs	
9. How was *need* defined?	
10. What kinds of needs were identified?	
11. Was the NA identified by orientation? (Examples: discrepancy, democratic, diagnostic, analytic)	
Data Collection and Analysis	
12. Were *data collection instruments* (DCIs) identified and described?	

(continued)

TABLE 10.3 RAP 3: Reading and Assessing Publications of a Needs Analysis (continued)	
13. Were DCIs provided?	
14. For each DCI was *reliability* discussed?	
15. For each DCI was *validation evidence* provided?	
16. As a result of data collection and analysis, did the author articulate needs?	
17. Were these needs reformulated as new *goals* or outcomes (see Criteria 2)?	
Strengths	
Weaknesses	
Citations in the Reference List of the Publication Were any articles or other publications in the reference list of interest to you? List here. Use the list to request or retrieve the publications.	
Bottom line: What did you learn about *needs analysis* and evaluation?	

TABLE 10.4 RAP 4: Reading and Assessing Publications *About* Needs Analysis	
Publication citation (authors, year, journal name, etc.)	
Was *needs analysis* (NA) defined?	
Synthesis A short synthesis of the publication Key points 1. 2. 3. 4. 5.	
Needs Analysis **Methodology** What points do the author(s) claim are essential for doing an NA? 1. 2. 3. 4. 5.	
Strengths	
Weaknesses	
Citations in the reference list of the publication Were any articles or other publications in the reference list of interest to you? List here. Use the list to request or retrieve the publications.	
Bottom line: What did you learn about *needs analysis* and evaluation?	

Annotated Example RAPs for Reading and Assessing Publications *of* an Evaluation

Here we provide two annotated example RAPs for reading and assessing publications *of* an evaluation. We understand that some terms and concepts brought up in the RAP template given previously are unfamiliar. And while we have a glossary in the book, we wanted to provide explanations, rationales, and examples embedded directly into the templates. The publication used as the example for a quantitative study is an article in a journal by Henry and Roseberry (1998; Table 10.5). The publication used as an example of a qualitative study is Pawan and Thomalla (2005; Table 10.6).

TABLE 10.5   Annotated RAP for a Publication of an Evaluation Using Quantitative Data

Publication citation (authors, year, journal name, etc.)	You need the sort of detail APA (American Psychological Association) or MLA (Modern Language Association) demands so that you and others can locate and retrieve the publication at a later date. *Example* Henry, A., & Roseberry, R. L. (1998). An evaluation of a genre-based approach to the teaching of EAP/ESP writing. *TESOL Quarterly, 32*(1), 147–156.
Short summary of publication	When reading large numbers of publications it is easy to mix them up in your memory. It also helps to summarize the publication to prepare for a presentation about the RAP or the publication to colleagues. *Example* An innovative genre-based approach to a writing course was evaluated using a quasi-experimental design. Two groups of 17 students each were randomly assigned to control and treatment groups and given a writing assignment using a particular genre. This writing sample was used as a pretest for both groups. After six hours of instruction over a three-week period, it was administered again as a posttest. Three instruments (a) motivation scores by raters, (b) move index scores, and (c) ratings from Roseberry's (1995) index of texture were used to compare results from the control and experimental groups in terms of motivation, moves, and texture. The results for motivation and texture were statistically significant, but the results for moves were not. It was concluded that, "a teaching approach focusing on rhetorical organization can be successful in an EAP/ESP teaching situation" (p. 154).
Basic Description	
1. Were course or program *goals* or *outcomes* discussed or analyzed?	Course goals are sometimes called outcomes, objectives, learning points, targets, aims, benchmarks, or criteria. Course goals need to be stated so a reader can understand what someone (the authors/evaluators or the course developer) thinks the course is supposed to accomplish. While a course evaluation can be used to assign worth to a many aspects of a course (including the course goals), there is a basic assumption that worth is also assigned in terms of whether a course accomplishes its goals. *Example* Course goals were not mentioned.

(continued)

TABLE 10.5   Annotated RAP for a Publication of an Evaluation Using Quantitative Data (continued)

*2. Was a *needs analysis* provided, discussed, or even mentioned?	A needs analysis (NA) refers to "techniques and procedures for collecting information to be used in syllabus design" (Nunan, 1988, p. 13). Brown (1995, p. 36) defines NA as "the systematic collection and analysis of all subjective and objective information necessary to define and validate defensible curriculum purposes that satisfy the language learning requirements of students within the context of particular institutions that influence the learning and teaching situation." An NA supplies the justification for the course, and in some respects, the reason for doing a course evaluation. A publication on course or program evaluation should at least mention a needs analysis. If we do not know what needs the course is answering, it would be difficult to understand the evaluation and apply the results. Look for whether the authors/evaluators explicitly use the term NA or describe what constitutes the problem the course addresses and why the problem is important (see Long, 2005b). This may speak to why the course or program evaluation was done in the first place. *Example* A needs analysis was not mentioned. The rationale for doing the course evaluation and the instructional intervention itself was discussed only indirectly in an introduction explaining the purpose of the writing instruction intervention: "to raise learners' awareness of both the rhetorical organization and the linguistic features closely associated with the genre" (p. 147). It was not made clear whether learners' greater awareness of rhetorical organization would make them better second language writers.
3. What was the duration of the course? What was the duration of the evaluation?	Duration refers to the time period covered by the course and by the evaluation itself. Many courses are a term or semester long (10–14 weeks), while a course evaluation may take place over only a few weeks (implying a cross-section "snapshot" approach), or for as long as two semesters (suggesting a longitudinal approach). If the time of the course is different than the course being evaluated, authors/evaluators should give both times. Beretta (1992) and Alderson (1992) call for the course or program evaluation study duration to be included, implying that long-term evaluations are more valued. *Example* Yes, on p. 148, course duration of 6 hours of instruction over three weeks was mentioned. While it is implied the data for the course evaluation was collected for the same duration, this is not explicitly stated.

(continued)

TABLE 10.5 Annotated RAP for a Publication of an Evaluation Using Quantitative Data (continued)	
4. Were course or program participants described?	For participants (students), we want to know to what extent these participants are similar to or different from our students? Beretta (1986a; 1986b) calls for an emphasis on generalizability (applicability to other situations) because he advocates that course or program evaluations should be helpful to others. *Example* Yes on pp. 149–150 there was a detailed description of the participants, how they were selected for the course evaluation, and what their second language levels were.
5. Were types of instruction in the course or program identified?	Type of instruction refers to "what the course is about" in terms of what it purports to teach, for example writing, academic listening, basic conversation. In other words, is it clear what is being evaluated? Norris and Ortega (2006) suggest type of instruction as a category of interest for a meta-analysis (a comparison of courses in terms of the type of instruction they use). The type of instruction also goes to generalizability in that readers can directly compare the instruction used in the course evaluation to their own courses. *Example* Yes this study focused on writing English for academic purposes. On pp. 151–152 the instruction and materials were described in detail, although samples of the materials were not provided. To be fair, this evaluation report appeared in a "Brief Reports and Summaries" section of a journal, meaning that the editors demanded brevity from the authors/evaluators.
6. Was it clear whether all or part of the course or program was evaluated?	This is related to Criterion 3, but gets at the idea of matching the course to the "coverage" of the course evaluation in a different way by looking at the scope of the program evaluation. In other words, were all aspects of the course observed, or just some specific part, such as only listening instruction (in a four-skills course) or final exam procedures (in a course which includes instruction and many types of assessments). Beretta (1986a; 1986b) advocates evaluating whole programs rather than bits and pieces. See, however Chapter 6 on *formative evaluation.* *Example* On p. 150, the course evaluation is described as being conducted "during the writing component" but not for the reading or oral skills part of the course.

(continued)

TABLE 10.5 Annotated RAP for a Publication of an Evaluation Using Quantitative Data (continued)

*7. Were *stakeholders* identified?	Stakeholders are persons who have an interest in the outcome of the evaluation, including students (see "participants" in Criterion 4), supervisors, policy makers, teachers of the course or program being evaluated, and colleagues. Beretta (1990, p. 4) calls for "a dialogue between evaluators and stakeholders" and a first step in any dialogue is to identify stakeholders. Beretta notes that evaluation is a form of policy research, and Alderson (1992) notes that because various stakeholders may have different values and interests in the evaluation, stakeholder identification is important to help sort out these interests. An evaluator might put stakeholder identification in or near the evaluation questions (EQs; see Criterion 8). Who the stakeholders are and the role they play in the evaluation may be described. *Example* Yes, but only the students. There were 34 first-year college students (17 in a control group and 17 in experimental group).
8. Were the purpose and *evaluation questions* (EQs) stated?	EQs are statements of the purpose, reason, or rationale for doing the course or program evaluation. Without a clearly stated rationale it is difficult to interpret the study (Alderson, 1992). Typically course evaluation purpose and EQs are found in the short section near the end of the introduction with the word "purpose" or "intent." *Example* Yes, but more in terms of the project being a piece of research rather than a course evaluation. The purpose (p. 148) was to determine to what extent genre-based instruction and materials improved the learners' ability to produce effective tokens of the genre in their writing. The EQs were stated as three hypotheses: (a) Genre-based instruction will result in significant improvement to achieving communicative goals; (b) Genre-based instruction will improve the subjects' ability to produce texts that conform to the allowable structure; (c) Genre-based instruction will improve the subjects' ability to texture their writing. There was limited grounding of the intervention in the research literature which provided a research-based rationale, but no rationale was given for doing the evaluation itself. The authors/evaluators implied a connection from this course evaluation to other unnamed second language educators "teaching the writing of short tourist information texts in an EAP (English for Academic Purposes) context" (p. 148).

(continued)

TABLE 10.5 Annotated RAP for a Publication of an Evaluation Using Quantitative Data (continued)

*9. Was an *evaluation model* or theory used or mentioned?	An evaluation model is a theory that outlines the parameters or orientation of a course or program evaluation. For instance, is an evaluation for accountability purposes or to inform and illuminate details of how a course works (see House, 1993)? Without an evaluation model, teachers/evaluators lose focus on their work as evaluation and are more likely to revert to a research orientation. *Example* No.
10. Was a *research design* identified and used?	A research design is how data are linked to research purpose to show a causal relationship between one variable (using new materials or instruction, etc.) and another variable (students' scores on a test after using the new materials; Griffee, 2012). Identifying the research design helps guide readers to understand the evaluation by establishing expectations about what is being tested or investigated and how well then the research findings aid in assigning worth to a course or some aspect of a course. Knowing something about the research design also helps readers assess the research itself, and thus its utility to a course evaluation. For instance, if a quasi-experimental research design is used then we can assess how well the author/evaluator identified and operationalized all of the variables and threats to the ability of the research to establish causality. Sometimes an evaluation report will mention a recognized design, such as experimental, case, or action research. More often, enough components of a design are present to allow a reader to decide which design is being used. *Example* Yes, quasi-experimental.
11. Was it clear whether this was a field study or a lab study?	As defined by Beretta (1986b), field study is "long-term, classroom-based inquiry into the effects of complete programs" and laboratory research is "short-term and only involves the testing of individual components of a theory in an environment in which extraneous variables are artificially held constant" (p. 296). Beretta (1986b) argues this distinction is important, because lab studies are not related to the real world, that is, the world program evaluation inhabits. *Example* Yes, it was a field study taking place in two working classrooms.

(continued)

TABLE 10.5   Annotated RAP for a Publication of an Evaluation Using Quantitative Data (continued)

Data Collection and Analysis

12. Were *data collection instruments* (DCIs) identified and described?	Data collection instruments (DCIs) are any means by which data are collected including paper and pencil forms such as questionnaires, or mental representations such as interview questions held in the head of the evaluator. Readers need to know how the data were collected to understand the findings. DCIs should be directly related to the evaluation questions (EQs). DCIs that are adequately described (or even provided) are easier to analyze as sufficiently related to the EQs or not. As Lynch (1992) recommends, always have a clear reason for any data collected, and that clear reason is your EQ. Descriptions of DCIs may be found in a materials or procedure section of a report. *Example* Yes. Three instruments were used: (a) a short writing assignment to all students in both groups; (b) grades for motivation on a scale by untrained raters; and (c) a move score was calculated, and a texture index.
13. Were DCIs provided?	We want to see the actual data collection instrument, as description alone often fails to convey to readers what was done. DCIs are often found as appendices to a report. This may be a questionnaire, or an interview, or a test. *Example* No DCIs were included in the publication.
14. For each DCI was *reliability* discussed?	*Reliability* indicates the level to which a DCI can be trusted to measure something (ability to write coherent paragraphs in the second language, etc.) consistently. DCIs with high reliability are likely those that have been carefully thought out against a well-defined purpose, and have been piloted and perfected. An evaluation report should have a description of what a DCI is designed to capture, and how it was developed to do that. For tests or questionnaires resulting in quantitative data some kind of reliability coefficient should be given, which will have a range from .00 to .99 (the higher the coefficient, the more reliable the DCI is). For subjective ratings of students' writing or speaking samples, the author/evaluators should report reliability coefficients between two raters of the same sample. For interview or observation protocols resulting in qualitative data, the author/evaluators should describe the procedures that would demonstrate how disinterested others would reach similar interpretations of the data, such as an external audit.

(continued)

TABLE 10.5 Annotated RAP for a Publication of an Evaluation Using Quantitative Data (continued)

	Example To some extent. In the measures section, the three DCIs were described in detail in terms of what second language knowledge or skills they were supposed to capture that may speak to validation evidence (see Criterion 15). No piloting information was given. For instrument A (motivation), interrater reliability was used and a coefficient of .60 was given without comment (p. 153) but which to this reader seemed low. Two more DCIs (move score and texture index) seemed to be subjective measures requiring two or more raters, but no interrater reliability coefficients were given. Thus while the DCIs may be intricately designed they may not capture data consistently, meaning that in one course evaluation it may appear students are improving but in a second course evaluation the same or similar students may not appear to improve.
15. For each DCI was *validation evidence* provided?	Validation evidence is anything that supports the idea that a DCI functioned as intended, and captured some predetermined second language knowledge or skill. In some ways evidence for reliability overlaps with validation evidence. One example of validation evidence is a detailed description of how a DCI was designed and piloted; another example is data triangulation (Alderson, 1992, p. 285; Long, 2005b) where three or more DCIs are used to independently confirm some change in learners. *Example* To some extent. The three DCIs were used to examine related aspects of second language writing improvement (triangulation). The design of the measures were described in sufficient detail (measures) such that they appeared to be related to the specialized instruction given to the students (teaching materials and teaching method).
16. If courses or programs were compared, were the DCIs *program-fair?*	*Program-fair evaluation* is the notion that if two or more courses or programs are being compared, the DCI (for example a test) must be used on students in all courses or programs (Beretta, 1986c). In other words, if program A is compared to program B, any DCI must assess both programs equally. It would not be fair to say one program "worked" and another did not simply because the same DCI was not administered to learners in the second program. Thus it must be made clear that each course or program being compared was evaluated using the same or similar DCIs.

(continued)

TABLE 10.5 Annotated RAP for a Publication of an Evaluation Using Quantitative Data (continued)	
	Example Yes probably. The same three DCIs were administered to both an experimental (intervention) and control (nonintervention) group.
Quantitative Data Collection and Analysis	
17a. Was each *statistical procedure* identified?	We would like to know the name of each statistical procedure used in the course or program evaluation. This is the first step in understanding what analyses were done and why. *Example* Yes, on p. 152 the authors/evaluators stated that Wilcoxon matched pairs signed ranks tests were used on group comparisons on all three DCIs.
18a. Were *statistical assumptions* stated and addressed?	Statistical assumptions are the requirements of the statistical procedure. Each statistical procedure was designed with certain types of data and conditions in mind. "While these assumptions are not always tenable, they should be presented and discussed along with the analysis" (Lynch, 1992, p. 93). If we use statistics in an inappropriate way, we may get results that do not actually tell us anything, even though they may seem to. Key terms such as assumptions or requirements should be mentioned and their applications to a given statistical procedure should be discussed. *Example* Yes, the authors/evaluations mentioned on p. 152 that they wanted to compare pretest and posttest scores on the DCIs on the same learners and that they knew the scores would have a non-normal distribution. Thus the statistical assumptions were met for the nonparametric Wilcoxon matched pairs signed ranks tests.
19a. Was there *statistical clarity*?	Statistical clarity means that the authors/evaluators stated in plain terms why the statistical procedure was used. Statistical clarity also means that each statistical procedure is explicitly related to an evaluation question (EQ). Look for wording like: "X procedure was used to establish W [whatever]. If Y [for example, a *p-value* at .05] is achieved, that would support EQ [number], in that [continue explanation]." *Example* Somewhat. In a statistical treatment section, the authors/evaluators made it clear which statistical procedures were used, but not directly what they were for. The relationship between the statistical procedure and its purpose was assumed rather than stated. While the

(continued)

TABLE 10.5 Annotated RAP for a Publication of an Evaluation Using Quantitative Data (continued)

	three EQs were stated in a different section, the statistical procedures were not related directly to the EQs.
20a. Was a *p-value* given? At what level was it set?	A *p-value* is the probability of demonstrating some relationship between two sets of scores or other quantitative results, given the null hypothesis (the predetermined assumption of "no change" or "no relationship"). A *p-value* is provided by most statistical software programs when doing a *statistical procedure* such as a *t*-test or ANOVA, or correlation. A *p*-value is a *cut point* the author/evaluator chooses beforehand that indicates the likelihood of some relationship between two sets of numbers as due to random chance. *P-values* are often set at .05 (suggesting there is only a 5% chance that some relationship between two sets of scores could be due to random chance). When the previous statistical procedure results in a *p-value*, for instance, .06 or .10, then the author/evaluator failed to meet the cut point and thus cannot claim that their finding is anything more than random chance or a "ghost in the numbers." Evaluation reports using quantitative data and statistical procedures need report a preset *p-value* along with a brief explanation as to why that *p-value* if differs from the largely accepted .05 (such as .025, etc.). *Example* Yes, authors reported a *p*-level set at .025 for one set of comparisons (Table 10.1) but did not explain why. .05 was set for another set of comparisons (Table 10.2). In both cases, the authors/evaluators were unable to reject the null hypothesis on some of their statistical procedures and so stated that.
21a. Was an indicator of practical significance such as *effect size* reported?	Effect size is a measure of practical significance. It indicates a difference in outcome, such as that between a group who received a treatment and a group who did not. *P-values* may seem to show that but do not. Rather *p*-values are a first step, yes/no type of decision to demonstrate that some difference between groups is not accidental. An effect size shows how important the difference is as in "effect size is the degree to which the null hypothesis is false" (Vogt, 1999, p. 94). Effect sizes range from .00 to .99, and the larger the number the greater the effect size. An effect size of .60 is quite large and suggests that 60% of the difference in scores can be explained by group membership ("got the treatment" versus "did not get the treatment"). The author/evaluator should provide an effect size and interpret it for readers.

(continued)

TABLE 10.5 Annotated RAP for a Publication of an Evaluation Using Quantitative Data (continued)

	Example No effect size was reported for the comparisons portrayed in Tables 10.1 and 10.2. Without an effect size we cannot judge how important the differences between the pretest and posttest, and genre and nongenre groups are. For example, for the motivation index, the difference between the genre group pretest (5.14) and the posttest (6.29) was 1.15 with a p-value of .002. A low p-value tells us that the difference is not the result of random chance, but is only an indication that "yes" this result is not an accident. If we could see an effect size of .50 or more, however, then we might claim that the difference between the pretest and posttest scores was meaningful and that some really did change within the students (perhaps due to the treatment).
Qualitative Data Collection and Analysis	
17b. Could you follow the sequences of how the data were collected and analyzed?	
18b. Was the author's role and status within the site explicitly described?	
19b. Were any forms of *peer review* used?	
20b. Were *areas of uncertainty* identified?	
21b. Was *negative evidence* sought, found, and reported?	
Evaluation Results	
*22. Were the *evaluation questions* (EQs) answered in a clear way?	We are looking for a specific answer to each EQ. In a results section look for a specific reference an EQ and some answer stating "yes" or "no," or "this study found that..." or "the results suggest that..." *Example* Yes. In a results section the authors/evaluators referenced their hypotheses and stated "all null hypotheses of no difference were rejected for these measures" (p. 153). They also offered a more concrete interpretation: "this level of significance does indicate a trend towards producing texts that conform more closely to the allowable move structure" (p. 153).

(continued)

TABLE 10.5   Annotated RAP for a Publication of an Evaluation Using Quantitative Data (continued)

*23. Were policy and/or pedagogical recommendations given?	Course or program publications should state clearly the recommendations based on the results. This criterion is unique to evaluation in that the purpose of doing an evaluation is to solve problems specific to a course or program. Evaluation is applied research (Beretta, 1986a) that must encounter the world of the plausible rather than the world of the possible. Research publications generally differ in that many authors simply conclude some finding is possible, that there may be some pedagogical implications in a general sense, and that more research is necessary.
	Example No policy or pedagogical recommendations were given. Rather, the findings were presented as research findings in terms of hypotheses to be accepted or rejected based on mean scores and p-values.
Strengths	We think readers can use this template to identify the strengths (or usefulness) of an evaluation publication for their own purposes, such as planning their own course evaluation The ultimate aim of assessing evaluation publications is not to pick apart the evaluation or research of another author, but rather to identify applicable or useful parts of an evaluation or research publication, and to better learn key elements of the genre of evaluation publications.
	Example We think the strengths of this publication were the use of multiple DCIs (data collection instruments; Criterion 12), and the use of appropriate statistical procedures for the data (Criteria 17a, 18a, 20a). The participants were described in detail (Criterion 4), and the instruction was described (Criterion 5). This was applied research (Criterion 11) that took place in working classrooms.
Weaknesses	We think readers can use this template to identify the weaknesses (or areas of less usefulness) of an evaluation publication from their own purposes, such as planning their own course evaluation. The aim here is to build up knowledge of what to avoid or improve on, and of course, better learn key elements of the genre of course or program publications.
	Example It was not clear if this publication was course evaluation or research thrown out into a decontextualized and unidentified world of purpose. On p. 148 the authors stated that "few if any attempts have been made to evaluate the approach" implying that the study was an

(continued)

TABLE 10.5 Annotated RAP for a Publication of an Evaluation Using Quantitative Data (continued)	
	evaluation. But on p. 155 the authors called for further research suggesting they may have seen their work as research, not evaluation. Further, no evaluation theory was given. The authors reported a low reliability coefficient between raters of $r = .60$ and did not report an effect size so we are left in doubt about the validity of their findings. No policy or pedagogical recommendations were provided.
Citations in the Reference List of the Publication Were any articles or other publications in the reference list of interest to you? List here. Use the list to request or retrieve the publications.	The best way to build up our library of citations (publications) relevant to our work as teachers/ evaluators is to "mine" the reference lists of publications we read. Do not avoid publications that seem "old" such as those published in the 1980s or 1990s. Old is not a logical, nor useful, assessment criterion for course or program evaluation publications. *Example* Two citations in the authors' reference list are of interest if one wants to know more about piloting genre-based writing modules, and adapting the authors' "texture index"(one of the DCIs used in the current publication) to use in one's own evaluation: Bhatia, V.K. (1993). *Analysing genre: Language use in professional settings.* London, England: Longman. Roseberry, R.L. (1995). A texture index: Measuring texture in discourse. *International Journal of Applied Linguistics, 5*, 205–223.
Bottom line: What did you learn about evaluation?	*Example* Without a needs analysis (NA), an evaluation theory, or policy or pedagogical recommendations, it was difficult to know if this publication was evaluation or research. We think writing this paper as a course evaluation would have made this publication more focused and relevant.

[*] Indicates that the criterion is considered necessary and unique for course or program evaluation.

TABLE 10.6   Annotated RAP for a Publication of an Evaluation Using Qualitative Data

Publication citation (authors, year, journal name, etc.)	*Example* Pawan, F. & Thomalla, T. G. (2005). Making the invisible visible: A responsive evaluation study of ESL and Spanish language services for immigrants in a small rural county in Indiana. *TESOL Quarterly 39*(4), 683–705.
Short summary of publication	*Example* The authors/evaluators were contacted by County Alliance for Community Education (CACE) in a rural county in Indiana (RCI) to do a *program evaluation* of current services provided to Spanish-speaking immigrants and to advise on possible changes. The authors/evaluators selected an evaluation model (Stake's responsive model; Stake, 1975) because it emphasizes interaction between evaluators and stakeholders. Interviews and other data were gathered (visits, observations of activities, analysis of documents in location). Two meetings were held with stakeholders to report results and clarify issues. Short-range and long-range policy recommendations were made.
Basic Description	
1. Were course or program *goals* or *outcomes* discussed or analyzed?	*Example* The program goals of CACE (who asked for the evaluation) were not explicitly stated, but on p. 684 the authors implied that CACE was concerned with "ESL services for immigrants and Spanish language services for service providers" and that such services be sufficient so as to avoid the immigrant group from being "underserved."
*2. Was a *needs analysis* provided, discussed, or even mentioned?	*Example* No needs analysis was explicitly mentioned, but an extensive consultation with stakeholders was reported. On p. 684, stakeholder CACE "saw a pressing need to evaluate ESL services for immigrants and Spanish language services for service providers." This concern was the justification for the evaluation. Another formulation of a need was a discussion of declining overall English-speaking resident populations, but increasing Spanish-speaking immigrant populations in rural counties in Indiana: "RCI will be a part of the trend and understands that it needs to be prepared" (p. 684).
3. What was the duration of the course? What was the duration of the evaluation?	*Example* There was no discussion of the duration of the program, nor of the evaluation.

(continued)

TABLE 10.6 Annotated RAP for a Publication of an Evaluation Using Qualitative Data (continued)

4. Were course or program participants described?	*Example* A general description of translators and students (both Mexican and American workers) were given. The existence of teachers was implied, but they were not described.
5. Were types of instruction in the course or program identified?	*Example* English- and Spanish-language services were described in Table 3 (p. 693) and also on p. 692. Specific types of instruction in English- and Spanish-language classes were not described.
6. Was it clear whether all or part of the course or program was evaluated?	*Example* Yes. All services were evaluated.
Purpose of the Evaluation	
*7. Were *stakeholders* identified?	*Example* Yes, on pp. 686, 688, and 689. The Spanish speakers/workers were largely from Mexico. Other stakeholders/interviewees were identified, but not described in detail.
8. Were the purpose and *evaluation questions* (EQs) stated?	*Example* The purpose was stated as "Immigrant trends in Indiana and the economic impact of these trends have on the state as a whole have resulted in an increasing number of calls for studies that investigate and evaluate language services rendered to meet the new immigrants' needs" (p. 685). Two EQs were stated on p. 685: What language services are currently offered to assist immigrants? What changes should be made?
*9. Was an *evaluation model* or theory used or mentioned?	*Example* Yes. Stake's (1975) responsive evaluation model was mentioned and reasons for its selection were given (pp. 685-686). This model was important for the evaluation in that it propelled the authors/evaluators to use "stakeholders' issues as conceptual organizers for inquiry in the evaluation" (p. 685). This became a way to plan who to interview and what issues to explore. To help organize their report, the authors/evaluators used a SWOT model (strengths, weaknesses, opportunities, and threats). No attribution was given for SWOT in the publication.
10. Was a *research design* identified and used?	*Example* Yes. Action research was identified on pp. 686 and 691, and mentioned briefly in the limitations of the study on p. 701, but it was not clear how the evaluation model (Stake's model) was seen to be overlapping with

(continued)

TABLE 10.6 Annotated RAP for a Publication of an Evaluation Using Qualitative Data (continued)

	A sampling method was described on p. 687. Figure 1 on p. 687 seemed to illustrate the evaluation model and sampling method but could also be taken as a research method (action research).
11. Was it clear whether this was a field study or a lab study?	*Example* Yes. It was a field study carried out in the offices and other locations where the stakeholders worked or did business.
Data Collection and Analysis	
12. Were *data collection instruments* (DCIs) identified and described?	*Example* Yes on pp. 689–690, interviews, visits, observations of activities, and analysis of documents in location were described in general terms.
13. Were DCIs provided?	*Example* For interviews, yes. Three questions were asked to the CACE stakeholders and two questions were asked to the immigrant participants on pp. 689–690. Protocols for visits, observations of activities, and analyses of documents were not made available.
14. For each DCI was *reliability* discussed?	*Example* Yes, on p. 690 triangulation as a reliability strategy was discussed: Redundancy of data increases "stability and consistency of information collected."
15. For each DCI was *validation evidence* provided?	*Example* Validation evidence was offered for interviews (members check, p. 691), but none for other DCIs.
16. If courses or programs were compared, were the DCIs *program-fair?*	*Example* Programs were not compared so this criterion is not applicable.
Quantitative Data Collection and Analysis	
17a. Was each *statistical procedure* identified?	
18a. Were *statistical assumptions* stated and addressed?	
19a. Was there *statistical clarity?*	
20a. Was a p-*value* given? At what level was it set?	
21a. Was an indicator of *practical significance* such as *effect size* reported?	

(continued)

TABLE 10.6   Annotated RAP for a Publication of an Evaluation Using Qualitative Data (continued)

Qualitative Data Collection and Analysis

17b. Could you follow the sequences of how the data were collected and analyzed?	When working with qualitative data, it is key that a reader can follow the sequences of how data were collected, processed, transformed, and displayed for specific conclusion drawing (Miles & Huberman, 1994, p. 277). This quality is "confirmability" and is concerned with assuring that data, interpretations, and outcomes of inquiries are rooted in contexts and persons apart from the evaluator, and are not simply figments of the evaluator's imagination (Guba & Lincoln, 1989, p. 242). According to this point of view, the integrity of the findings is rooted in the data themselves, and not in the method. Look for descriptions of procedures for data collection, processing, transformation (such as converting learner comments into frequencies or categories), and display.
	Example
	Somewhat. This publication was more informative about the interview data collection process than it was about the other methods of data collection. From pp. 687–690 the authors/evaluators described collecting the interview data, noting that based on the results "we then established standards for evaluation" (p. 689). Descriptions of how data were processed or transformed were not given other than to report "the evaluators used the standards . . . to elicit and organize information from interviewees" (p. 692). It was not clear how the authors chose to display their interview results on p. 693 (Table 3).
18b. Was the author's role and status within the site explicitly described?	According to LeCompte and Goetz (1982, p. 38), researchers "must clearly identify the researchers' role and status within the group being investigated." This is important because of social roles and interactions of researchers and informants (stakeholders in this case). The role of the researcher may affect what questions they ask of whom, and what answers stakeholders may be comfortable giving. Thus "interviews [and other forms of social contacts providing data] may be more reflective of the social relationship between interviewer and informant, than they are of any personal reality the informant may want to express" (Gorsuch, 2002, p. 33).
	Example
	Yes, the authors/evaluators described the role on p. 685, and again throughout the study, for example on p. 686 discussing their meetings with stakeholders. The authors took as their model Stake (1975) in noting that

(continued)

TABLE 10.6 Annotated RAP for a Publication of an Evaluation Using Qualitative Data (continued)

	"responsive evaluators' roles are thus not to straighten out stakeholders' thinking or their values, but to help stakeholders make decisions most relevant to their needs" (Pawan & Thomalla, 2005, p. 686).
19b. Were any forms of *peer review* used?	Peer review means a process where a person with sufficient knowledge to understand the evaluation, but who is also not directly involved, reviews your data (Miles & Huberman, 1994, p. 277). A peer reviewer can be asked: Can you trace a path from my raw data to my conclusions? Are my conclusions plausible? Can you think of alternative conclusions? Do you think my conclusions are not only plausible, but correct? *Example* Somewhat. The authors did a "member check" where they asked stakeholders to read their own interview transcripts "to check for any misrepresentation" (p. 691). On p. 695 the authors also noted "the researchers and stakeholders jointly conducted a SWOT analysis of language services" suggesting that stakeholders were involved in data analysis at some point.
20b. Were *areas of uncertainty* identified?	Credibility is parallel to internal validity (Guba & Lincoln, 1989, p. 236). It means answering the question: Is what the stakeholders think is going on the same as what the author/evaluator thinks is going on? *Example* Yes, the authors/evaluators had a lengthy discussion of "Limitations of the Study" (pp. 700–701), and noted that in separate interviews with "immigrant worker and family members" (stakeholders) they found much similarity between their findings and the perceptions of the stakeholders. At the same time they admitted that some stakeholders might not have said everything they wished to say because they were contacted through their place of work and may have feared losing their jobs (p. 701).
21b. Was *negative evidence* sought, found, and reported?	Negative evidence is data that might disconfirm a key assertion (Miles & Huberman, 1994, p. 277). "If the researcher lacks evidence that a deliberate search was made for potentially disconfirming data while in the field setting, this weakens the plausibility of the conclusions and leaves the researcher liable to charges of seeking only evidence that would support favorite interpretations" (Erickson, 1986, p. 140). *Example* Yes. The SWOT analysis (p. 691) provided an opportunity for authors/evaluators to identify negative

(continued)

TABLE 10.6 Annotated RAP for a Publication of an Evaluation Using Qualitative Data (continued)

	evidence for their descriptions of the language services offered by the hosting agency.
Evaluation Results	
*22. Were the *evaluation questions* (EQs) answered in a clear way?	*Example* Yes and no. EQ1 is answered on p. 692, but authors do not use language to explicitly tell readers they are answering their EQ ("The answer to EQ1 is…" or "To answer the first question we found that…").
*23. Were policy and/ or pedagogical recommendations given?	*Example* Yes. Multiple recommendations were given on pp. 699–700 in a "Recommendations" section.
Strengths	*Example* They included (a) the mention of an evaluation model that apparently guided the evaluation (Criterion 9), and (b) detailed descriptions of the extensive interactions with stakeholders including interviews with the immigrants (Criteria 12, 13, 15) and (c) long-term and short-term policy recommendations (Criterion 23).
Weaknesses	*Example* They included (a) Other than interviews, data sources were not described (Criteria 12, 13, 15), (b) The action research design was not clearly identified and documented (Criterion 10), and (c) Answers to the EQs (called research questions in this publication) were not identified clearly (Criterion 22).
Citations in the Reference List of the Publication Were any articles or other publications in the reference list of interest to you? List here. Use the list to request or retrieve the publications.	*Example* Two citations in the authors' reference list are of interest if one wants to know more about a responsive evaluation model: Curran, V., Christopher, J., Lemire, F., Collins, A., & Barret, B. (2003, March). Application of responsive evaluation in medical education. *Medical Education, 37*(3), 256–266. Green, J. C., & Amba, T. A. (Eds.). (2001). *Responsive evaluation: New directions for evaluation, no. 92.* San Francisco, CA: Jossey-Bass. One citation is of interest if one wants to know what sorts of documents should be read to build up an argument for an evaluation purpose: Johnson-Webb, K. D. (2001). Midwest rural communities in transition: Hispanic immigration. *Rural Development News, 25*(1). Ames, IA: North Central Regional Center for Rural Development.

(continued)

TABLE 10.6 Annotated RAP for a Publication of an Evaluation Using Qualitative Data (continued)	
Bottom line: What did you learn about evaluation?	*Example* It is hard to write a clear course or program evaluation report. Because we deal with large amounts of information from multiple stakeholders we can sometimes write without clearly identifying our topic. This can inhibit our readers from understanding what we are doing.

* Indicates that the criterion is considered necessary and unique for course or program evaluation.

APPLICATION TASKS: Asking and Answering Questions About RAPs, Retrieving Articles, and Completing a RAP

First task idea: With colleagues or classmates, go through the annotated RAPs and create a list of questions on topics or concepts in the RAPs you are uncertain about. You can either find the answers together in the glossary (or from a senior colleague or graduate course instructor), or decide on a plan of action to get further information to answer your questions.

Second task idea: To check your own understanding of the articles used in the previous annotated RAPs, retrieve the two articles (Henry & Roseberry, 1998; Pawan & Thomalla, 2005). Read through them, and in terms of the criteria in the RAPs add any notes or revisions needed to the annotations. In other words, add your own understandings and knowledge to the annotations.

Third task idea: Find a publication that you believe portrays a course or program evaluation, or a needs analysis and complete the appropriate RAP using the templates given previously. You will get better at this the more times you try it! It helps to present the publication using the criteria in a RAP during a regular working teachers' meeting or a graduate class you might be taking. Most professionals welcome knowing about a publication that may directly help them, particularly if a colleague "digests" it for them.

References

Alderson, J. C. (1992). Guidelines for the evaluation of language education. In J. C. Alderson & A. Beretta (Eds.), *Evaluating second language education* (pp. 274–304). Cambridge, England: Cambridge University Press.

Alderson, J. C., & Beretta, A. (1992). (Eds.). *Evaluating second language education* (pp. 274–304). Cambridge, England: Cambridge University Press.

Beretta, A. (1986a). Toward a methodology of ESL program evaluation. *TESOL Quarterly, 20*(1), 144–155.

Beretta, A. (1986b). A case for field-experimentation in program evaluation. *Language Learning, 36*(3), 295–309.

Beretta, A. (1986c). Program-fair language teaching evaluation. *TESOL Quarterly, 20*(3), 431–445.

Beretta, A. (1990). The program evaluator: The ESL researcher without portfolio. *Applied Linguistics, 11*(1), 1–15.

Beretta, A. (1992). Evaluation of language education: An overview. In J. C. Alderson & A. Beretta (Eds.), *Evaluating second language education* (pp. 5–24). Cambridge, England: Cambridge University Press.

Brown, J. D. (1989). Language program evaluation: A synthesis of existing possibilities. In R. K. Johnson (Ed.), *The second language curriculum* (pp. 222–241). Cambridge, England: Cambridge University Press.

Brown, J. D. (1995). *The elements of language curriculum.* Boston, MA: Heinle & Heinle.

Bruning, R., Flowerday, T., & Trayer, M. (1999). Developing foreign language frameworks: An evaluation study. *Foreign Language Annals, 32*(2), 159–171.

Erickson, F. (1986). Qualitative methods in research on teaching. In M. Wittrock (Ed.), *Handbook on research and teaching* (pp. 119–161). New York, NY: MacMillan.

Gorsuch, G. (2002). Making art out of fragments: An accessible vision? *Asia Pacific Journal of Language in Education, 5*(1), 29–36.

Griffee, D. T. (2012). *An introduction to second language research methods: Design and data.* Retrieved from http://www.tesl-ej.org/wordpress/

Guba, E. G., & Lincoln, Y. S. (1989). *Fourth generation evaluation.* Newbury Park, CA: Sage.

Henry, A., & Roseberry, R. L. (1998). An evaluation of a genre-based approach to the teaching of EAP/ESP writing. *TESOL Quarterly, 32*(1), 147–156.

House, E. (1993). *Professional evaluation: Social impact and political consequences.* Newbury Park, CA: Sage.

Jasso-Aguilar, R. (2005). Sources, methods and triangulation in needs analysis: A critical perspective in a case study of Waikiki hotel maids. In M. Long (Ed.), *Second language needs analysis* (pp. 127–169). Cambridge, England: Cambridge University Press.

LeCompte, M. D., & Goetz, J. P. (1982). Problems of reliability and validity in ethnographic research. *Review of Educational Research, 52*(1), 31–60.

Long, M. H. (2005a). *Second language needs analysis.* Cambridge, England: Cambridge University Press.

Long, M. H. (2005b). Methodological issues in learner needs analysis. In M. H. Long (Ed.), *Second language needs analysis* (pp. 19–76). Cambridge, England: Cambridge University Press.

Lynch, B. (1992). Evaluating a program inside and out. In J. C. Alderson & A. Beretta (Eds.), *Evaluating second language education* (pp. 61–99). Cambridge, England: Cambridge University Press.

Miles, M. B., & Huberman, A. M. (1994). *Qualitative data analysis* (2nd ed.). Thousand Oaks, CA: Sage.

Norris, J., & Ortega, L. (Eds.). (2006). *Synthesizing research on language learning and teaching.* Philadelphia, PA: John Benjamins.

Nunan, D. (1988). *Syllabus design.* Oxford, England: Oxford University Press.

Pawan, F., & Thomalla, T. G. (2005). Making the invisible visible: A responsive evaluation study of ESL and Spanish language services for immigrants in a small rural county in Indiana. *TESOL Quarterly 39*(4), 683–705.

Richards, J. C. (2001). *Curriculum development in language teaching.* Cambridge, England: Cambridge University Press.

Roseberry, R.L. (1995). A texture index: Measuring texture in discourse. *International Journal of Applied Linguistics, 5,* 205–223.

Stake, R. (1975). *Evaluating the arts in education.* Columbus, OH: Charles E. Merrill.

Vogt, W. P. (1999). *Dictionary of statistics & methodology* (2nd ed.). Thousand Oaks, CA: Sage.

APPENDIX $\overline{\underline{A}}$

A Bibliography of *Evaluation*

Adair-Hauck, B., Willingham-McLain., L., & Youngs, B., (1999) Evaluating the integration of technology and second language learning. *CALICO Journal 17*(2).

Alderson, J. C., & Beretta, A. (Eds.). (1992). *Evaluating second language education*. Cambridge, England: Cambridge University Press.

Antón, M. (2009). Dynamic assessment of advanced second language learners. *Foreign Language Annals, 42*(3), 576–598.

Arnold, N. (2009). Online extensive reading for advanced foreign language learners: An evaluation study. *Foreign Language Annals, 42*(2), 340–366.

Bacha, N. (2001). Writing evaluation: What can analytic versus holistic essay scoring tell us? *System, 29*(3), 371–383.

Baniabdelrahman, A. A. (2010). The effect of the use of self-assessment on EFL students' performance in reading comprehension in English. *TESL-EJ, 14*(2). Retrieved from http://www.tesl-ej.org/wordpress/issues/volume14/ej54/ej54a2/

Barkaoui, K. (2010). Do ESL essay raters' evaluation criteria change with experience? A mixed-methods, cross-sectional study. *TESOL Quarterly, 44*(1), 31–57.

Barrette, C. (2004). Assessment, testing, and evaluation: An analysis of foreign language achievement test drafts. *Foreign Language Annals, 37*(1), 58.

Evaluating Second Language Courses, pages 243–250
Copyright © 2016 by Information Age Publishing
All rights of reproduction in any form reserved.

Beretta, A. (1990). Implementation of the Bangalore project. *Applied Linguistics, 11*, 321–327.

Beretta, A. (1992). What can be learned from the Bangalore evaluation. In J. C. Alderson & A. Beretta (Eds.), *Evaluating second language education* (pp. 250–273). Cambridge, England: Cambridge University Press.

Beretta, A., & Davies, A. (1985). Evaluation of the Bangalore project. *English Language Teaching Journal, 39*(2), 121–127.

Blyth, C., & Davis, J. (2007). Using formative evaluation in the development of learner-centered materials. *CALICO Journal, 25*(1), 48–68.

Brandl, K. K. (2000). Foreign language TAs' perceptions of training components: Do we know how they like to be trained? *The Modern Language Journal, 84*, 355–371.

Brindley, G. (1998). Outcomes-based assessment and reporting in language programs: A review of the issues. *Language Testing, 15*(1), 45–85.

Brindley, G. (2001). Outcomes-based assessment in practice: Some examples and insights. *Language Testing, 18*(4), 393–407.

Bruning, R., Flowerday, T., & Trayer, M. (1999). Developing foreign language frameworks: An evaluation study. *Foreign Language Annals, 32,* 159–171.

Burstein, L., & Guiton, G. W. (1984). Methodological perspectives on documenting program impact. *Advances in Special Education, 4,* 21–42.

Burton, J. (1998). A cross-case analysis of teacher involvement in TESOL research. *TESOL Quarterly, 32*(3), 419–446.

Camhi, P. J., & Ebsworth, M. E. (2008). Merging a metalinguistic grammar approach with L2 academic process writing: ELLs in community college. *TESL-EJ, 12*(2). Retrieved from http://www.tesl-ej.org/wordpress/issues/volume12/ej46/ej46a1/

Chuo, T-W. I. (2007). The effects of the WebQuest writing instruction program on EFL learners' writing performance, writing apprehension, and perception. *TESL-EJ, 11*(3). Retrieved from http://www.tesl-ej.org/wordpress/issues/volume11/ej43/ej43a3/

Coleman, H. (1992). Moving the goalposts: Project evaluation in practice. In J. C. Alderson & A. Beretta (Eds.), *Evaluating second language education* (pp. 222–249). Cambridge, England: Cambridge University Press.

Collins, L., Halter, R., Lightbown, P., & Spada, N. (1999). Time and the distribution of time in L2 instruction. *TESOL Quarterly, 33*(4), 655–680.

Crandall, E., & Basturkmen, H. (2004). Evaluating pragmatics-focused materials. *ELT Journal, 58*(1), 38–49.

Datnow, A. (2000). Power and politics in the adoption of school reform models. *Educational Evaluation and Policy Analysis, 22*(4), 357–374.

Davies, P. (2009). Strategic management of ELT in public educational systems: Trying to reduce failure, increase success. *TESL-EJ, 13*(3). Retrieved from http://www.tesl-ej.org/wordpress/issues/volume13/ej51/ej51a2/

Dheram, P., & Rani, N. (2008). From experience to learning: An appraisal of the questionnaire and workshop as research methods in ESL. *TESL-EJ, 12*(3).

Retrieved from http://www.tesl-ej.org/wordpress/issues/volume12/ej47/ej47a5/

Dushku, S. (1998). ELT in Albania: Project evaluation and change. *System, 26*(3), 369–388.

Ellis, R. (1998). Evaluating and researching grammar consciousness-raising tasks. In P. Rea-Dickins & K. Germaine, *Managing evaluation and innovation in language teaching* (pp. 220–252). New York, NY: Addison Wesley Longman.

Ellwood, C., & Nakane, I. (2009). Privileging of speech in EAP and mainstream university classrooms: A critical evaluation of participation. *TESOL Quarterly, 43*(2), 203–230.

Edstrom, A. (2006). L1 use in the L2 classroom: One teacher's self-evaluation. *The Canadian Modern Language Review, 63*(2), 275–292.

Elder, C. (2009) Reconciling accountability and development needs in heritage language education: A communication challenge for the evaluation consultant. *Language Teaching Research, 13*(1), 15–33.

Fan, M., & Xunfeng, X. (2002). An evaluation of an online bilingual corpus for the self-learning of legal English. *System, 30*(1), 47–63.

Fattash, M. (2010). Congruity or disparity: Teachers' assessment of the new Palestinian English language school curriculum. *TESOL Journal, 2*, 189–206.

Fenton-Smith, B., & Torpey, M.J. (2013). Orienting EFL teachers: Principles arising from an evaluation of an induction program in a Japanese university. *Language Teaching Research, 17*(2), 228–250.

Fisher, D., & Frey, N., (2010). Unpacking the language purpose: Vocabulary, structure, and function. *TESOL Journal, 1*(3), 315–337.

Garrett, P., & Shortall, T. (2002) Learners' evaluations of teacher-fronted and student-centered classroom activities. *Language Teaching Research, 6*(1), 25–57.

Garza, T., (1991). Evaluating the use of captioned video materials in advanced foreign language learning. *Foreign Language Annals, 24*(3), 239–258.

Gascoigne, C. (2004). Assessment, testing, and evaluation: Examining the effect of feedback in beginning L2 composition. *Foreign Language Annals, 37*(1), 71.

Griffee, D. T. (1993). Textbook and authentic dialogues: What's the difference? *The Language Teacher, 27*(10), 25–33.

Griffee, D. T. (2002). Portfolio assessment: Increasing reliability and validity. *The Learning Assistance Review, 7*(2), 5–17.

Griffee, D. T., & Gevara, J. R. (2011). Standard setting in the post-modern era for an ITA performance test. *Texas Papers in Foreign Language Education, 15*(1), 3–16. Retrieved from http://studentorgs.utexas.edu/flesa/TP-FLE_New/Index.htm

Griffee, D. T., Gorsuch, G.J, Britton, D., & Clardy, C. (2009). Intensive second language instruction for international teaching assistants: How much is effective? In G. Ollington (Ed.), *Teachers and teaching: Strategies, innovations and problem solving* (pp. 187–205). Hauppage, NY: Nova Science.

Gorsuch, G. (2009). Investigating second language learner self-efficacy and future expectancy of second language use for high-stakes program evaluation. *Foreign Language Annals, 42*(3), 505–540.

Gorsuch, G., & Sokolowski, J. A. (2007). International teaching assistants and summative and formative student evaluation. *Journal of Faculty Development, 21*(2), 117–136.

Gottlieb, M. (2006). *Assessing English language learners: Bridges from language proficiency to academic achievement.* Thousand Oaks, CA: Corwin.

Gray, S. (2012). From principles to practice: Collegial observation for teacher development. *TESOL Journal, 3*(2), 231–255.

Harris, J. (2009) Late-stage refocusing of Irish-language programme evaluation: Maximizing the potential for productive debate and remediation. *Language Teaching Research, 13*(1), 55–76.

Henning, G. (1982). Growth-referenced evaluation of foreign language instructional programs. *TESOL Quarterly, 16*(4), 467–477.

Henry, A., & Roseberry, R. (1998). An evaluation of a genre-based approach to the teaching of EAP/ESP writing. *TESOL Quarterly, 32*(1), 147–156.

Hussin, H. (2006). Dimensions of questioning: A qualitative study of current classroom practice in Malaysia. *TESL-EJ, 10*(2). Retrieved from http://www.tesl-ej.org/wordpress/issues/volume10/ej38/ej38a3/

Ishihara, N. (2009). Teacher-based assessment for foreign language pragmatics. *TESOL Journal, 43*(3), 445–470.

Jacques, S., Combs, M., McMurray, M., Awwad, R., Loomis, R., & Suffi, K. (2009). *Self-study report for commission on English language programs accreditation.* Retrieved from http://www.auk.edu.kw/iep/accreditation/accr_ss_report_intro.pdf

Jamieson, J., Chapelle, C., & Preiss, S. (2005). CALL evaluation by developers, a teacher, and students. *CALICO Journal, 23*(1), 93–138.

Johnson, K., Kim, M., Ya-Fang, L., et al. (2008). A step forward: Investigating expertise in materials evaluation. *ELT Journal, 62*(2), 157–163.

Johnson, R. K. (Ed.). (1989). *The second language curriculum.* Cambridge, England: Cambridge University Press.

Kamhi-Stein, L. (2000). Looking to the future of TESOL teacher education: Web-based bulletin board discussions in a methods course. *TESOL Quarterly, 34*(3), 423–455.

Kato, F. (2009) Student preferences: Goal-setting and self-assessment activities in a tertiary education environment. *Language Teaching Research, 13*(2), 177–199.

Kennedy, C. (1988). Evaluation of the management of change in ELT projects. *Applied Linguistics, 9*(4), 329–342. doi: 10.1093/applin/9.4.329

Kiely, R. (2001) Classroom evaluation: Values, interests and teacher development. *Language Teaching Research, 5*(3), 241–261.

Kiely, R. (2006) Evaluation, innovation, and ownership in language programs. *The Modern Language Journal, 90,* 597–601.

Kiely, R. (2009) Small answers to the big question: Learning from language programme evaluation. *Language Teaching Research, 13*(1), 99–116.

Kiely, R., & Askham, J. (2012). Furnished imagination: The impact of preservice teacher training on early career work in TESOL. *TESOL Quarterly, 46*(3), 496–581.

Kubanyiova, M. (2006). Developing a motivational teaching practice in EFL teachers in Slovakia: Challenges of promoting teacher change in EFL contexts. *TESL-EJ, 10*(2). Retrieved from http://www.tesl-ej.org/wordpress/issues/volume10/ej38/ej38a5/

Leshem, S., & Bar-Hama, R. (2008). Evaluating teaching practice. *ELT Journal, 62*(3), 257–265.

Lewkowicz, J., & Nunan, D. (1999). The limits of collaborative evaluation. *TESOL Quarterly, 33*(4), 681–700.

Llosa, L., & Slayton, J. (2009) Using program evaluation to inform and improve the education of young English language learners in U.S. schools. *Language Teaching Research, 13*(1), 35–54.

Long, M. H. (1984). Process and product in ESL program evaluation. *TESOL Quarterly, 18*(3), 409–425.

Long, M. H. (2005). *Second language needs analysis.* Cambridge, England: Cambridge University Press.

Lorenzo, F., Casal, S., & Moore, P. (2010). The effects of content and language integrated learning in European education: Key findings from the Andalusian bilingual sections evaluation project. *Applied Linguistics, 31*(3), 418–442. doi: 10.1093/applin/amp041

Lozano, A. S., Hyekyung, S., Padilla, A. M., & Silva, D. M. (2002). Evaluation of professional development for language teachers in California. *Foreign Language Annals, 35,* 161–170.

Lynch, B. (1992). Evaluating a program inside and out. In J. C. Alderson & A. Beretta (Eds.), *Evaluating second language education* (pp. 61–99). Cambridge, England: Cambridge University Press.

Lynch, B. (1996). The role of program evaluation in applied linguistics research. *Issues in Applied Linguistics, 2*(1), 84–86.

Machado de Almeida Mattos, A. (2000). A Vygotskian approach to evaluation in foreign language learning contexts. *ELT Journal, 54*(4), 335–346.

Madyarov, I. (2016). Designing a workable framework for evaluating distance language education. *CALICO Journal, 26*(2), 290–308.

Maftoon, P., Moghaddam, M. Y., Gholebostan, H., & Beh-Afarin, S. R. (2010). Privatization of English education in Iran: A feasibility study. *TESL-EJ, 13*(4). Retrieved from http://www.tesl-ej.org/wordpress/issues/volume13/ej52/ej52a8/

Martin, W. M., & Lomperis, A. E. (2002). Determining the cost benefit, the return on investment, and the intangible impacts of language programs for development. *TESOL Quarterly, 36*(3), 399–429.

Maurizio, O. M. A., & Yvette, P. (1995). Internet resources and second language acquisition: An evaluation of virtual immersion. *Foreign Language Annals, 28*(4), 551–563.

Mitchell, R. (1992). The 'independent' evaluation of bilingual primary education: A narrative account. In J. C. Alderson & A. Beretta (Eds.), *Evaluating second language education* (pp. 100–140). Cambridge, England: Cambridge University Press.

Morris, M. (2006). Addressing the challenges of program evaluation: One department's experience after two years. *Modern Language Journal, 90*(4), 585–588.

Songtao, Mo., & Zhao, L. (2012) Reflective note on evaluation methods in management distance learning courses. *Academy of Educational Leadership Journal, 16*(4), 19–26.

Morris, M. (2006). Addressing the challenges of program evaluation: One department's experience after two years, *The Modern Language Journal, 90*, 585–588.

Munro, J. M., & Derwing, T.M. (1998). The effects of speaking rate on listener evaluations of native and foreign-accented speech. *Language Learning, 48*(2), 159–182.

Murdoch, G. (2000). Introducing a teacher-supportive evaluation system. *ELT Journal, 54*(1), 54–65.

Newman, F. M., Smith, B., Allensworth, E., & Bryk, A. S. (2001). Instructional program coherence: What it is and why it should guide school improvement policy. *Educational Evaluation and Policy Analysis, 23*(4), 297–321.

Nkosana, L. (2008) Attitudinal obstacles to curriculum and assessment reform. *Language Teaching Research, 12*(2), 287–312.

Noels, K. A., et al. (1999). Perceptions of teachers' communicative style and students' intrinsic and extrinsic motivation. *The Modern Language Journal, 83,* 23–34.

Norris, J. (2009) Understanding and improving language education through program evaluation: Introduction to the special issue. *Language Teaching Research, 13*(1), 7–13.

Palmer, A. (1992). Issues in evaluating input-based language teaching programs. In J. C. Alderson & A. Beretta (Eds.), *Evaluating second language education* (pp. 141–166). Cambridge, England: Cambridge University Press.

Pardo-Ballester, C. (2012). CALL evaluation: Students' perception and use of LoMasTv. *CALICO Journal, 29*(3), 532–547.

Pawan, F., & Thomalla, T. (2005). Making the invisible visible: A responsive evaluation study of ESL and Spanish language services for immigrants in a small rural county in Indiana. *TESOL Quarterly, 39*(4), 683–705.

Peacock, M. (2009) The evaluation of foreign-language-teacher education programmes. *Language Teaching Research, 13*(3), 259–278.

Poehner, M., Lantolf, J. (2005) Dynamic assessment in the language classroom. *Language Teaching Research, 9*(3), 233–265.

Rea-Dickins, P., & Germaine, K. (1998). The price of everything and the value of nothing: Trends in language programme evaluation. In P. Rea-Dickins & K. Germaine (Eds.), *Managing evaluation and innovation in language teaching: Building bridges* (pp. 3–19). London, England: Longman.

Reinders, H., & Lewis, M. (2006). An evaluative checklist for self-access materials. *ELT Journal, 60*(3), 272–278.

Reinders, H., & Lazaro, N. (2007). Current approaches to assessment in self-access language learning. *TESL-EJ, 11*(3). Retrieved from http://www.tesl-ej.org/wordpress/issues/volume11/ej43/ej43a2/

Riazi, A. M., & Mosalanejad, N. (2010). Evaluation of learning objectives in Iranian high-school and pre-university English textbooks using Bloom's taxonomy. *TESL-EJ, 13*(4). Retrieved from http://www.tesl-ej.org/wordpress/issues/volume13/ej52/ej52a5/

Ross, S. J. (1992). Program-defining evaluation in a decade of eclecticism. In J. C. Alderson & A. Beretta (Eds.), *Evaluating second language education* (pp. 167–196). Cambridge, England: Cambridge University Press.

Ross, S. J. (2003). A diachronic coherence model for language program evaluation. *Language Learning, 53*(1), 1–33.

Saif, S. (2010). A needs-based approach to the evaluation of the spoken language ability of international teaching assistants. *Canadian Journal of Applied Linguistics (CJAL), 5*(1).

Sakui, K. (2004). Wearing two pairs of shoes: Language teaching in Japan. *ELT Journal, 58*(2), 155–163.

Schulz, R. A. (2001). Cultural differences in student and teacher perceptions concerning the role of grammar instruction and corrective feedback: USA-Colombia. *The Modern Language Journal, 85*, 244–258.

Scriven, M. (1967). The methodology of evaluation. In R. W. Tyler, R. M. Gagne, & M. Scriven (Eds.), *Perspectives of curriculum evaluation* (pp. 39–83). Chicago IL: Rand McNally.

Shadish, W., Cook, T., & Leviton, L. (1991). *Foundations of program evaluation.* Newbury Park, CA: Sage.

Shepard, L. (2000). The role of assessment in a learning culture. *Educational Researcher, 29*(7), 1–14.

Slimani, A. (1992). Evaluation of classroom interaction. In J. C. Alderson & A. Beretta (Eds.), *Evaluating second language education* (pp. 197–221). Cambridge, England: Cambridge University Press.

Stewart, T. (2007). Teachers and learners evaluating course tasks together. *ELT Journal, 61*(3), 256–266.

Stockwell, G. (2010). Using mobile phones for vocabulary activities: Examining the effect of the platform. *Language Learning & Technology, 14*(2), 95–110.

Su, S-W. (2010). Motivating and justifiable: Teaching western literature to EFL students at a university of science and technology. *TESL-EJ, 14*(1). Retrieved from http://www.tesl-ej.org/wordpress/issues/volume14/ej53/ej53a2/

Sugarman, J. (2008). Evaluation of the dual language program in the North Shore School District 112, Highland Park, IL. Center for Applied Linguistics.

Sugarman, J., Hoover, J., & Nier, V. (2009). Evaluation of the dual language program at the Edward Bain school of language and art. Center for Applied Linguistics.

Sullivan, J. H. (2006). The importance of program evaluation in collegiate foreign language programs. *The Modern Language Journal, 90,* 590–593.

Thaine, C. (2004). The assessment of second language teaching. *ELT Journal, 58*(4), 336–345.

Tribble, C. (2000). Designing evaluation into educational change processes. *ELT Journal, 54*(4), 319–328.

Vandergrift, L., & Bélanger, C. (1998). The national core French assessment project: Design and field test of formative evaluation instruments at the intermediate level. *The Canadian Modern Language Review, 54*(4), 553–578.

Vandergrift, L. (2000). Setting students up for success: Formative evaluation and FLES. *Foreign Language Annals, 33,* 290–303.

Velazquez-Torres, N. (2006). How well are ESL teachers being prepared to integrate technology in their classrooms? *TESL-EJ, 9*(4). Retrieved from http://www.tesl-ej.org/wordpress/issues/volume9/ej36/ej36a1/

Vellenga, H. (2004). Learning pragmatics from ESL & EFL textbooks: How likely? *TESL-EJ, 8*(2). Retrieved from http://www.tesl-ej.org/wordpress/issues/volume8/ej30/ej30a3/

Walker, E. (2010). Evaluation of a support intervention for senior secondary school English immersion. *System, 38*(1), 50–62.

Warschauer, M., & Ware, P. (2006) Automated writing evaluation: defining the classroom research agenda. *Language Teaching Research, 10*(2), 157–180.

Weigle, S. C., Boldt, H., & Valsecchi M. I. (2003). Effects of task and rater background on the evaluation of ESL student writing: A pilot study. *TESOL Quarterly, 37*(2), 345–354.

Woodall, B. (2010). Simultaneous listening and reading in ESL: Helping second language learners read (and enjoy reading) more efficiently. TESOL Journal, *1*(2), 186–205.

Wu, W., & Xu, J. (2010). *A comprehensive evaluation on China's EFL learners' autonomous learning competence.* E-Business and Information System Security (EBISS), 2010 Second International Conference, Wuhan, China. doi: 10.1109/EBISS.2010.5473758

Yang, W. (2009) Evaluation of teacher induction practices in a U.S. university English language program: Towards useful evaluation. *Language Teaching Research, 13*(1), 77–98.

Zhu, W., & Flaitz, J. (2005). Using focus group methodology to understand international students' academic language needs: A comparison of perspectives. *TESL-EJ, 8*(4). Retrieved from http://www.tesl-ej.org/wordpress/issues/volume8/ej32/ej32a3/

APPENDIX B

A *Bibliography* About *Evaluation*

Alderson, J. C. (1992). Guidelines for the evaluation of language education. In J. C. Alderson & A. Beretta (Eds.), *Evaluating second language education* (pp. 274–304). Cambridge, England: Cambridge University Press.

Alderson, J. C., & Scott, M. (1992). Insiders, outsiders and participatory evaluation. In J. C. Alderson & A. Beretta (Eds.), *Evaluating second language education* (pp. 25–60). Cambridge, England: Cambridge University Press.

Beretta, A. (1986). Toward a methodology of ESL program evaluation. *TESOL Quarterly, 20*(1), 144–155.

Beretta, A. (1986). Program-fair language teaching evaluation. *TESOL Quarterly, 20*(3), 431–445.

Beretta, A. (1986). A case for field-experimentation in program evaluation. *Language Learning, 36*(3), 295–309.

Beretta, A. (1990). The program evaluator: The ESL researcher without portfolio. *Applied Linguistics, 11*(1), 1–15.

Beretta, A., & Davies, A. (1985). Evaluation of the Bangalore project. *English Language Teaching Journal, 39*(2), 121–127.

Berner, M., & Bronson, M. (2005). A case study of program evaluation in local government: Building consensus through collaboration. *Public Performance & Management Review, 28*(3), 309–325.

Evaluating Second Language Courses, pages 251–255

Berwick, R. F. (1989). Needs assessment in language programming: From theory to practice. In R. K. Johnson (Ed.), *The second language curriculum* (pp. 48–62). Cambridge, England: Cambridge University Press.

Bigelow, M. (2009). Testing. [Review of the book *Validity evaluation in language assessment* by J. M. Norris]. *The Modern Language Journal, 93,* 469–470.

Black, P. (2009). Formative assessment issues across the curriculum: The theory and the practice. *TESOL Quarterly, 43*(3), 519–524.

Blue, G., & Grundy, P. (1996). Team evaluation of language teaching and language courses. *ELT Journal, 50*(3), 244–253.

Brindley, G. (1998). Outcomes-based assessment and reporting in language programs: A review of the issues. *Language Testing, 15*(1), 45–85.

Brindley, G. (2001). Outcomes-based assessment in practice: Some examples and insights. *Language Testing, 18(4),* 393–407.

Brown, J. D. (1989). Language program evaluation: A synthesis of existing possibilities. In R. K. Johnson (Ed.), *The second language curriculum* (pp. 222–241). Cambridge, England: Cambridge University Press.

Brown, J. D. (1995). Language program evaluation: Decisions, problems and solutions. *Annual Review of Applied Linguistics, 15,* 227–248.

Brown, J. D., & Hudson, T. (1998). The alternatives in language assessment. *TESOL Quarterly, 32*(4), 653–675.

Burstein, L., & Guiton, G. W. (1984). Methodological perspectives on documenting program impact. *Advances in Special Education, 4,* 21–42.

Coleman, H. (1988). Analyzing language needs in large organizations. *English for Specific Purposes, 7,* 155–69.

Cronbach, L. J. (1982). *Designing evaluations of educational and social programs.* San Francisco, CA: Jossey-Bass.

Cumming, A. (1987). What is a second-language program evaluation? *The Canadian Modern Language Review/La Revue Canadienne Des Langues Vivantes, 43*(4), 678–700. Retrieved from http://search.proquest.com/docview/58106442?accountid=7098

Daloglu, A., & Marsh, F. (2007). Teacher-student partnership in evaluating and revising a multidisciplinary sustained-content English language course. *Applied Language Learning, 17*(1/2), 15–31. Retrieved from http://search.proquest.com/docview/85671029?accountid=7098

Datnow, A. (2000). Power and politics in the adoption of school reform models. *Educational Evaluation and Policy Analysis, 22*(4), 357–374.

Diamond, R. M., & Sudweeks, R. R. (1980). A comprehensive approach to course evaluation. *Journal of Instructional Development, 4*(1), 28–34.

Ellis, R. (1998). Evaluating and researching grammar consciousness-raising tasks. In P. Rea-Dickins & K. Germain, *Managing evaluation and innovation in language teaching* (pp. 220–252). New York, NY: Addison Wesley Longman.

Ephratt, M. (1992). Developing and evaluating language courseware. *Computers and the Humanities, 26*(4), 249–259.

Fraenkel, J. R., & Wallen, N.E. (2000). *How to design & evaluate research in education* (6th ed.). New York, NY: McGraw-Hill.

Gaea, L. (1977). Program evaluation: An empirical study of individualized instruction. *American Educational Research Journal, 14*(3), 277–293.

Gaies, S. J. (1992). *An approach to the evaluation of ELT prep programs.* ERIC database (ED369276)

Gaber, J. (2000). Meta-needs assessment. *Evaluation and Program Planning, 23,* 139–147.

Genesee, F., & Upshur, J. A. (1996). *Classroom-based evaluation in second language education.* Cambridge, England: Cambridge University Press.

Gorsuch, G. (2009). Investigating second language learner self-efficacy and future expectancy of second language use for high-stakes program evaluation. *Foreign Language Annals, 42*(3), 505–540.

Gottlieb, M. (2006). *Assessing English language learners: Bridges from language proficiency to academic achievement.* Thousand Oaks, CA: Corwin.

Guba, E. G., & Lincoln, Y. S. (1981). *Effective evaluation.* San Francisco, CA: Jossey-Bass.

Harris, J. (2009). Late-stage refocusing of Irish-language programme evaluation: Maximizing the potential for productive debate and remediation. *Language Teaching Research, 13*(1), 55–76.

Henning, G. (1982). Growth-referenced evaluation of foreign language instructional programs. *TESOL Quarterly, 16*(4), 467–477.

House, E. R. (1993). *Professional evaluation: Social impact and political consequences.* Newbury Park, CA: Sage.

Johnson, R. K. (Ed.). (1989). *The second language curriculum.* Cambridge, England: Cambridge University Press.

Knight, T. O., Johnson, S. R., & Finley, R. M. (1987). Extension program evaluation using normative decision models. *American Journal of Agricultural Economics, 69*(2).

Llosa, L., & Slayton, J. (2009). Using program evaluation to inform and improve the education of young English language learners in U.S. schools. *Language Teaching Research, 13*(1), 35–54.

Long, M. H. (1984). Process and product in ESL program evaluation. *TESOL Quarterly, 18*(3), 409–425.

Long, M. H. (Ed.). (2005). *Second language needs analysis.* Cambridge, England: Cambridge University Press.

Lynch, B. (1996). The role of program evaluation in applied linguistics research. *Issues in Applied Linguistics, 2*(1), 84–86.

Lynch, B. (1996). *Language program evaluation: Theory and practice.* Cambridge, England: Cambridge University Press.

Mathison, S. (2008). What is the difference between evaluation and research, and why do we care? In N. L. Smith & P. R. Brandon (Eds.). *Fundamental issues in evaluation.* New York, NY: Guilford.

McNamara, T. (2001). Language assessment as social practice: Challenges for research. *Language Testing, 18*(4), 333–350.

Memet, M. (1999). Evaluation of language teacher and course by learners. *Les Cahiers De l'Apliut, 18*(3), 107–119. Retrieved from http://search.proquest.com/docview/85696727?accountid=7098

Mitchell, R. (1990). Evaluation of second language teaching projects and programmes. *Language Culture and Curriculum, 3*(1), 3–17. Retrieved from http://search.proquest.com/docview/85513911?accountid=7098

Mohr, L. (1992). *Impact analysis for program evaluation.* Thousand Oaks, CA: Sage.

Murphy, D. (2000). Key concepts in ELT: Evaluation. *ELT Journal, 54*(2), 210–212.

Newman, F. M., Smith, B., Allensworth, E., & Bryk, A. S. (2001). Instructional program coherence: What it is and why it should guide school improvement policy. *Educational Evaluation and Policy Analysis, 23*(4), 297–321.

Norris, J. M. (2008). *Validity evaluation in language assessment.* New York, NY: Peter Lang.

Patton, M. Q. (2008). Utilization-focused evaluation. In S. Mathison (Ed.), *Encyclopedia of evaluation* (pp. 429–432). Thousand Oaks, CA: Sage.

Rea-Dickins, P., & Germaine, K. (1998). The price of everything and the value of nothing: Trends in language programme evaluation. In P. Rea-Dickins & K. Germaine (Eds.). *Managing evaluation and innovation in language teaching: Building bridges,* (pp. 3–19). London, England: Longman.

Richards, D. (1997). Program evaluation in TESOL. *Prospect, 12*(1), 4–19.

Ross, S. (2003). A diachronic coherence model for language program evaluation. *Language Learning, 53*(1), 1–33.

Scriven, M. (1967). The methodology of evaluation. In R. W. Tyler, R. M. Gagne, & M. Scriven (Eds.), *Perspectives of curriculum evaluation* (pp. 39–83). Chicago, IL: Rand McNally.

Shadish, W., Cook, T., & Leviton, L. (1991). *Foundations of program evaluation.* Newbury Park, CA: Sage.

Shepard, L. (2000). The role of assessment in a learning culture. *Educational Researcher, 29*(7), 1–14.

Smith, N. L., & Brandon, P. R. (2008). *Fundamental issues in evaluation.* New York, NY: Guilford.

Stumpf, S. A. (1979). Assessing academic program and department effectiveness using student evaluation data. *Research in Higher Education, 11*(4), pp. 353–363.

Tagliante, C. (1993). Evaluation in a program of language training for specific objectives. *Le Francais Dans Le Monde,* 124–135.

TESOL. (2008). *Standards for ESL/EFL teachers of adults.* [Reviewed in *TESL Quarterly, 43*(3) p. 560.]

Tribble, C. (2000). Designing evaluation into educational change processes. *ELT Journal, 54*(4), 319–327.

Vilela, E.g., (2009). CALL evaluation for early foreign language learning: A review of the literature and a framework for evaluation. *CALICO Journal, 26*(2), 363–389.

APPENDIX C

A Bibliography of *Needs Analysis*

Alalou, A. (2001). Reevaluating curricular objectives using students' perceived needs: The case of three language programs. *Foreign Language Annals 34*(5), 453–469.

Baştürkmen, H., & Al-Huneidi, A. (1996). *Refining procedures: A needs analysis project at Kuwait University.* ERIC database. (ED413762).

Bosher, S., & Smalkoski, K. (2002). From needs analysis to curriculum development: Designing a course in health-care communication for immigrant students in the USA. *English for Specific Purposes 21*, 59–79.

California Department of Education (2015). *California's school nutrition personnel: Training and education needs assessment.* Sacramento, CA: Author. Retrieved from http://www.cde.ca.gov/pd/fs/ne/documents/tenareport.pdf

Cameron, R. (1998). A language-focused needs analysis for ESL-speaking nursing students in class and clinic. *Foreign Language Annuals, 31*(2), 203–218.

Chan, V. (2001, July). Determining students' language needs in a tertiary setting. *English Teaching Forum, 39*(3), 16–27.

Chia, H., Johnson, R., Chian, H., & Olive, F. (1999). English for college students in Taiwan: A study of perceptions of English needs in a medical context. *English for Specific Purposes, 18*(2), 107–119.

Chur-Hansen, A., Elliott, T. E., & Klein, N. C. (2007). Assessment of English-language proficiency for general practitioner registrars. *Journal of Continuing Education in the Health Professions, 27*(1), 36–41.

Coleman, H. (1988). Analyzing language needs in large organizations. *English for Specific Purposes, 7,* 155–169.

Edwards, N. (2000). Language for business: Effective needs assessment, syllabus design and materials preparation in a practical ESP case study. *English for Specific Purposes, 19,* 291–296.

Elisha-Primo, I., Sandler, S., Goldfrad, K., Ferenz, O., & Perpignan, H. (2010). Listening to students' voices: A curriculum renewal project for an EFL graduate academic program. *System: An International Journal of Educational Technology and Applied Linguistics. 38*(3), 457–466.

Fixman, C. S. (1990). The foreign language needs of U.S.-based corporations. In R. Lambert., & S. Moore (Eds.), *Foreign language in the workplace, annals of the American Academy of Political and Social Science, 511,* 25–46.

Flowerdew, L. (2010). Devising and implementing a business proposal module: Constraints and compromises. *English for Specific Purposes, 29*(2) 108–120.

Gilabert, R. (2005). Evaluating the use of multiple sources and methods in needs analysis: A case study of journalists in the autonomous community of Catalonia (Spain). In M. H. Long (Ed.) *Second language needs analysis* (pp. 182–199). Cambridge, England: Cambridge University Press.

Holme, R., & Chalauisaeng, B. (2006). The learner as needs analyst: The use of participatory appraisal in the EAP reading classroom. *English for Specific Purposes, 25*(4), 403–419.

Iwai, T., Kondo, K., Lim, D. S. J., Ray, G. E., Shimizu, H., & Brown, J. D. (1999). *Japanese language needs analysis.* Honolulu, HI: University of Hawaii, Second Language Teaching & Curriculum Center. Retrieved from http://www.nflrc.hawaii.edu/NetWorks/NW13/

Jacobson, W. H. (1986). An assessment of the communication needs of nonnative speakers of English in an undergraduate physics lab. *English for Specific Purposes 5,* 189–195.

Krohn, N. (2009). The Hebrew language needs of future conservative rabbis: A needs analysis. *Journal of Jewish Education, 75*(3), 258–289.

Lambert, C. (2010). A task-based needs analysis: Putting principles into practice. *Language Teaching Research, 14*(1), 99–112.

Lee, Y., Altschuld, J. W., & White, J. L. (2007). Problems in needs assessment data: Discrepancy analysis. *Evaluation and Program Planning, 30*(3), 258–266.

Lepetit, D., & Cichocki, W. (2002). Teaching languages to future health professionals: A needs analysis study. *Modern Language Journal, 86*(3), 384–96.

Orikasa, K. (1989). A needs analysis for an EFL program in Japan: A systematic approach to program development. *University of Hawaii Working Papers in ESL, 9*(1), 1–47.

Schmidt, R. (1981). Needs assessment in English for specific purposes: The case study. In L. Selinker, E. Tarone & V. Hanzelli (Eds.), *English for academic and technical purposes: Studies in honor of Louis Trimble* (pp. 199–210). Rowley, MA: Newbury House.

Wozniak, S. (2010). Language needs analysis from a perspective of international professional mobility: The case of French mountain guides. *English for Specific Purposes, 29*(4), 242–252.

Zghoul, M. R., & Hussein, R. F. (1985). English for higher education in the Arab world: A case study of needs analysis at Yarmouk University. *The ESP Journal, 4*, 133–152.

Zhu, W., & Flaitz, J. (2005). Using focus group methodology to understand international students' academic language needs: A comparison of perspectives. *TESL-EJ. Teaching English as a Second or Foreign Language, 8*(4), 1–11.

A *Bibliography* About *Needs Analysis*

Altschuld, J. W., & Witkin, B. R. (1995). *Planning and conducting needs assessments: A practical guide.* Thousand Oaks, CA: Sage.

Altschuld, J. W., & Witkin, B. R. (2000). *From needs assessment to action.* Thousand Oaks, CA: Sage.

Berwick, R. (1989). Needs assessment in language programming: From theory to practice. In R. K. Johnson (Ed.), *The second language curriculum* (pp. 48–62). Cambridge, England: Cambridge University Press.

Bray, L., & Swan, A. (2008). Second language needs analysis. *Language Teaching, 41*(20), 299–309.

Brindley, G. (1989). The role of needs analysis in adult ESL programme design. In R. K. Johnson (Ed.), *The second language curriculum* (pp. 63–78). Cambridge, England: Cambridge University Press.

Brown, J. D. (1995). Needs analysis. In J. Brown, *The elements of language curriculum* (pp. 35–70). Boston, MA: Heinle & Heinle.

Brown, J. D. (2009). Foreign and second language needs analysis. In M. H. Long & C. J. Doughty (Eds.), *The handbook of language teaching* (pp. 267–293). New York, NY: Wiley & Sons.

Bosher, S., & Smalkoski, K. (2002). From needs analysis to curriculum development: Designing a course in health-care communication for immigrant students in the USA. *English for Specific Purposes 21*, 59–79.

Evaluating Second Language Courses, pages 261–263

Cameron, R. (1998). A language-focused needs analysis for ESL-speaking nursing students in class and clinic. *Foreign Language Annuals, 31*(2), 203–218.

Chambers, E. (1980). A re-evaluation of needs analysis in ESP. *The ESP Journal, 1*(1), 25–33.

Frye, A. W., & Hemmer, P. A. (2012). Program evaluation models and related theories: AMEE Guide No. 67. *Medical Teacher, 34*(5), 288–299. doi: 10.3109/0142159X.2012.668637

Hutchinson, T., & Waters, A. (1987). Needs analysis. In T. Hutchinson & A. Waters, *English for specific purposes: A learning-centred approach* (pp. 53–64). Cambridge, England: Cambridge University Press.

Jordan, R. R. (1997). Needs analysis. In R. R. Jordan, *English for academic purposes* (pp. 20–42). Cambridge, England: Cambridge University Press.

Long, M. H. (2005). Methodological issues in learner needs analysis. In M. H. Long (Ed.), *Second language needs analysis* (pp. 182–199). Cambridge, England: Cambridge University Press.

Macalister, J. (2012). Narrative frames and needs analysis. *System: An International Journal of Educational Technology and Applied Linguistics, 40*(1), 120–128.

Mackay, R. (1978). Identifying the nature of the learner's needs. In R. Mackay & A. Mountford (Eds.), English for specific purposes (pp. 21–42). London, England: Longman.

McCawley, P. (2009). *Methods for conducting an educational needs assessment: Guidelines for cooperative extension system professionals.* Moscow, ID: University of Idaho. Retrieved from http://www.cals.uidaho.edu/edComm/pdf/BUL/BUL0870.pdf

McKillip, J. (1987). *Need analysis: Tools for the human services and education.* Newbury Park, CA: Sage.

Mouzakitis, G. (2009). *Since everybody needs needs analysis why do we fail to investigate?* Proceedings of the European Conference on E-Learning, Bari, Italy, (pp. 400–405).

Nation, I. S. P., & Macalister, J. (2010). *Language curriculum design.* New York, NY: Routledge.

Richards, J. C. (2001). Needs analysis. In J. C. Richards, *Curriculum development in language teaching* (pp. 51–88). Cambridge, England: Cambridge University Press.

Roberts, C. (1982). Needs analysis for ESP programmes. *Language Learning and Communication, 1*(1), 105–120.

Ross, J. A. (2008). Cost-utility analysis in educational needs assessment. *Evaluation and Program Planning, 31*(4), 356–367.

Stufflebeam, D. L., McCormick, C. H., Brinkerhoff, R. O., & Nelson, C. O. (1985). *Conducting educational needs assessments.* Boston, MA: Kluwer-Nijhoff.

Thomsett, J., Leggett, B., & Ainsworth, S. (2011). TESOL in context: Authentic workplace learning for pre-service teachers. *TESOL in Context, 21*(2), 4–22.

Watanabe, Y., Norris, J. M., & Gonzalez-Lloret, M. (2009). Identifying and responding to evaluation needs in college foreign language programs. In J. M. Norris, J. M. Davis, C. Sinicrope, & Y. Watanabe (Eds.), *Toward useful program evaluation in college foreign language education* (pp. 5–56). Honolulu: University of Hawaii at Manoa, National Foreign Language Resource Center.

West, R. (1994). Needs analysis in language teaching. *Language Teaching, 27*(1), 1–19.

Witkin, B. R., & Altschuld, J. W. (1995). *Planning and conducting needs assessment: A practical guide.* Thousand Oaks, CA: Sage.

Glossary

Areas of uncertainty is a term used in qualitative data collection and refers to the deliberate self-questioning of a teacher/evaluator about the validity of his or her findings with reference to the beliefs and perceptions of stakeholders. In other words, is what the teacher/evaluator thinks is going on in a course, the same as what stakeholders think is going on?

Assessment refers to data collection instruments (tests, questionnaires, interviews, observations, etc.) and data collection protocols used to answer the question of whether learner outcomes have come about (e.g., Did students' vocabulary knowledge improve?). Assessment is also used to answer evaluation questions that are posed by a teacher/evaluator.

Communicative language learning theory refers to a set of beliefs that holds that a second language is mostly effectively learned through interaction of learners, or interaction between more and less proficient second language speakers while working on a mutual task, or problem.

Construct refers to the theoretical model of the ability, the attitude, or the perception, that a data collection instrument, such as a test, is thought to be measuring. For tests, constructs might be grammatical accuracy in second language writing, or vocabulary learning for the purposes of reading short narrative texts, or communicative appropriateness in email exchanges.

Construct validity refers to the extent to which a test or quiz, or other data collection instrument captures the abilities, attitudes, or perceptions

Evaluating Second Language Courses, pages 265–272
Copyright © 2016 by Information Age Publishing
All rights of reproduction in any form reserved.

the user intends for it to capture. The process of arguing for construct validity involves using strategies that will result in validation evidence.

Content validity refers to the extent to which a test or quiz reflects the content presented and practiced in a course, not only in a surface topical sense, but also in the sense that learners are doing things with the second language on a test that are similar to what they do in class or during homework. In this second respect, content validity has to do with constructs.

Course evaluation is a process by which we collect information and assign a judgment of worth to a course or parts of a course.

Course logic refers to the assumptions of how a curriculum (classes, materials, teaching, etc.) is supposed to bring about desired outcomes.

Course logic table is an organizing graphic used to bring together elements of a course logic study, including findings from an impact model and an organizational chart done for a course.

Criterion-referenced tests refer to tests that are designed and used for specific learners in a specific course. Criterion-referenced tests are designed to measure learner achievement of prespecified course outcomes (or goals) and may be used for diagnostic purposes while a course is still underway.

A curricular innovation is some principled change to a course to bring about some worthwhile change in students' learning or other stated outcome. Examples are increasing the time classes meet or how often they meet, or diversifying the type of vocabulary exercises used.

Curriculum refers to all the ways a course or program responds to a perceived learner need. This includes class exercises, textbooks, handouts, lectures, how often classes are scheduled to meet and for how long, teaching methods, etc.

Cut-points or **cut-scores** are prespecified numerical values on a test used to decide grades, or passing or failing performances.

Data collection instrument (DCI) is any means by which data are collected for a course evaluation, including paper and pencil forms such as questionnaires, quizzes, or interview questions.

Data collection protocol refers to a working plan for specific kinds of data collection, and may include an actual data collection instrument, such as a questionnaire, a quiz, or a list of questions for an interview, but also simply listing what documents to collect, for example lesson plans, class handouts, photocopied pages of textbooks, etc.

Decision points are an array of specific suggestions for teachers focused on the elements of the curriculum that were investigated in accordance with the evaluation questions (EQs).

Domain theory is published theory in specific second language learning or education content areas which explains and predicts how second language learning takes place and/or how and why pedagogical interventions may be related to, or affect, second language learning.

Effect size is a measure of the practical significance of results from a statistical procedure. Effect size indicates a difference in outcome, such as that between a group who received a treatment and a group who did not. P-values may seem to show that but do not. Rather p-values are a first step yes/no type of decision to demonstrate that some difference between groups is not accidental. An effect size shows how important the difference is.

Evaluation is a process by which we collect information and assign a judgment of worth to parts of a course, an entire course, or several related courses that comprise a program.

An **evaluation model** refers to beliefs about what the components of a course or program are, such as outcomes and assessment, and how they relate to each other. An evaluation model guides the planning and processes of an evaluation.

Evaluation purpose refers to the orientation of an evaluation. For instance, is an evaluation for accountability purposes, or to inform and illuminate details of how a course works?

Evaluation questions (EQs) are posed by a teacher/evaluator to explicitly state the purpose and rationale for the course evaluation.

Foreign language refers to any language taught in places where it is not consistently or widely used outside the classroom, such as French, German, or Russian taught in the United States, and English or Chinese taught in Russia or Japan.

Formative evaluation is a process whereby stakeholders (often students in a course) are asked to comment on a course currently underway for the purpose of changing or improving some aspect of the course. Formative evaluation can also be used at the end of a course to consider changes to a future course. Formative evaluation also includes quiz scores, or learner or teacher observations or comments that suggest that specific processes in the course are promoting learner achievement of outcomes, or are not as effective as they could be.

Goals for a course or program are sometimes called outcomes, objectives, learning points, targets, aims, benchmarks, or criteria. Goals are statements of what a course or program is supposed to accomplish, and in terms of modern conceptions of curriculum may be stated in terms of what knowledge, skills, or attitudes learners in the course should learn.

Impact model is used as an initial point in a course logic study. It refers to a visual model prepared by teachers/evaluators to show what he or she believes is the causal sequence between curriculum and outcomes. The evaluator stipulates inputs, what they think will cause outcomes-focused learning, and to create a predicted short- and long-term effect.

Memo is a word processing document or notebook in which a teacher/evaluator keeps brief daily notes about the evaluation in process.

Needs analysis is the process of collecting data on learner needs from stakeholders and from the political, social, and educational environment (referred to later in this book as the world) in which the stakeholders live and operate.

Negative evidence is data that might disconfirm a key assertion arising from the collection of interpretation of qualitative data. Negative evidence must be sought by a teacher/evaluator to ensure that he or she is not simply seeking or noticing data that strengthen his or her desired interpretation.

Norm-referenced tests refer to tests that are designed to compare general language proficiency across courses and programs. Norm-referenced tests are not directly connected to any one second or foreign language program or course.

Objectives for a course or program are sometimes called outcomes, goals, learning points, targets, aims, benchmarks, or criteria. Objectives are statements of what a course or program is supposed to accomplish, but is spelled out is somewhat more specific, classroom-based terms than overall aims. Objectives may be stated in terms of what knowledge, skills, or attitudes learners in the course should learn.

An **organizational chart** is used as a second point in a course logic study. It refers to a model-based process by which an evaluator thinks through the activities of a course to define who does the activities (course coordinator, teachers, or students) and why the activities are done.

Outcomes refer to the aims, goals, and objectives of a course. They are statements of what ought to come about in terms of learner knowledge, ability, or attitude as a result of participating in a course. Statements of outcomes may be found on course syllabuses or program websites, and are named as course purposes or mission statements.

Outcome validation is a formal process whereby teachers/evaluators investigate course or program outcomes by investigating their origins, their history, and their role in a course or program. Teachers/evaluators should be particularly interested in whether and how stakeholders understand the outcomes, and whether the outcomes align with the values and concerns of stakeholders.

A ***p*-value** is the probability of demonstrating some relationship between two sets of scores or other quantitative results, given the null hypothesis (the predetermined assumption of "no change" or "no relationship"). A p-value is provided by most statistical software programs when doing a statistical procedure such as a t-test, ANOVA, or correlation. A p-value is a cut-point a teacher/evaluator chooses beforehand that indicates the likelihood of some relationship between two sets of numbers as due (or not) to random chance.

Peer review is a data and data interpretation review process used to ensure that a teacher/evaluator is collecting data appropriate to the purposes of a course evaluation and is making reasonable interpretations of the data. Peer review involves having a person with sufficient knowledge to understand a course evaluation to do the review. At the same time, he or she may not be directly involved in the evaluation.

Piloting is a rehearsal for data collection done with the intent to improve a data collection instrument, or make needed adjustments to a data collection protocol.

Program evaluation is a process by which we collect information and assign a judgment of worth to several related courses that comprise a program.

Program-fair evaluation is the notion that if two or more courses or programs are being compared, the data collection instrument (for example a test) must be used on students in all courses or programs. It would not be fair to say one program "worked" and another did not simply because some intervention was not used in the second program and the same data collection instrument (DCI) was not administered to learners in the second program.

Reading and assessing evaluation publications (RAP) is a template in Chapter 9 which is useful for assessing and building up knowledge of the evaluation literature. RAPs are used for finding information relevant for doing our own course evaluation and for insights on writing effective course evaluation reports for dissemination.

Reliability indicates the level to which a DCI can be trusted to measure something (ability to write coherent paragraphs in the second language, etc.) consistently. For tests or questionnaires where quantitative data is generated, teachers/evaluators can estimate a reliability coefficient with a range from .00 to .99 (the higher the coefficient, the more reliable the DCI is). For interview or observation protocols resulting in qualitative data, teachers/evaluators can use procedures that demonstrate how disinterested others would similar interpretations of the data (e.g., "Yes, it looks to me also that the teacher interrupted the student four times.").

Research design is an operating model or blueprint for a research project that includes a specific approach to how research questions will be answered. Experimental design is the most familiar example, and others are time-series and case study.

Second language refers to a language taught in places where the language is consistently and widely used, such as English in the United States and United Kingdom, or Turkish in Turkey. Second language also refers more generally to the cognitive learning processes involved in learning another language, in other words, what happens inside learners' heads.

Stakeholders refer to anyone who has an interest in the outcomes of a course including students, teachers, researchers, administrators, parents, and future employers.

Statistical assumptions are the requirements of a given statistical procedure. Each statistical procedure was designed with certain types of data and conditions in mind. Correlation, for instance, assumes that the two variables being correlated have a normal distribution and have the same number of observations (e.g., 20 scores are being correlated with 20 scores on another measure).

Statistical clarity means that there is a plainly seen and stated reason a statistical procedure is used. For instance, "A t-test comparison was used to compare students' test scores at the beginning of the semester and at the end of the semester."

Statistical procedure refers to a statistical analysis done to quantitative data. Common statistical procedures are estimating descriptive statistics (mean, standard deviation, etc.), correlation, or t-test comparisons.

Summative evaluation refers to evaluation that has the purpose of judging the worth of a course either during a course, or after the course has been taught, for the purpose of accountability.

A **syllabus** is a document, typically focused on a single course, which outlines information about the course, such as required materials, and includes a statement of course goals or outcomes. In the historical second language curriculum literature, a syllabus is more specifically the specification of what content or skills are to be focused on in a course, and in what order (e.g., a grammatical syllabus that specifies grammar forms, or a functional syllabus that specifies communicative functions).

Teaching methods are organized "teaching actions" taken by classroom teachers according to stated principles about the nature of language, learning, and teaching. Historical (and yet still current) teaching methods are the Grammar-Translation Method, the Direct Method, and the Audio-Lingual Method. Direct Method teachers, for example, use only the second language in the classroom, and engage learners in long, interactive spoken question-and-answer sessions designed to introduce and reinforce grammar points inductively.

Teacher theory refers to the private, implicit, action-oriented beliefs that teachers hold about how to teach in specific classroom contexts.

Test-taker bias refers to a characteristic of some persons in a group that might affect their test scores, especially if it is unidentified and not taken into account. These include gender, being late for a test, degree of test preparation, cognitive style, sickness at the time of the test, and differential responses to a test environment.

Test washback refers to the effect of a test on teaching and learning in classrooms at a local, regional, or even national level.

Triangulation refers to the practice of collecting data on the same construct, evaluation question, or area of inquiry from multiple points of view. This may mean using different data collection instruments, or interviewing several different stakeholders.

Unintended consequences refers to both positive and negative effects of a course that a teacher/evaluator or course designer did not think of beforehand. For instance, a teacher may develop a course using extensive reading (learners read many easy books to increase fluency) but then may find that learners' writing also becomes less complex in terms of lexical and grammatical choices.

Validation is a process whereby a data collection instrument is designed, piloted, revised, and used with much forethought, consideration, and afterthought as to what is being measured.

Validation evidence is anything that supports the idea that a data collection instrument functioned as intended, and captured some predetermined second or foreign language knowledge or skill, or teacher attitude, or student perception (whatever is being investigated). Triangulation (comparing the results from two or more DCIs thought to measure similar things) is one strategy for providing validation evidence.

The **world** is something outside the course or program, but which is relevant to the course in the sense that it affects the course by making the course necessary or shaping what the course ends up being.

Printed in the USA
CPSIA information can be obtained
at www.ICGtesting.com
JSHW010259260124
55775JS00006B/24